The Economics of Firm Productivity

Productivity varies widely between industries and countries, but even more so across individual firms within the same sectors. The challenge for governments is to strike the right balance between policies designed to increase overall productivity and policies designed to promote the reallocation of resources towards firms that could use them more effectively. The aim of this book is to provide the empirical evidence necessary in order to strike this policy balance. The authors do so by using a micro-aggregated dataset for 20 EU economies produced by CompNet, the Competitiveness Research Network, established some 10 years ago among major European institutions and a number of EU productivity boards, national central banks and national statistical institutes, as well as academic institutions. They call for pan-EU initiatives involving statistical offices and scholars to achieve a truly complete EU market for firm-level information on which to build solidly founded economic policies.

CARLO ALTOMONTE is Associate Professor of Economics at Bocconi University and visiting fellow at Bruegel. He has acted as consultant for a number of international institutions, including the United Nations Conference on Trade and Development (UNCTAD), the European Commission and the UK Parliament.

FILIPPO DI MAURO is Chair of CompNet. He has been an economist and research manager in several central banks, including the Bank of Italy, the US Federal Reserve Board and the European Central Bank.

The Economics of Firm Productivity

Concepts, Tools and Evidence

CARLO ALTOMONTE
Bocconi University

FILIPPO DI MAURO
CompNet-IWH

CAMBRIDGE
UNIVERSITY PRESS

CAMBRIDGE
UNIVERSITY PRESS

University Printing House, Cambridge CB2 8BS, United Kingdom

One Liberty Plaza, 20th Floor, New York, NY 10006, USA

477 Williamstown Road, Port Melbourne, VIC 3207, Australia

314–321, 3rd Floor, Plot 3, Splendor Forum, Jasola District Centre,
New Delhi – 110025, India

103 Penang Road, #05–06/07, Visioncrest Commercial, Singapore 238467

Cambridge University Press is part of the University of Cambridge.

It furthers the University's mission by disseminating knowledge in the pursuit of
education, learning, and research at the highest international levels of excellence.

www.cambridge.org
Information on this title: www.cambridge.org/9781108489232
DOI: 10.1017/9781108774277

First published 2022

A catalogue record for this publication is available from the British Library.

Library of Congress Cataloging-in-Publication Data
Names: Altomonte, Carlo, author. | Di Mauro, Filippo, author.
Title: The economics of firm productivity : concepts, tools and evidence /
    Carlo Altomonte, Filippo di Mauro.
Description: New York : Cambridge University Press, [2022] |
    Includes bibliographical references and index.
Identifiers: LCCN 2021060130 (print) | LCCN 2021060131 (ebook) |
    ISBN 9781108489232 (hardback) | ISBN 9781108702164 (paperback) |
    ISBN 9781108774277 (epub)
Subjects: LCSH: Industrial productivity. | Industrial management. |
    Organizational change. | International finance. |
    BISAC: BUSINESS & ECONOMICS / Industrial Management
Classification: LCC HD56 .A4548 2022 (print) | LCC HD56 (ebook) |
    DDC 338.4/5–dc23/eng/20220204
LC record available at https://lccn.loc.gov/2021060130
LC ebook record available at https://lccn.loc.gov/2021060131

ISBN 978-1-108-48923-2 Hardback

Contents

Figures

Tables

About the Authors

Carlo Altomonte

Carlo Altomonte is Associate Professor of economics at Bocconi University and a non-resident fellow at Bruegel. He received his BA in international economics at Bocconi University, and his MSc in economics and PhD in applied economics at University College London/KU Leuven (UCL/KUL). He is the director of the Globalization and Industry Dynamics unit at the Baffi Carefin Centre of Research at Bocconi University, and a non-resident fellow at Bruegel. He has been a visiting scholar at the Centre of Economic Performance of the London School of Economics and at the research department of the European Central Bank. He has been a visiting professor at the Paris School of Economics (Panthèon-Sorbonne, Paris, France) and KU Leuven (Belgium), and has held short teaching courses at the Wagner School of Government (New York University (NYU)), Keio University (Tokyo), Fudan University and CEIBS (Shanghai), among others. His main areas of research and publication are European economic policy, industrial economics and economic geography, theory of multinational corporations and foreign direct investment. He has published in several academic journals, including the *International Journal of Industrial Organization, Journal of Industrial Economics, Journal of Economic Geography, Journal of International Business Studies, Economic Policy, European Economic Review, Review of World Economics and Oxford Bulletin of Economics and Statistics.* http://faculty.unibocconi.eu/carloaltomonte/

Filippo di Mauro

Filippo di Mauro is the founder and Chairman of the Competitiveness Research Network (CompNet), a leading forum for productivity research and provider of a top standard firm-level based dataset.

During the period 2016–2021, he was visiting professor at the Business School of the National University of Singapore (NUS) and consultant for the Monetary Authority as well as the Economic Development Board of Singapore. At present he is co-Principal Investigator of the CISCO-NUS Corporate laboratory on "Accelerated Digital Economy". He has more than 30 years of experience as economist and research manager in central banks, including the Bank of Italy (1984–1990, 1996–1998), the US Federal Reserve Board (2010) and the European Central Bank (ECB) (1998–2016). He has also worked at the Asian Development Bank (1990–1994) and the International Monetary Fund (IMF) (1986–1988, 1994–1996). He joined the ECB at the start of its operations in 1998, where he directed until 2010 the international economic analysis and global forecasts in its Department of Economics. The Division he led was also responsible to analyse the developments of the euro and the euro area competitiveness at the early stage of the EU common currency. His present research interests include firms concentration and resource reallocation, and the interaction between productivity and global value chains. He has published in academic journals such as the *Journal of Applied Econometrics, Journal of International Money and Finance and Economic Policy.* An economics graduate of University of Rome, he holds an MA and a PhD in economics from the University of Chicago and the American University, respectively.
http://filippodimauro.com

Preface

Productivity is an essential concept in almost every field related to economics and management. As Paul Krugman wrote in *The Age of Diminishing Expectations* (1994),

Productivity isn't everything, but in the long run it is almost everything. A country's ability to improve its standard of living over time depends almost entirely on its ability to raise its output per worker.

As we slowly exit the nightmare of the 2020 COVID-19 pandemic, enhancing productivity is even more critical. The crisis has battered global economic activity in an unprecedented way. Entire sectors have been forced to cease trading, and unemployment has risen to record levels. Governments, central banks and international organisations have responded promptly and massively to the shock, sheltering firms and employees from its impact. This will, however, inevitably further slow aggregate productivity, at least in the short run.

Thus, the debate on how to raise productivity is again in the headlines, and that is the subject of this book. We believe that any useful insight must be based on detailed granular information compiled at the level of the firm. To that end, we will draw from research and the dataset produced by the Competitiveness Research Network (Comp-Net, www.comp-net.org), a leading European research initiative that the authors founded a decade ago.

Using this data, we provide the conceptual framework and tools to analyse aggregate productivity, taking into account how it varies across firms. We identify and study a wide range of potential drivers of firm performance, explaining why productivity diverges across and within countries and industries.

The firm-level perspective provides critical insights to assess the impact of policy, most notably after a shock such as COVID-19, whose impact was felt differently in different countries and sectors, as well as firms within those sectors. Unfortunately despite the progress made, additional European Union (EU)-wide efforts need to be made to collect and analyse data to ensure that the analysis is sufficiently deep, accurate and, most important, timely. We thus appeal to European institutions and research fellows to make a stronger case for better and more reliable firm-level data, which are also truly comparable across EU countries. It has never been more valuable.

Acknowledgements

This book owes a great amount of gratitude to our editor at Cambridge University Press, Phillip Good. We would not have committed to such an ambitious project without his support and encouragement.

We are tremendously indebted to all the Competitiveness Research Network (CompNet) researchers who provided a wide range of research inputs from which we could draw; in particular, we are grateful to all the authors of the CompNet modules and the 2020 Firm Productivity Report. Hence, we thank Annalisa Ferrando, Matteo Iudice, Sven Blank, Marie-Hélène Felt, Philipp Meinen, Katja Neugebauer and Iulia Siedschlag (Financial Module); Cristina Fernández, Roberto García, Paloma Lopez-Garcia, Benedicta Marzinotto, Roberta Serafini, Juuso Vanhala and Ladislav Wintr (Labour Module); Antoine Berthou, Emmanuel Dhyne, Matteo Bugamelli, Ana-Maria Cazacu, Calin-Vlad Demian, Peter Harasztosi, Tibor Lalinsky, Jaanika Meriküll, Filippo Oropallo and Ana Cristina Soares (Trade Module); Johannes Amlung, Tommaso Bighelli, Roman Blyzniuk, Marco Christophori, Jonathan Deist, Mirja Hälbig, Peter Haug, Matthias Mertens, Verena Plümpe, Annalisa Ferrando, Tibor Lalinsky, Philipp Meinen, Ottavia Papagalli, Roberta Serafini, Sergio Inferrera and Marc Melitz (the 2020 Firm Productivity Report); and Daniele Aglio, Eric Bartelsman and Chad Syverson (CompNet authors).

We likewise thank all the data providers who helped put together the data used for the analysis presented in this book and who, over the years, have been producing so far eight rounds of data: Tibor Lalinsky, Martin Suster, Satu Nuri, Juuso Van Hala, Matjaz Koman, Nataša Todorović Jemec, Katja Gattin Turkalj, Aurelija Proskute, Eva Pereira, Guida Nogueira, Massimiliano Ferrari, Elizabeth Steiner, Romain Cometx, Ivan Sutoris, Judit Rariga, Andreas Kuchler, Shari Stehrenberg, Michael Polder, Jan Baran, Madalin Viziniuc, Alexandru Leonte, Andreas Poldahl and Caisa Bergman.

Finally, we owe a great amount of gratitude to our team of young researchers affiliated with CompNet-IWH, Bocconi University and the National University of Singapore: Daniele Aglio, Mirja Hälbig, Duy Hoang, Sergio Inferrera, Marco Lo Faso and Paolo Mengano. They provided critical input in the drafting of the book and its annexes, as well as formatting and putting together the whole book.

1 Introduction

Studying productivity and sensibly advising on best policies for its enhancement is a tricky affair. Two are the main challenges. First, productivity diverges widely and persistently between – and most notably within – countries and industries. It is a constant empirical regularity across the globe that there are only a few firms (even within narrowly defined sectors) which are highly productive. Most of them instead are struggling just to make it, while several others will inexorably exit their respective markets. This implies that there is not such a thing as an "average" firm performance, with meaningful implications, but rather a small set of exceptionally performing firms and the remaining others. Understanding why – and under which circumstances – such "stars" exist and what are the conditions under which others could follow is the key to interpret and foster productivity developments at the country and sector level, which is what ultimately counts for overall economic welfare. Connecting the micro and macro perspective is, however, the second challenge productivity research has to face. Put simply, there are not good enough data to do that, particularly in Europe. Data at the firm level are often solely available at the individual country level and with rather severe restrictions on their use, because of their confidentiality. Cross-country analysis is therefore severely hampered, since the available datasets at the national level are very uneven in terms of firms' coverage, and thus hardly comparable.

To tackle such issues, since early 2010 the two of us have been engaged in the creation of the Competitiveness Research Network – CompNet – a large European initiative with two main objectives: (i) developing a forum for discussion on productivity research and (ii) setting up a truly comparable European Union (EU) dataset of productivity indicators, based on firm-level information of top quality.

In this book, we aim at providing the intuitions and all the necessary tools to analyse firms' productivity, taking into account their heterogeneity. At the same time, we will attempt to identify and study a wide range of potential drivers of firms' performance, which could help explaining why it diverges across and within countries and industries. To this end, we will extensively use the research work and the dataset generated by CompNet. Our ultimate objective is to show how rich and critical information we can gather by taking a firm-level perspective, but also point out that despite the progress made, additional EU-wide efforts need to be made on the data front to ensure sufficient depth and accurateness.

1.1 Overall Feature/Intellectual Underpinnings

The concept of "granularity" in the economic literature captures the idea that economic phenomena, rather than being the result of a homogeneous process carried out by atomistic, indistinguishable agents, can be driven to a great extent by a few outstanding individuals or firms that play a dominant role in regional and national economic performance. In most countries, a handful of firms are responsible for a large part of economic activity, including export sales and foreign direct investment. Within narrowly defined (four-digit Standard Industrial Classification [SIC]) US manufacturing industries, Syverson (2004) found that firms in the 90th percentile of the (total factor) productivity (TFP) distribution are on average 1.92 times more productive than the 10th percentile. In other words, though producing the same products with the same endowments of labour and capital, the top productive firms are able to produce twice as much as the least productive firms. These within-industry differences are significantly larger than the difference in average TFP measured across industries. The situation is not different in Europe. As shown by Mayer and Ottaviano (2007), in European countries on average about 1% of these "Happy Few" firms produce more than 75% of output or of foreign sales. An even greater within-industry heterogeneity has been reported in China and India, with average 90th to 10th decile ratios in terms of productivity in excess of 5:1 (Hsieh and Klenow, 2009).

The finding that a handful of firms determine to a great extent the aggregate economic outcomes has two important policy implications. First, it underlines how countries are subject to the actions of a few dozen firms. For instance, Gabaix (2011) estimated that even for the US economy, the business cycle movements of the largest 100 firms explain a third of the aggregate movements in output growth.

The impact is a fortiori much greater for smaller countries or regions that accommodate only one or a few of those "top" enterprises. Di Giovanni et al. (2014) look at the universe of French firms between 1990 and 2007, decomposing aggregate sales fluctuations (in both domestic and foreign markets) and identifying reactions to macro, sectoral and firm-specific idiosyncratic shocks. Similar to the findings of Gabaix (2011) for the US, they confirm the substantial contribution of firm-specific shocks to aggregate volatility in France, with the magnitude of the effect of firm-level shocks being similar to those of sectoral and macroeconomics shocks, common to all firms. Second, the presence of heterogeneous firms in an economy provides a major additional channel through which aggregate productivity and thus competitiveness can be boosted. Recent literature (Bartelsman et al., 2013; Hopenhayn, 2014; Gopinath et al., 2017) takes advantage of the availability of cross-country competitiveness indicators built from firm-level data to show that a significant part of the differences in productivity between countries can be accounted for by differences in allocative efficiency. That is, aggregate productivity in a country might, in part, be lagging behind because capital and labour are not allocated efficiently between firms within an industry. In other words, some technology or policy-induced frictions in factor markets might prevent productive inputs from flowing into the firms that would use them in the most productive way. Removing these frictions thus provides a potential new channel for boosting aggregate productivity, i.e., the reallocation of resources away from poorly performing firms towards the most productive firms, with gains that in some cases can be quantified as an additional 30%, with proportional impacts on potential output (Bartelsman et al., 2013). CompNet research shows that this is particularly the case for the euro area, with major policy implications: "the type of policies that could release an upward shock to potential growth are not just those focused on price flexibility. They include [...] on the TFP side, policies that encourage the reallocation of resources – which could be powerful in the euro area given the wide and skewed distribution between the least and most productive firms".[1]

---

[1] Mario Draghi, speech on "Structural Reforms, Inflation and Monetary Policy", ECB Forum on Central Banking, Sintra, 22 May 2015, available at www.ecb.europa.eu/press/key/date/2014.

Much of the subsequent research in international trade has been undertaken within this integrated "new trade theory" framework, which has become a standard paradigm of analysis. Yet, traditional models based on the representative firm setup are not able to explain a significant number of empirical findings. Indeed, traditional economic analysis used to build on the role of countries and sectors rather than firms within countries and sectors, which are, however, the actors who produce, trade and compete among themselves. If the underlying structure of firms is not properly taken into account, aggregate variables might undermine their reliability as indicators of average performance.

This observation has since led many economists to adopt a different perspective. As a result, seminal empirical works in the 1990s – such as the work by Olley and Pakes (1996a) on the US telecommunications sector – departed from a representative firm's setting to focus on firms within sector, in order to keep into account the role of firms' productivity heterogeneity to explain aggregate productivity growth. Since then, the economic literature has found that, using firm-level information, similar aggregate productivity growth might be the result of very different dynamics at the firm level.[2] This finding related to the high heterogeneity and skewness of the firm productivity distribution has several implications for economic analysis and policy, and represents the feature which will be more thoroughly analysed and disentangled in this book.

One implication of such high dispersion and skewness is that there are obviously two major meta-drivers of firm productivity.

- Some are common to all firms as deployed in a specific territory or sector. This includes infrastructures, logistic efficiency, institutions, barriers to entry, market structures, the degree of competition and the like. Such elements tend to influence the average productivity of all the firms present in that specific market/regions.
- Some other pertains instead to firm specific characteristics; something that makes the firm "special". This includes that peculiar mix of innovative content, managerial capacity, marketing and such.

---

[2] For a review of preliminary empirical results on firm heterogeneity and trade, see Tybout (2021) and Bernard et al. (2003).

Overall, assuming that the aim of societies is the maximisation of their respective economies productivity, the role of governments is to draw a right balance between policy measures aimed at increasing the overall productivity (of the relevant country or sector) and others promoting a reallocation of resources – within that country or sectors – towards the firms that could use them most productively. It is the role of empirical research to provide the necessary evidence to tilt the balance in one direction or the other. This represents also the main objective of this book, i.e., disentangling the different drivers of productivity and collect evidence on the extent to which different factors and alternative strategies may matter when policies are actually put in place.

The second implication is that the response to external shocks – or to policies – of any economy will be strictly dependent on the overall constellation of firms that populate such economy. Take as an example the exchange rate fluctuations and their overall impact on export performance. It is by now a rather consolidated result in the most recent empirical literature that the impact will be much stronger for smaller and less productive firms, than for large and more productive ones. For the latter, the exchange rate may represent just a small driver of firms' results. And obviously such differentiated impact will be also observable for other potential productivity drivers, availability of external finance, cost of labour force and so on. A critical conclusion of such dimension is that – yet again – it is up to empirical research to provide the right quantitative context on which to base policies, following a correct assessment of likely outcomes.

1.2 Relevance for Policy Institutions

Awareness of firm heterogeneity and its implications for effective policy making is widely increasing among major institutions, also because of substantial improvements in the availability of novel datasets in which firm-level or individual-product-level information is disaggregated. For instance, for central banks such as the European Central Bank (ECB), when looking at transmission mechanisms of monetary policy, it is key to bear in mind that firms react differently to changes in factors such as money supply or loans availability. The need to identify the drivers of productivity and competitiveness is even more relevant when domestic or international public institutions are involved in designing (and monitoring the implementation of) structural reforms, such as the International Monetary Fund (IMF), the European Commission, as well as the ECB. For instance, similar types of structural reforms will have different outcomes depending upon the prevailing constellation of firms characterising that sector or country (e.g., in terms of size of operations, firms' financial stance, export orientation) as well as the institutional environment surrounding those firms (e.g., product market access, labour market flexibility). There is an increasing awareness among researchers and practitioners that firm-level information must therefore – at the very least – be used to complement traditional aggregated information at the country and sector level in order to improve the policy toolkit. And efforts are being made to that end by all concerned institutions – as we will mention later.

1.3 Overall Content/Gap Bridging

Against this background, this book aims at handling the issue of what drives aggregate productivity by taking a firm-level (micro) empirical perspective. Its ultimate objective is to provide a toolkit of conceptual underpinnings and of empirical evidence which could help improve policy analysis and formulation. In line with a growing literature, the book will also attempt to bridge the wide gap which still exists between the micro and macro perspective. A gap that – as previously implied – can be a source of quite considerable errors in policy formulation.

In looking at productivity drivers, the book will have in mind the two previously mentioned dimensions of productivity. These are related to firm-specific characteristics such as size, organisation and technological capacity. But they are also related to other critical external conditions that firms have to confront – labour market regulation, financial constraints and so on – which are of paramount importance as drivers of firm productivity.

1.4 Overall Structure/Value Added

Overall, the book will provide a solid and comprehensive, yet not overly voluminous, handbook of the economics of productivity, taking a firm-level approach. The novelty of the book with respect to other existing books (see Annex 1 for a brief summary of existing books on the topics, including a brief outline of content) is that it will put upfront its micro-foundation, both at the conceptual and empirical level. The interaction with the macro perspective of course will not be forgotten, but will form more a critical part of the final chapters of the book, rather than its initial starting point. This is a stark departure from the traditional approach, which mostly considers firm-level analysis as additional, supportive information – e.g., "case study" material – rather than the bulk of the framework.

In terms of overall structure, the book will include in a first chapter after the introduction a stylised theoretical micro-founded model on which to base the analysis and facilitate the discussion throughout the book. It will then present some of the most relevant ways to define and measure productivity so that the reader will have a comprehensive view of the challenges that researchers have to face when dealing with productivity analysis.

The bulk of the book, however, will be composed of empirical evidence. For that, the book will draw extensively from the research results produced by members of CompNet, the Competitiveness Research Network.

The tight connection between the authors of this book and the members of CompNet has permitted a close participation of the economists in the network to the output of this book, including facilitating the process of obtaining the permission of using part of their research as supporting material.

2 | Basic Concepts

2.1 Productivity

In recent decades, the topic of firm productivity has increasingly gained attention from academics and in the policy debate. Macro-economists find that productivity growth is the source of almost all per capita income differences across countries, and so a new strand of research has emerged, dedicated to understanding the drivers of this growth (Syverson, 2011). Trade economists identify firm productivity as the most important determinant of export activity (Melitz, 2003) and foreign direct investment of multinational enterprises (Helpman et al., 2004). Labour economists are exploring the impact of workers' human capital on productivity differences (Bloom and Van Reenen, 2007). Micro-economists are developing new methods to correctly measure productivity to improve our understanding of firm behaviour and market efficiency.

In this chapter, we try to explain what productivity is and how it can be estimated. We will also provide some practical examples and computing codes. Let's start with one definition (of the many possible definitions) of productivity.

Productivity is the effectiveness of productive effort, especially in industry, as measured in terms of the rate of output per unit of input. (Oxford Dictionary)

In other words, productivity measures how efficiently production inputs such as intermediates, energy, labour or capital are bundled together to produce an output. A typical (economic) measure of this efficiency is the ability of the production process to generate *value added*, that is, the increase in value in the final output of production compared to the value of the materials used in the production process by a firm.

In this sense, it is necessary to distinguish the productivity of a single production factor such as labour (this is what we call "factor productivity") from the ability of a firm to combine the bundle of inputs at its disposal to create new value. This is "total factor productivity" (TFP), also known as "multi-factor productivity".

2.2 Factor Productivity

Usually in economic models, a firm operates under a production function that transforms two inputs of production – labour and capital – into an output – a product or a service.

"Labour" is an aggregate term for all the people employed by the firm. It can be disaggregated by the level of skills of the workforce. We typically differentiate between high- and low-skilled labour, or between white- and blue-collar workers. We can also distinguish the type of task performed by workers, for example between managerial and production tasks.

"Capital" includes all human-made goods used in the production process, including machinery, tools and buildings. These are termed "tangible" assets. It can also include other type of goods or services, such as software or data that contribute to the production process, identified as "intangible" assets.

We can easily determine factor productivity using balance-sheet data from individual firms. This is simply a non-parametric indicator created by taking the ratio between a firm's final output and the production factor on which we want to focus.

It can be expressed in a simple formula as follows:

$$[Factor]\ Productivity_{it} = \frac{Output_{it}}{[Factor]\ Input_{it}}, \qquad (2.1)$$

where [Factor] is the name of the factor of production whose productivity we want to assess (labour, for example), i indicates a given firm for which we are computing the index, and t is the period considered, usually a given year.

This formula is simple and intuitive, but it raises several methodological issues and gives us problems if we just attempt to drop in raw data. In this section, we will discuss complications in computing the numerator – output measures – and in later sections we will discuss the possible denominators.

The numerator of Equation 2.1, a firm's output, can be expressed by two different indicators: total revenue (or sales) or value added. Both have advantages and limitations.[1]

- Total revenue, or sales, is generally the most easily accessible information in business registers.[2] If we want to employ revenue or sales for the measuring productivity – that is, use them as proxies of output – we should transform them from nominal values (measured in current prices) into real values. This means we can distinguish between variations in quantity, which we are seeking, and the rise and fall of prices.

  Let's assume, for example, that an enterprise registers a 2% increase in its (nominal) sales in a year. Taking this value as it is, we would see a directly proportionate increase in productivity if inputs were to remain constant. But what if the increase in nominal sales is due to inflation causing an increase in prices, while the quantities produced remained constant? We would wrongly interpret a simple price effect as an increase in productivity.

  For this reason, we have to exclude the influence of this price effect. The most straightforward way to perform this transformation would be to divide the nominal values that we extracted from balance sheets by an appropriate price index, typically retrieved from national statistics.[3] In formula,

$$\frac{Nominal\ Value}{Price\ Index} = Real\ Value.$$

  The second issue when we use revenue or sales as a proxy of output is that these measures also include the value of the intermediate products used by the firm in the production process.

---

[1] Bobbold (2003) offers a detailed description of the advantages and disadvantages of using gross output and value-added measures.

[2] Firms may post figures on revenue that differ from the sales-only figures, because supplementary income sources and one-off events appear in the balance sheet. At times, sales "turnover" is also used as a measure. For the purpose of this book, turnover can be considered equivalent to revenue. Revenue is shown usually as the top item in an income (profit and loss) statement.

[3] In principle, price indexes are industry specific, and thus one should use the index of the industry in which the firm operates. A clear and useful guide on this topic has been provided by the Federal Reserve Bank of Dallas and can be found at this link: www.dallasfed.org/research/basics/nominal.aspx.

So, if we construct factor productivity using revenue or sales, we would be including some value that was created outside the firm. To solve this problem, we prefer to compute productivity measures using value added as a proxy of output.

- Value added is computed as total revenue minus intermediate inputs, and so by definition it eliminates the over-representation of a firm's final production when we use revenues or sales as a proxy for output. For this reason, although information on intermediate consumption at the firm level is not as easy to find as total revenue data, value added is used in most empirical studies. We have to consider that this proxy is also calculated in nominal terms and deflate nominal value-added measures using the appropriate (industry-specific) price index as before.

Labour Productivity

The productivity of the labour input has been studied extensively for many years. It is a very good indicator of a firm's performance, as well as a fair indication of labour market efficiency. It is also the basis of some determinants of demand-side indicators such as wages, consumption and savings.

Information on the labour input is generally available in accounting and fiscal registries. The most widespread indicator is the number of employees, although in some countries it is not mandatory to report these data in balance sheets.

An alternative proxy of the labour input at the firm level is the total amount of wages paid to the workforce. This wage bill is a common item in balance sheet information, as it measures labour costs. The disadvantage of using the wage bill as a proxy for the labour input is that, once again, it is a nominal variable. But, this time, there is no obvious price index to be used as a deflator.[4] And so, if available, the number of employees is the preferred proxy of the labour input, as it does not embed any price bias.

---

[4] In principle, one could use a measure of the average wage in a given industry/year as a price index, and thus retrieve the estimated number of workers, but the same information on the average wage is typically not reported by official statistics, and potentially distorted by social charges, etc.

While the number of employees is a straightforward measure, its validity for productivity purposes relies on two assumptions:

1. There is no discrimination among workers' qualifications or tasks.
2. All employees have the same work schedule.

We are forced to make the first assumption because we have limited knowledge of each employee's skill level. If we wanted to find this out, we would need to acquire a large amount of additional personal information on each employee of the firm, researching college qualifications and postgraduate degrees, previous work experience, specialisation and so on. This is typically not available in business registries.[5]

Moreover, we would need to perfectly identify the amount of revenue that each employee is generating. This is an extremely difficult exercise and can be done only for small samples of firms for which detailed information about workforce composition and revenues is available. Some datasets may capture a basic distinction between white- and blue-collar workers.[6]

Our assumption of identical working schedules implies counting every employee as "one unit" of labour, notwithstanding that employee's contract. For example, some will work full-time, and others work part-time. In principle, we could weight every employee by the amount of hours actually worked – but again, this information is not available in business registries. Instead, we can make the reasonable assumption that a standard use of part-time hours against overtime working hours might balance out. If this was the case, the number of employees should produce a fairly accurate representation of the actual number of hours worked in each firm, in normal circumstances.

Beware, though: when there are flexible work schedules, zero-hours contracts and short-time work schemes, using the number of employees as a proxy might lead us to overestimate the labour input. This results in a downward bias in labour productivity estimates for a given level of output.

---

[5] This information is becoming increasingly available through the development of Linked Employer-Employee Data (LEED), which track every worker, and her personal characteristics, during her entire career across different firms. See Abowd et al. (2008) for more information on the use of these data.

[6] The economic literature has analysed in a number of studies the different impacts of different kinds of employees. For example, a recent stream of literature analyses how managerial capacity affects firm productivity (for example, Bloom and Van Reenen, 2007).

Capital Productivity

Use of capital is another common benchmark to measure firm's productivity. Besides providing insights on firm performance, it allows us to analyse the capital structure of the firm in detail. This is important because every year managers decide on their investment strategy – in the terms we are using, the units of capital they buy or sell.

At first this looks straightforward. But even the definition of capital raises more issues than the convoluted definition of labour. Capital stock is generally measured in two different ways: by its book value, or by applying the perpetual investment method (PIM).

The book value proxies the capital stock with *tangible* fixed assets (machinery and equipment, land, buildings and so on), reported as an item of the balance sheet.

The PIM measures the capital stock by taking the initial capital stock and adding successive annual investments, then subtracting depreciation. More specifically, the capital in the second year of activity would be as follows:

$$K_2 = (1 - \delta)K_1 + I_1, \tag{2.2}$$

where K_1 and K_2 represent the capital stock in the first year and in the second, respectively. The term δ is the depreciation rate. I is the investment expenditure, which can be available separately as a balance sheet item or calculated as the difference between the (non-deflated) book value of assets between two years.

The law of motion of capital stock can then be generalised as follows:

$$K_{it} = (1 - \delta_i)K_{i,t-1} + I_{i,t-1}. \tag{2.3}$$

The PIM approach is more precise than relying on book value, but it raises some issues:

- It requires a measure of the initial capital stock.
- Depreciation rates are usually not available at the firm level and are replaced with industry-aggregated ones, introducing a further degree of approximation.

More importantly, both the PIM and the book value lead to measures of the capital stock that are defined, once again, in nominal terms. So, once more, we need to eliminate the *price effect*. This means that capital stock measures have to be adjusted by using appropriate deflators. These are generally not available at the firm level. Worse, it is not obvious which industry-aggregated deflator to employ, because it is not clear what the "unitary" price of capital is. This may create important biases in the measure of capital productivity. We deal with these in more detail in Section 3.2.

Another common issue in capital measurement concerns *intangible* assets. The term "intangible" capital generally includes computerised information (software, databases), innovative property (research and development (R&D) expenses, designs) and economic competencies (training, market research, branding). Most of these assets are not accounted for in standard accounting conventions, not least because measuring them is arduous.

Nonetheless, rapid technological development and the rise of the digital economy since the mid-1990s suggest an increased role of intangible assets as drivers of productivity. Even before the financial crisis hit in 2008, both in the US and in Europe, investment in this kind of capital had already overtaken investment in traditional assets such as plants and machinery. Some authors refer to "capitalism without capital" (Haskel and Westlake, 2018), meaning that intangible-rich economies may have started to behave differently from tangible-rich ones.

This is mostly due to four characteristics of intangible capital: scalability, sunkenness, spillovers and synergies:

- Scalability means that intangible assets can be used repeatedly and in multiple places at the same time, unlike tangible assets.
- Sunkenness has to do with irrevocable costs: investment in intangible capital is hard to recover, and thus it is ex ante harder to finance, as its possible use as collateral is limited.
- Spillovers mean that intangible investment can be used by others.
- Synergies may occur between an intangible investment and other investments, or between intangibles and human capital.

Retrieving information on the intangible assets of a firm level from balance-sheet data is hard to do, although measures of intangibles have been constructed at the macro level for a number of countries.[7]

---

[7] At the micro level, see the discussion in Covarrubias et al. (2019). At the macro level, see Corrado et al. (2018), who use a newly revised and updated release

In the remainder of this book, we will repeatedly encounter the rising importance of intangibles in the productivity debate, especially when analysing the link between productivity and market power in Chapter 9.

2.3 Production Function and Total Factor Productivity

In 1957, at the beginning of the academic debate on productivity, Robert Solow introduced a pioneering concept in the work that three decades later would earn him a Nobel Prize: the concept of technical change. He pointed out that, keeping constant labour and capital accumulation as inputs, any increase in output can derive only from a shift in the way firms produce.

Let's first introduce the concept of the *production function*, which expresses the relation between inputs and output. More specifically, it measures how a firm transforms the bundle of inputs at its disposal into final products to be sold on the market. A generic production function will have the following expression:

$$Y = A * f(X). \tag{2.4}$$

We have two elements determining a firm's output. The term $f(X)$ represents a generic function $f(\cdot)$ of the vector of inputs, X. We will discuss it at more length in Chapter 3. The term A includes all technological changes occurred over time. Mathematically, the term acts as a multiplier of the value of inputs transformed into output. Hence, if $A = 1$, a given combination of inputs X produces a given output Y_1; but if $A > 1$, the *same amount* of inputs X could be associated to an output $Y_2 > Y_1$, due to technical change.

This A is known as **multi-factor productivity** or **total factor productivity (TFP)**. It is an index of a firm's efficiency in producing output with a given set of inputs. A firm with higher A than its competitor would be able to produce more with the same inputs, or the same with fewer inputs. In both cases, we say that the firm had a higher TFP than its rival.

The problem for the policymaker is that we cannot observe this TFP directly. It has to be estimated using information on the firm's

of the INTAN-Invest dataset for the market sector for 18 European countries and the US to analyse the diffusion of intangible investment within countries.

production structure: its output and inputs. Also, there is no common definition of TFP. It would not be obvious what TFP is in our firm, because many factors could be responsible for the "boosting" effect on output (the firm might have superior technology, more skilled managers, higher intensity of R&D or many other advantages). As a result, TFP is sometimes referred to as "a measure of our ignorance"(Hulten, 2001).

Hence, the standard procedure for measuring TFP consists of computing the "Solow residual" of the production function. This is the difference between a firm's actual output and its *predicted* output: that is, the average output that we would predict given the amount of inputs the firm was using. TFP estimation involves a number of critical steps, and we will explore those in detail in Chapter 3.

2.4 Productivity and Growth Accounting

Productivity has become quite a popular notion in the economic policy debate in recent decades as it was widely acknowledged that its rate of growth is one of the major drivers of overall economic performance.

We can use *growth accounting*, that is, the breakdown of economic growth into specific factors, to estimate the magnitude of productivity's contribution. In its simplest form, we can write output Y as the quantity of labour employed L times the average labour productivity Y/L, measured as the output produced by one unit of labour.

At the macro level, output Y is proxied by national income or GDP, while the quantity of labour employed L is measured by the total number of hours worked in an economy, a figure available in national statistics. We can then write the identity:

$$Y = L * \frac{Y}{L}. \tag{2.5}$$

In this basic framework, growth is given by the first-order derivative (with respect to time) of national income Y. It can therefore be written as the sum of two components: the **growth of employment**, times the average productivity of the labour force, plus the **change in labour productivity**, times labour employed. Formally:

$$\frac{dY}{dt} = \frac{dL}{dt} * \frac{Y}{L} + \frac{d\left(\frac{Y}{L}\right)}{dt} * L, \tag{2.6}$$

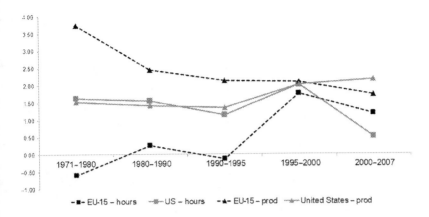

Figure 2.1 Employment and productivity growth in EU-15 vs US: 1970–2007.
Source: Adapted from Sapir et al. (2004). Data sourced from the Organisation for Economic Co-operation and Development (OECD) productivity database

where the term $\frac{dL}{dt}$ represents the change in the total number of hours worked, and the term $\frac{d\left(\frac{Y}{L}\right)}{dt}$ is the change in output per hour worked: that is, the change in labour productivity.

In the simple framework in Equation 2.6, income growth arises from the combination of growth in the quantity of labour and (labour) productivity growth. Figure 2.1 decomposes economic growth in these two terms and looks at how they have evolved over time in two key markets, the US and the European Union (in this case, the EU-15) from the 1970s to just before the Global Financial Crisis (GFC) of 2008–2009.

The figure shows that in the 1970s, both the EU-15 and the US had a similar growth rate of around 3% per year. However, while the US growth rates derived equally from productivity and labour growth (around 1.5% each), the growth of the EU stemmed entirely from productivity growth (3.5%), as a result of a process of technological catch-up and increasing integration. In fact, rigid institutions made a negative contribution (−0.5%) of labour inputs to growth rates in the EU.

The situation started to improve after the mid-1990s, when most European countries implemented structural reforms leading to an increase of the labour contribution to growth. At the same time, however, productivity growth in Europe started to slow down, off-setting the gains achieved through labour market reforms.

If we look at the term $\frac{dL}{dt}$ – the change in the total number of hours worked – in greater detail, we can better understand how the different components of growth have shaped the relative economic well-being of EU and US citizens, and the role played by structural reforms. The number of hours worked in an economy is a function of the employment rate (how many people participate in the labour market as a share of the working age population) and the number of working hours per person employed (how working hours are regulated in the economy). Rearranging these terms, we find that gross domestic product (GDP) per capita (output divided by population) can be decomposed as a function of the employment rate, the total number of hours worked by each individual and labour productivity.

Table 2.1 displays a cross-country comparison of GDP per capita, productivity and other labour market measures in 1970 and 2000, again for the US and the EU-15. All US values are normalised to 100.

The table shows that over this period the EU has experienced a constant gap in GDP per capita compared to the US, with the European average stuck at 70–75% of the US figure. The drivers of this gap change over time. In the 1970s, nearly all the difference in GDP levels in the US and Europe could be accounted for by differences in productivity. Afterwards, productivity in Europe grew more than in the US (see Figure 2.1). At the same time, however, the total number of hours worked in Europe started to decrease. This was due to both a reduction in the number of hours worked by each individual and in employment rates across Europe. These trends were caused by increasingly rigid labour market institutions that limited the number of hours worked; and generous pension systems that limited the employment rate, especially among those aged between 55 and 65.

Therefore, from the 1970s and during the 1980s the gap between European and US GDP per capita remained constant as higher productivity gains in Europe were undercut by labour market failures. The labour market alone explains the gap between Europe and the US until at least the beginning of the 1990s.

Since the mid-1990s, several European countries implemented reforms which managed to fix the poor dynamics of their labour markets. As a result, the employment rate started to increase

Table 2.1. *Productivity vs labour gap across countries – 1970–2000 (USA = 100).*

	GDP/head population		GDP/working hours		Working hours per person employed		Employment/ working age population		Working age population/ population	
	1970	2000	1970	2000	1970	2000	1970	2000	1970	2000
Austria	65.2	79.3	53.7	95.7	101.6	80.8	120.3	97.4	99.4	105.2
Belgium	68.3	75.3	66.2	113.7	107.5	82.7	94.2	78.7	101.8	101.8
Denmark	84.6	83.9	77.2	95.5	87.3	82.0	120.6	103.4	104.1	103.6
Finland	61.6	73.2	52.9	91.9	93.8	87.1	115.9	87.9	107.0	104.0
France	73.2	70.7	73.2	105.2	99.4	82.0	102.2	83.5	98.4	98.2
Germany	78.7	74.2	70.8	93.4	100.9	81.6	107.2	92.2	102.8	105.5
Greece	42.8	47.6	42.9	60.3	112.4	103.5	85.9	72.9	103.5	104.7
Ireland	41.9	81.7	39.2	97.7	116.2	90.5	98.9	88.8	93.1	104.1
Italy	65.0	73.5	74.7	104.0	97.9	87.0	85.2	77.5	104.2	104.8
Netherlands	76.3	79.4	74.8	104.9	93.5	71.7	108.0	100.1	101.1	105.3
Portugal	34.7	51.6	24.8	54.1	107.7	93.5	130.3	94.9	99.8	107.4
Spain	49.8	57.5	47.1	73.2	105.8	97.1	98.9	76.2	101.1	106.2
Sweden	83.8	71.0	76.4	83.1	89.5	86.4	115.9	99.2	105.7	99.8
United Kingdom	70.8	70.2	58.7	80.3	103.5	88.0	114.8	97.9	101.5	101.5
EU-15	69.0	70.3	64.8	90.7	101.0	85.6	103.6	87.6	101.7	103.4
USA	100	100	100	100	100	100	100	100	100	100

Source: Sapir et al. (2004).

again across Europe, while the individual number of hours worked decreased only slightly. On balance, the total number of hours worked increased. Labour market dynamics in the EU remained positive, at least until the Global Financial Crisis; but the overall income gap between the EU and US did not close, because at this time productivity growth was slower in Europe than in the US.

During the GFC of 2008–2009, the EU and US also experienced different dynamics of adjustment, as shown in Figure 2.2. It decomposes growth in the EU and US for every year since 1995.

The negative growth shock of 2008–2009 translated into a large negative productivity shock for the EU (left panel), while the US adjusted much more through a reduction in their labour input (right panel). This is typical of more flexible labour market institutions in the US, which allowed firms to absorb demand shocks by laying off workers. This kept labour productivity (that is, value added per worker) relatively high in the short term. On the contrary, relatively

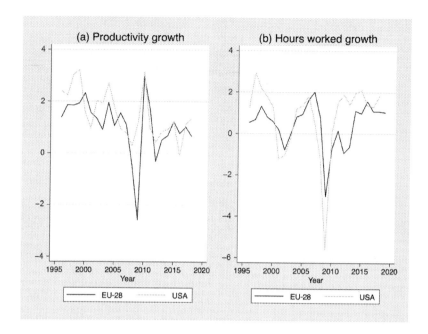

Figure 2.2 Employment and productivity growth in EU-15 vs US: 1995–2019.
Source: OECD productivity database

rigid labour markets in the EU prevented a severe downward adjustment in the labour force. The demand shock translated instead into negative productivity growth rates.

After the shock, both the EU and the US were ultimately able to resume similar levels of labour input and productivity growth, although the double dip in economic activity in Europe caused by the 2010–2012 debt crisis prevented employment growth adjusting as swiftly as in the US, as shown in the panel on the right.

Both the EU and the US exited from the GFC with significantly lower rates of labour productivity growth (left panel), a phenomenon often referred to as "secular stagnation" (for example, in Midrigan et al., 2016).

We can further disentangle our growth accounting framework by using a more complex production function with multiple production factors. In this context, production is a function of capital K, labour L, intermediate inputs M and technological change or TFP A. This results in a production function of the form $Y = f(K, L, M, A)$

Under the assumptions of Hicks-neutral technological change – competitive factor markets in which each factor is priced at its marginal cost – full input utilisation and constant returns to scale, the growth of output can be represented as the cost-share weighted growth of inputs and technological progress. Considering a log-linear form of the previous production function, and taking its change over time yields:

$$\Delta ln Y_t = \phi_t^K \Delta ln K_t + \phi_t^L \Delta ln L_t + \phi_t^M \Delta ln M_t + \Delta ln A_t, \qquad (2.7)$$

where $\phi_{it}^K = \frac{P_{it}^K K_{it}}{P_{it}^Y Y_{it}}, \phi_{it}^L = \frac{P_{it}^L L_{it}}{P_{it}^Y Y_{it}}, \phi_{it}^M = \frac{P_{it}^M M_{it}}{P_{it}^Y Y_{it}}$ represent the average share of input i in real output.

The terms in Equation 2.7 represent the contribution to output growth by the growth in capital, labour, intermediate inputs and technological change, respectively. In this framework, the share of production growth accounted for by capital and intermediate inputs is given by the product of its share in total costs and growth rate. As before, the contribution of labour can be partitioned into changes in hours worked and changes in the composition of labour. Any residual output growth is finally accounted for by the TFP term A, which therefore represents changes in unmeasured – for example, intangible – inputs.

Figure 2.3 illustrates graphically the results of this output decomposition between 2000 and 2014. It uses averages for these years in a number of EU countries, and distinguishes the contribution of capital in ICT assets from non-ICT assets. There is clearly cross-country variation: average yearly growth rates range from 2% in Austria to −1% in Italy. This period includes the Global Financial Crisis and the subsequent EU debt crisis. The reduction of hours worked reduced value-added growth in all countries. The impact of TFP growth is instead positive in all countries except Italy.

In Altomonte et al. (2017), a similar decomposition, but instead distinguishing the years before and after the crisis, shows that the post-crisis period in Europe has been characterised by a general slowdown in the average growth rate. In most countries, this was driven by a collapse in the contribution of TFP and a decrease of non-ICT capital deepening, in turn a direct consequence of the fall in corporate investment.

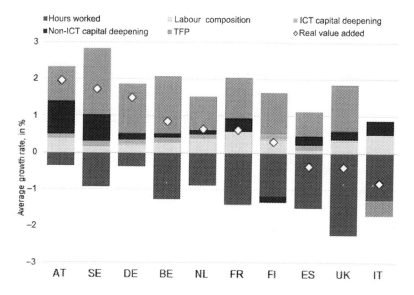

Figure 2.3 Growth accounting decomposition, selected EU countries, 2000–2014 averages.

Source: Reproduced from Altomonte et al. (2017)

In Finland, Spain and Italy, the depressive effects of the crisis were deeper, leading to a remarkable reduction of hours worked caused by job dismissal and firm closure. This further worsened the situation.

2.5 Firm Heterogeneity and TFP

All the evidence on growth accounting that we have used so far relies on aggregate indicators, such as GDP, employment rate, total number of hours worked or gross fixed capital formation. However, as already pointed out in the Introduction, the economic literature in the last decade has made it very clear that, because of granularity, any analysis trying to assess the drivers of economic growth at the level of country, industry or region should also make use of indicators derived from the aggregation of firm-level information.

Luckily, nowadays we can avail ourselves of a number of firm-level datasets which we will examine in Chapter 5.

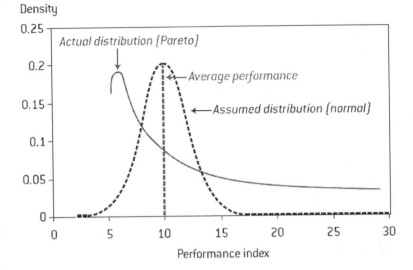

Figure 2.4 Firm heterogeneity.

Source: Reproduced from Altomonte et al. (2011b)

Firm-level analysis of productivity, however, needs to acknowledge two facts.

First, we have to familiarise ourselves with the idea that beyond the aggregate variables that we normally use in our macro-analyses, there is no "representative" or "average" firm, but rather a statistical distribution of **heterogeneous firms**.

Second, we also need to consider the *shape* of the statistical distribution of firm-level features. For example, consider the distribution of a variable such as productivity across firms. There is plenty of evidence in the economic literature (Bernard et al., 2011a, or Mayer and Ottaviano, 2007, for example) that many measures are asymmetrically distributed, with a relatively dense initial part of the distribution and a thin right tail (Figure 2.4).[8]

---

[8] These distributions are in general known as power distributions, with the class of Pareto distributions being the most commonly used.

The figure shows that firm performance in a sector or region is not centered around an *average* performance level with bad and good firms distributed left and right of the mean in equal numbers. In reality, there are many relatively bad firms, plus a few good firms at the right-hand tail of the distribution – the firms known as the *happy few* (Mayer and Ottaviano, 2007).

This heterogeneity has important implications for the accuracy with which we are able to assess the drivers of economic growth. In general, performance indicators issued by statistical offices start with firm-level observations, but are are derived as averages. Compare the two distributions in Figure 2.4. The same mean average can represent wildly different distributions in the underlying population.

So an aggregate performance measure calculated as an unweighted mean of the individual firm's distribution would be upward biased, as the median of the actual distribution (that is, where 50% of firms are) would be lower. This is typical of power (or Pareto) distributions. Using this type of calculation to estimate the underlying competitive position of an entire industry or country would be misleading. This makes a case that we should always use aggregation functions that correctly weight individual observations based on their actual representativeness in the sample when deriving aggregate statistics, or, at least, for using median rather than average values when discussing aggregate indicators for policy making.

And if different industries or countries also have different underlying distributions of the measured performance, aggregation without weighting across industries (to retrieve country averages) or countries (to retrieve EU-wide averages) may introduce a further bias.

So let's bring the concept of firm heterogeneity into our measure of aggregate productivity A. To do that, we need a firm-level production function of the following form:

$$Y_i = A_i * f(X_i), \tag{2.8}$$

where i represents each firm in the population.

Once we have obtained the relevant firm-level indicator of productivity A_i as the residual of the production function, we need to aggregate it to provide an useful representation of a specific industry or country. To that extent, we can use a firm's output or input shares $0 \leq s \leq 1$ in a country or industry S to compute weighted averages. Aggregate productivity will be the weighted average of all firms belonging to that set S:

$$A = \sum_{i \in S} s_i * A_i. \tag{2.9}$$

If we derive aggregate productivity as the weighted sum of individual firm productivity, aggregate productivity trivially increases if the productivity of all firms increases. But it also increases if proper weight is given to more productive firms (the same reasoning applies to economic growth). In other words, productivity is related to the efficiency of the *allocation* of economic activities across agents. We explore this important insight later, starting with some technical detail in Chapter 4.

We can also link this to the effectiveness of policy in enhancing competitiveness. Research has shown that firms react very differently to shocks depending on their specific characteristics – notably size, industrial organisation, technology and research content, market conditions, entry and exit barriers in their sector and trade frictions.

Policies should aim to catalyse the dynamic transition of more-productive firms rather than just working on the *average* performance of the sector. A successful policy for competitiveness would generate a *thicker* right-hand tail of the distribution.

Policies aimed at fostering the internal growth of firms via more efficient product and factor markets (cross-firm competition and agglomeration, removal of financial constraints and better access to capital, wage-setting mechanisms more in line with individual firms' productivity) help to reallocate resources towards better-performing firms, increasing the aggregate level of competitiveness. Policies designed to support weaker firms may result in barriers to growth and even more thickening of the left-hand tail of the performance distribution.

2.6 Other Firm-Level Performance Measures

Given an adequately representative dataset based on individual firm balance sheets, using income statements or profit-and-loss statements we can construct other aggregate figures traditionally used in economic analysis – but now with the additional benefit of the information contained in their underlying distributions. For reference, Box 2.1 summarises the typical framework of a firm's balance sheet. In the reminder of this chapter we analyze some of the other firm-level performance measures.

Imports and Exports

Information on the current account, or net exports, is a typical component of macro-indicators. It is not straightforward to extract the same information at a disaggregated level from balance sheet data. Accounting standards do not oblige firms to distinguish domestic sales from exports, or imported intermediates from those they source locally. If we want to work with disaggregated trade data, it is necessary to merge firm-level information with customs data on individual transactions: each trade transaction is associated to a value-added tax (VAT) code in that country, which maps to a legal entity.

Aggregating all the trade transactions for each legal entity, and then merging balance sheet data associated to that legal entity (if, of course, the legal entity is required to produce a balance sheet), produces a dataset in which it is possible, for example, to associate the trade exposure of a given firm (volume of exports, number of countries exported to, average export size per country) to its characteristics (size, productivity and so on).

If we manage to do this, the reward is that we can link the standard analysis of gains from trade to firm-level data and firm behaviour, something that, starting from the work of Melitz (2003), forms the foundation of modern international trade theory. Thanks to the increasing availability of data on the international transactions of firms, it is also possible to analyse in detail the emerging role of global value chains (GVCs) in the international economy. We explore trade and the link to firm performance in Chapter 8.

Access to Finance

Financial measures are another important class of macro-indicators that can be used to analyse the growth performance of countries. Firm-level data can be retrieved easily from balance sheets: bank loans, for example, or liquidity or debt ratios.

Besides the financial information directly available in a firm's balance sheet, another important indicator is the degree of accessibility to credit markets. A firm is *financially constrained* when it has in principle the ability to use funds productively but cannot get access to external financing from the formal financial system. As a result, due to restricted access to credit, there will a suboptimal allocation of capital and missed growth opportunities.

Much research has focused on accessibility to financial markets and its impact. Numerous studies estimate the extent to which reliance on internal financing affects firm performance as measured by investment, exporting, inventory management or firm growth.[9]

Researchers have developed measures of finance constraints using information retrievable from balance sheets, such as net worth, liquidity, interest and coverage. The data are typically used to proxy for a firm's financial health in a structural model of performance outcomes, and thus used as proxies of the likelihood of obtaining access to external finance.[10] Finance constraints have also been assessed by linking firm growth to the differential cost of capital between external financing sources.[11]

More recently, some datasets merge information from bank credit registries, in which all credit transactions between firms and banks are recorded, with firm balance sheets. This is a precise measure of credit constraint, as these datasets typically record whether a firm has asked for credit, and whether it was successful. The aggregation process is similar to the way in which statistical agencies measure imports and exports. The confidentiality of credit data is typically higher, though, and so the firm-level data in type of information are usually less accessible. One example of such project is the Analytical Credit Datasets (Anacredit), developed within the ECB (Israel et al., 2017), that provides detailed harmonised (across countries) information on individual bank loans in the euro area.

---

[9] Examples are Fazzari et al. (1988), Hubbard (1998), Love (2003) and Bond and Soderbom (2013). Reviews of this literature include Chirinko (1993) and Guariglia (2008).

[10] Contributions in this literature are Whited (1992), Bond and Meghir (1994), Kaplan and Zingales (1997), Bond et al. (2003), Whited and Wu (2006), Hadlock and Pierce (2010) and Mulier et al. (2016).

[11] Examples are Kashyap et al. (1993), Huang (2003), Bougheas et al. (2006), Guariglia and Mateut (2010) and O'Toole et al. (2014).

Since detailed firm surveys have recently become available, one effective method to measure financing constraints is to use information on firm perceptions of access to finance as an obstacle to growth and expansion (perceived financing constraints) and responses on credit applications and rejections (actual financing constraints).[12] All these financial dimensions of firm-level data, and their implication for firms' performance, are explored in detail in Chapter 6.

Markup

Market efficiency and the extent of competition are also key indicators of aggregate performance. Typically we estimate these through indicators of firm concentration in market shares. That means that any indicator of this type must use some information at the firm-level.

Representative datasets with balance sheet information mean that it is possible to measure the *markup* of individual firms, defined as the percentage difference between the output price set by the firm and the marginal costs that it bears. If a firm sells an additional unit of output at 120, and it costs 100 to make that same additional unit, then the markup would be $(120 - 100)/100 = 20\%$.

Another way to express markup is by indicating the amount by which the cost of a product has to be increased to match the selling price. The previous example would have a markup of 1.2.

Markups are used as a proxy of a firm's market power. In Economics 101, we learn that the two extreme scenarios of competition in the market are perfect competition and monopoly. In the first case, every firm has virtually no market power, and in this case price equals marginal cost, so markups are zero. A monopolistic firm can set prices above costs and so influence the market directly and autonomously.

The simplest indicator of a firm's markup is the Lerner Index. Initially proposed in Lerner (1934), the index – also referred to as markup ratio – measures the difference between firm's price and marginal costs (MC) over price, that is, $(P - MC)/P$.

Unfortunately though, neither the individual P nor the associated MC is retrievable from balance sheets. Research proxies them with variable costs:

$$L_i = \frac{sales_i - varcost_i}{sales_i} = \frac{(p * q)_i - (c * q)_i}{(p * q)_i} = \frac{(p_i - c_i)}{p_i}, \quad (2.10)$$

---

[12] Examples are Beck et al. (2006), Byiers et al. (2010), Ferrando and Griesshaber (2011) and Clarke et al. (2012).

where p_i and c_i are firm i's (approximated) price and marginal costs, respectively, and *varcost* are a firm's variable costs measured as cost of employees plus costs for materials. Chapter 4 provides an extensive overview of more complex indicators of market efficiency and their limitations as well as some examples of empirical applications. Chapter 9 looks in detail at the issue of market power.

Box 2.1   Balance Sheet and Income Statement

Firm-level data have two main sources: accounting books and surveys. While surveys do not have a standard format and can be subject to severe customisation, accounting books follow strict guidelines. Here is a brief overview of what balance sheets and income statements are and how to use them.

A *balance sheet* (also known as a statement of financial position) is a formal document that follows a standard accounting format showing the same categories of assets and liabilities regardless of the size or nature of the business. It summarises the financial position of an enterprise at a given moment, providing a financial snapshot of the firm. It is the main source of firm-level data used by economists. Unlike surveys, balance sheets are homogenised over time and across firms, and strict legal rules guarantee data reliability.

The balance sheet reflects the status of enterprise's assets (the economic resources owned by the enterprise), liabilities (debts owned to creditors) and equity (the owner's investment in the enterprise). The elements included are *balanced* following this identity:

$$Assets = Liabilities + Equity$$

This fundamental identity must always exist, because the assets represent what the enterprise owns, while liabilities and equity indicate how much was supplied by both creditors and owners.

In contrast to the balance sheet, an *income statement* (also known as a profit loos (PL) oss account) shows the enterprise's financial progress over a given period of time. Elements included in an income statement also follow a fundamental identity:

$$Revenues - Expenses = Profit\ (or\ Loss)$$

Revenues are the resources, primarily cash, coming into the enterprise as a result of selling products or rendering services. Expenses, on the other side, are the resources used by the enterprise to produce goods or services. The rationale is very intuitive: if revenues are greater than expenses, the business realises profits; if expenses exceed revenue, the business realises a loss from operations.

Table 2.2. *Example of a balance sheet.*

Assets		Liabilities	
Current assets:		Current liabilities:	
Cash	59,770	Notes payable	48,563
Marketable securities	87,466	Trade accounts payable	207,887
Accounts receivable	559,144	Payrolls	411,362
Inventory	618,120	Income taxes	124,684
Prepaid expenses	49,986	Total current liabilities	792,496
Total current assets	**1,374,486**	Long-term liabilities	431,350
Fixed assets:		**Total liabilities**	**1,223,846**
Land	25,807		
Buildings	716,076		
Machinery and equipment	1,010,770	**Shareholders' equity**	**1,103,190**
Less allowances for depreciation	800,103		
Total fixed assets	**952,550**		
Total assets	**2,327,036**	**Total liabilities and equity**	**2,327,036**

In Tables 2.2 and 2.3 we provide two examples of balance sheet and income statement to show how they look in practice. Please note that this information does not reflect any real firm.

On the Assets side, we can distinguish the following:

- *Cash*.
- *Marketable securities*: Temporary investments (generally 90 days) of excess or idle cash; listed at cost or market value since they are converted into cash within one year.
- *Accounts receivable*: Money owned to the company by debtors, generally for the purchase of goods and services.
- *Inventory*: The value of products that have been completed and are in storage waiting to be sold (finished goods), products that have been partially completed (work in process) and raw materials.
- *Prepaid expenses*: The value of items that the company has paid for in advance, such as insurance premiums.

Table 2.3. *Example of an income statement*

Revenues

Net sales	3,787,248	
Other income	42,579	
Total revenues		**3,829,827**

Expenses

Cost of goods sold	2,796,459	
Administrative and selling expenses	637,509	
Interest expenses	47,516	
Other expenses	0	
Total expenses		**3,503,545**
Earnings before income taxes		326,282
Income taxes		152,039
Net earnings		**174,243**

- *Fixed assets*: Tangible elements that will provide benefits to the company for one or more years. Fixed assets consist of three categories: land, buildings, machinery and equipment. They are reported on the balance sheet at purchasing cost and adjusted for yearly depreciation accumulated. The latter is the estimated decline in the useful value of an asset due to gradual wear and tear.

On the Liabilities side, we can distinguish the following:

- *Notes payable*: Money owed to banks or other lending institutions; generally short-term loans (up to one year) used to finance short-term needs.
- *Trade accounts payable*: Money owed to vendors for the purchase of goods and services.
- *Payrolls*: Money that institutions owe to people who have performed services, including salaries owed to employees, holidays remuneration, attorney fees, insurance premiums and pension funds.
- *Income taxes*: Money owed to the Tax Department; may sometimes be deferred and paid later but must always be paid.
- *Long-term liabilities*: Obligations, usually loans, that are due to be paid not in the current year but in some future period. The amount specified in the balance sheet is equal to the total amount borrowed.

The final major section, shareholders' equity, summarises the owners' investment in the business. Individuals and institutions become owners of a company by purchasing shares of the company's stock. Equity increases as more people purchase stock and the company retains increased profit.

On the Revenues side, we distinguish the following:

- *Net sales*: All sources earned by the company from the sale of its products and services.
- *Other income*: Generally resources from such sources as interest on bank accounts, cash dividends from investments in other firms and interest on bonds.

Within Expenses, we find the following:

- *Cost of goods sold*: All expenses incurred while making the products sold during the period, including the cost of materials, labour and factory overhead (rent, utilities and maintenance).
- *Administrative and selling expenses*: The costs of running and promoting the business, including items such as wages, advertising costs and sales commissions.
- *Interest expenses*: The interests paid by the company during the year on money that it borrowed.
- *Other expenses*: This would include any other unusual expenses incurred by the company to run the business not otherwise accounted for the preceding tables (for example, research and development expenses and organizational costs).

Box 2.2   Benchmarking New Zealand's Frontier Firms

New Zealand's productivity growth has been stagnant for 20 years. This is puzzling: New Zealand is considered to have strong policy fundamentals. To better assess the drivers behind this phenomenon, we focus on the empirical analysis of performance of New Zealand firms relative to comparable small, advanced economies (SAE) in the EU.

New Zealand's average labour productivity levels in the sample period suggest a relative productivity of 53% of the SAE average (Figure 2.5). Despite being half as productive as the EU sample, New Zealand's firms showed no sign of catching up. The labour productivity growth rate was broadly similar to the average comparable rate for the other SAEs (0.51% per annum compared to 0.49% per annum).

So, we examine firm tiers (Figure 2.6). New Zealand's laggard firms show gradual improvements in relative productivity, from 52% in 2003 to 65% in 2016. This upward trend was mainly driven by large

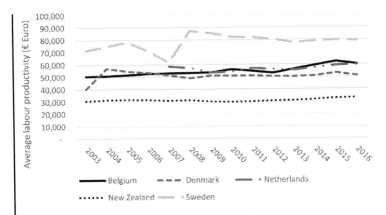

Figure 2.5 Average labour productivity levels across SAEs.
Source: Adapted from Zheng et al. (2021)

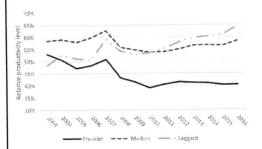

Figure 2.6 Relative labour productivity, by laggard, median and frontier firms.
Source: Adapted from Zheng et al. (2021)

productivity declines in SAEs: −1.1% per annum on average compared to an increase of 0.6% per annum in New Zealand. The performance of New Zealand's median firms remained stable relative to the corresponding labour productivity levels across the SAEs – averaging 54.6%. The productivity of New Zealand's national frontier steadily declined relative to that of frontier firms in SAEs, from 51.5% in 2003 to 43.5% in 2016. This relative drop reflected slower average productivity growth among New Zealand frontier firms, 0.4% per annum compared to 1.7% per annum in SAEs.

The productivity slowdown in many OECD countries, including New Zealand, has been attributed in part to a slowdown in the pace of

Figure 2.7 A simplified framework of technology diffusion.
Source: Adapted from OECD (2015)

frontier technology diffusion (Figure 2.7), leading to a widening
productivity gap between non-frontier firms and global frontier firms[13]
(OECD, 2015).

To quantify the cross-country and within-country technology
diffusion processes, we can regress the change in annual labour
productivity of firms that are not at the SAE frontier against two
factors:

- The lagged productivity gap between the SAE frontier and national
  frontier
- The lagged productivity gap within a country between frontier and
  non-frontier firms

These factors are used as proxy measures of the effects for
cross-country and within-country technology diffusion, respectively.

Table 2.4 shows the results of our model. In all specifications, the
estimated within-country diffusion is greater than the estimated
cross-country diffusion. For example, based on the results in the first
column for the full sample, a 1% increase in the gap between the SAE
frontier and the national frontier is associated with 0.047% labour
productivity growth for non-frontier firms in the following year. The
corresponding estimate for within-country diffusion is a 0.175%
increase in labour productivity growth for non-frontier firms. These
results suggest that the diffusion process is expensive and difficult to
transmit over distance. Many international frontier technologies are
tacit, non-codified and not available to all firms.

New Zealand and the SAE countries have similar speeds of
technology diffusion within the country. But for cross-country
diffusion, New Zealand has a statistically insignificant coefficient.
We might expect this, given New Zealand's location.

[13] Global frontier firms are the globally most productive firms in advanced
economies. Specifically, these frontier firms are the 100 most globally
productive firms in terms of multi-factor productivity in each industry
(OECD, 2015).

Table 2.4. *Regression estimates on technology diffusion models.*

Variables	All	New Zealand	Other SAE
$\beta 1$: Cross-country diffusion	0.047*** (0.007)	0.000 (0.007)	0.062*** (0.008)
$\beta 2$: Within-country diffusion	0.175*** (0.019)	0.233*** (0.053)	0.168*** (0.020)
Observations	3004	583	2421
R squared	0.725	0.622	0.729
ρ	−0.165	−0.182	−0.182

Adapted from Zheng et al. (2021).

3 | *Productivity Estimation*

In Chapter 2, we introduced the basic concept of productivity and the difference between factor (labour or capital) productivity and total factor productivity (TFP).

In this chapter, we will discuss in detail the theory behind the measurement of TFP and the problems caused by the way we specify the production function. We will also analyse the most common econometric techniques for estimating productivity.[1]

As we have seen, TFP is generally estimated as a residual – the difference between a firm's actual output Y_t and its *predicted* output, $\hat{Y}_t$. This requires a two-step procedure: first, we predict the value of output based on information on a firm's use of inputs, a theoretical framework explaining how the inputs are combined, and a consistent empirical estimation that measures this combination. Then we take the difference between the (correctly estimated) predicted output and the actual (observed) output. This residual will explain which part of the actual output we are not able to explain by looking at the way that firms have used inputs. This is our definition of total factor productivity.

3.1 Specifying the Production Function

We start by specifying a production function: a functional relationship between a firm's output on the left-hand side, and the set of inputs it uses on the right-hand side. When we do this, we set up the theoretical framework needed to analyse a firm's decisions and dynamics. For simplicity and clarity, we will use a standard Cobb–Douglas (CD) production function as a basis for our discussion.[2]

---

[1] For a comprehensive review of this topic, see Van Beveren (2012).
[2] The CD production function is a very simple functional form that has been used for several decades to represent the process of producing output. We are

A CD production function can be expressed as

$$Y_{it} = A_{it} K_{it}^{\beta_k} L_{it}^{\beta_l} M_{it}^{\beta_m}, \tag{3.1}$$

where Y_{it} is firm i's physical output in period t; K_{it}, L_{it} and M_{it} are the firm's inputs (capital, labour and materials), with their β factor productivities, respectively; and A_{it} is the efficiency level of firm i in period t.

According to this equation, A_{it} represents firm's productivity – the item we aim at estimating. Now consider the log-linear version of equation 3.1:

$$y_{it} = ln(A_{it}) + \beta_k k_{it} + \beta_l l_{it} + \beta_m m_{it}, \tag{3.2}$$

where the logarithm of A_{it} can be expressed as the sum of β_0, that is, the mean efficiency level across firms over time, an observable time- and firm-specific deviation from that mean, v_{it}, and an unobservable idiosyncratic component u_{it}^q. Our productivity measure $\omega_{it} = \beta_0 + v_{it}$ represents the observable part of A_{it}, whereas u_{it}^q is an independent and identically distributed (iid) random variable.

Therefore, substituting into Equation 3.2, we get the following:

$$y_{it} = \beta_k k_{it} + \beta_l l_{it} + \beta_m m_{it} + \omega_{it} + u_{it}^q. \tag{3.3}$$

To estimate TFP, we can start from the estimation of the input coefficients in Equation 3.3, which implies retrieving the (predicted) output elasticity $\hat{\beta}$ associated to each input (see Section 3.3 for more details); we can then use predicted output elasticities to evaluate predicted (log)output as $\hat{y}_{it} = \hat{\beta}_l l_{it} + \hat{\beta}_k k_{it} + \hat{\beta}_m m_{it}$; we calculate the predicted (log)TFP, $\hat{\omega}_{it}$, as the residual difference between actual and predicted (log)output:

$$\hat{\omega}_{it} = \hat{\beta}_0 + v_{it} = y_{it} - \hat{\beta}_k k_{it} - \hat{\beta}_l l_{it} - \hat{\beta}_m m_{it} - u_{it}^q \tag{3.4}$$

If the estimation procedure is unbiased, the residual difference between actual output and predicted output yields the term $\hat{\omega}_{it}$, our proxy of firm-level TFP, plus an iid error term u_{it}^q. The productivity

well aware that a CD does not perfectly reproduce the reality of the production process of individual firms. It nevertheless provides a very simple and clear framework to explain the theory of production functions, and it fits aggregate data (at the country or industry level) fairly well.

level that proxies our multiplicative index of technical change, $A_i t$, is the exponential of $\hat{\omega}_{it}$, in other words, $\hat{\Omega}_{it} = exp(\hat{\omega}_{it})$.

However, it might also be the case that some additional error component remains in the difference between actual and predicted output, on top of TFP and the iid term. This might create problems in the measurement of firm-level productivity, and so we will turn to that next.

3.2 Methodological Issues in Production Function Estimation

In order to estimate TFP at the firm level, we need to consult the balance sheet for information on the firm's output (sales, for example) and inputs (data such as number of employees, tangible assets to proxy capital or material costs). We deflate nominal variables – see the previous chapter for how to do this – meaning we could then pool firm-level information in a *panel* structure. This would include data on different firms observed repeatedly over time, as in Equation 3.3, and so we can use it to estimate factor productivities $\hat{\beta}$ across firms and time using appropriate estimators. From here it is possible to predict a firm's output, and then TFP as a residual with respect to actual output (Equation 3.4).

But methodological issues might arise, leading to incorrect estimates of $\hat{\beta}$ and, in turn, biased measures of TFP. So what problems might we encounter?

Simultaneity Bias

Equation 3.3 could be estimated in principle through a pooled ordinary least squares (OLS) estimator for panel data. In an OLS framework, however, all terms on the right-hand side of the equation – in this case, the firm's inputs and productivity – must be exogenous. In particular, productivity is a residual, and so it is technically a component of the regression error in the estimated production function, alongside the iid term. If there is correlation between an input (a regressor) and productivity (the regression error), this will leads to a bias in the estimated coefficient of the same input (the output elasticity $\hat{\beta}$).

Marschak and Andrews (1944) were the first to note that a firm's input choices are unlikely to be exogenous to its other (unobserved) characteristics: if a firm experiences a positive productivity shock, for example, then its managers are likely to increase inputs. This implies there is a positive correlation between inputs and unobserved productivity shocks, and that introduces an upward bias in the estimation of output elasticities $\hat{\beta}$ for those inputs that are freely adjustable (see De Loecker, 2007, for a detailed discussion). This problem is known as *simultaneity bias* in production function estimation. In Section 3.3, we discuss a number of techniques able to offset this bias.

Selection Bias

As first discussed by Wedervang (1965), the second major econometric issue when estimating production functions is *selection bias*. This distortion happens when we do not consider how firms enter and exit markets.[3] A firm's decision to operate or exit often depends on its productivity. But firm-level samples tend to be "balanced panels" – datasets in which, in each period, there are roughly the same number of firms. This biases productivity estimates upward, because they include only surviving (more efficient) firms. Productivity estimations should rely, whenever possible, on an "unbalanced panel", data representative also of the entry and exit dynamics of firms. At least in principle, we must also consider the probability of entry and exit decisions.[4]

Omitted Price Bias

In Section 2.2, we saw that we need real quantities rather than nominal values when we use firm-level information for economic analysis. So, if we want accurate productivity estimates, we need to extract prices from total revenues and input expenditures. Information on firm-level prices is rarely available, and so researchers are often forced to use average industry prices as deflators. On one hand, this is a good proxy for physical production, but on the other hand it generates a potential *omitted price bias*.

---

[3] Firm-level databases (especially commercial ones) often exclude firms that have stopped operating after a given number of years.

[4] An extensive description of this bias, and a first attempt to take it into account, can be found in Olley and Pakes (1996a).

The most straightforward bias is on output prices. A firm's total production (and thus its input use) is, of course, correlated with the final price that it can charge. If firm-specific prices are not the (average) industry price index used as deflator, we may have that some unobserved price component is correlated with input use. This ends up in the error term of the production function estimation, inducing a bias in the estimation of output elasticity $\hat{\beta}$, for the same reasons as for the simultaneity bias.

Formally, we can see how the production function changes by including nominal output deflated with an industry price index:

$$
\begin{aligned}
\tilde{r}_{it} &= y_{it} + p_{it} - \bar{p}_t \\
&= \beta_k k_{it} + \beta_l l_{it} + \beta_m m_{it} + \omega_{it} + u_{it}^q + (p_{it} - \bar{p}_t),
\end{aligned}
\tag{3.5}
$$

where $\tilde{r}_{it}$ is the deflated output, p_{it} is the firm-level specific price, and $\bar{p}_t$ is the (average) price index of the industry. Subtracting deflated output from predicted output in order to calculate TFP, as in Equation 3.4, instead yields in Equation 3.5 a residual which is "contaminated" with the price effect $(p_{it} - \bar{p}_t)$.

If input choices are correlated with firm-level prices, in other words, if $E(x_{it}(p_{it} - \bar{p}_t)) \neq 0$, where $x_{it} = (l_{it}, m_{it}, k_{it})$, then the estimates of $\hat{\beta}$ are going to be biased, with the sign of the bias depending on the correlation between the price charged by the firm and the chosen level of inputs as a function of the firm's output.[5] A similar reasoning applies for input prices.[6]

It is not easy to eliminate omitted price bias. For this reason, the literature has started to distinguish two measures of firm-level productivity (Foster et al., 2008): revenue productivity, *TFP-R*, is productivity estimated through the standard industry-specific deflators for which some price component remains in the error term; and physical productivity, *TFP-Q*, is productivity estimated through the use of a firm-specific price deflator. Physical productivity is a closer proxy to the true technical efficiency of the firm.

As discussed in De Loecker (2011), not controlling for unobserved prices is problematic when we are trying to create reliable point

---

[5] See De Loecker (2011) for a detailed discussion.

[6] For an extensive discussion on this topic, please refer to Klette and Griliches (1996), Foster et al. (2008), Katayama et al. (2009), De Loecker (2011) and De Loecker et al. (2016).

estimates for productivity. But, if the goal is to correlate a standard measure of TFP-R with other firm-level covariates, we don't need to worry about omitted price bias because this bias typically does not affect the sign of the correlation.[7]

Multiproduct Firms

Firms produce a range of different products but, when we retrieve information on firm revenues from balance sheets, we implicitly assume that all the firm's products are the same. If products differ in production technology or demand, this assumption may bias TFP estimations. For instance, each product might require a different combination of inputs, or might face a different demand.

The way in which prices of each product change over time might differ too, generating an omitted price bias at the product level. If we want to correctly account for multiproduct firms, we need production data for each product, and we cannot find that data in standard datasets. If these data became available, then we should do our analysis at the product level and aggregate our results for each firm.

If our goal was to link every unit of output to the inputs used to generate it, we would also need to find out the costs that are shared over the whole production system (the fixed cost component), and what costs refer to each single product. Such an exercise, however, presents strong limitations in terms of data availability and theoretical framework, although this is an area in which research is progressing. Specialised research such as Bernard et al. (2010, 2011b, 2014), De Loecker (2011), Smeets and Warzynski (2013) and Mayer et al. (2014) will provide more detail on this.

3.3 Estimation Strategies

The endogeneity of input choices (that is, the simultaneity bias) has inspired the creation of many refined methods beyond simple OLS for the estimation of TFP. Here we discuss and summarise those most commonly used.[8]

---

[7] For a more detailed discussion on this topic, please refer to De Loecker et al. (2016).

[8] For an introduction to the topic, see Van Biesebroeck (2007).

Fixed Effects

The most straightforward method to overcome simultaneity bias would be to adopt a fixed effects (FE) model, which involves including a set of dummy variables for each individual firm in the estimation. With a fixed intercept at the firm level, we can estimate the coefficient of interest by exploiting only the variation of the same firm over time, or the *within* variation. With FE, we avoid comparing the input–output relation of a firm that has received an unobserved productivity shock at time t with that of another firm that has not received it – we do not exploit the *between* variation for identification. This eliminates the source of the bias.

This approach, first proposed by Mundlak (1961) and Hoch (1962), has the drawback that we do not use a large part of the information in the data. FE exploits only the within-variation of firms over time, and in micro-datasets this tends to be much lower than the cross-sectional variation, as typically we observe thousands of firms for a short period. Often the number of available years is not even enough for proper identification, leading to weakly identified coefficients.[9]

Instrumental Variables

The idea behind the instrumental variables (IV) approach to TFP estimation is to find appropriate instruments to predict endogenous inputs. Such instruments must satisfy three conditions to be econometrically valid:

(1) They are correlated with the endogenous variables (k_{it}, l_{it} and m_{it} in our case).
(2) They cannot enter directly in the target equation, which is Equation 3.3.
(3) They cannot be correlated with the error term (in our case firm productivity: $\omega_{it} + u_{it}^q$).

---

[9] The latter, of course, does not imply that firm-FE cannot be used when dealing with TFP analyses. On the contrary, once reliable measures of TFP at the firm level are obtained (as described later), certain research questions (the effect of a trade shock on productivity would be one) often require exclusion of the unobserved compositional effect of given firms from the analysis, allowing the researcher to identify only the within-variation over time.

The theory of production suggests a natural choice as instruments for endogenous inputs: input prices.[10] Input prices directly influence input choices (1) and in principle do not enter into the production function (2). For similar reasons, output prices are a possible instrument. Note, however, that the non-correlation condition between input (output) prices and productivity requires, in principle, perfectly competitive input (output) markets (3), as the market power of the firm would result into deviations from equilibrium prices affecting productivity estimates ($\hat{\omega}_{it}$). Although this could technically be overcome by using appropriate estimation techniques (see in particular De Loecker, 2011, or Morlacco, 2019) for a detailed discussion), the IV approach has not been used much. Ackerberg et al. (2007) identify four possible explanations for this:

(1) Input prices are often not reported by firms. Labour costs, when available, are an average of all workers (see Section 2.2), and so provide poor information on the skills of the firms labour force.

(2) Inputs prices change too little over time to provide enough variance for a proper econometric estimation. Even if variations were providing enough information, we would need to make the assumption that this variation is exogenous, not a change in the firm's market power.

(3) Adopting an IV strategy would also imply that productivity evolves exogenously over time. In the strategy, we assume that ω_{it} is not influenced by input choices.

(4) Finally, using prices as instruments only addresses simultaneity bias and not selection bias. A firm's choice to exit the market is included in the model, and therefore there might still be a bias in input coefficients. For example, we might expect firms facing higher input prices to be more likely to exit.

For these reasons, the IV approach to TFP estimation using prices as instruments has not been widely used. Research has instead focused on the use of alternative instruments – some combination of lagged input choices which, under certain assumptions could be used to map directly productivity through a non-parametric functional form (typically approximated by a nth-order polynomial expansion).

---

[10] See Ackerberg et al. (2007) for more information.

This has generated a number of so-called *semi-parametric* techniques, in which the mapping of productivity through exogenous (lagged) inputs allows one to correctly identify (through a standard, parametric estimation) the coefficient of interest of the endogenous inputs. The remaining coefficient of the other inputs used to map productivity are instead identified non-parametrically. In what follows, we discuss the most common semi-parametric methods.

The Olley and Pakes (1996a) Approach

In 1996, Steven Olley and Ariel Pakes were the first to develop in an estimation algorithm ("OP" from now on) that explicitly takes into account the simultaneity and selection bias in TFP estimation. Although these issues were first discussed in the 1950s, theirs was the first attempt to deal with them when estimating production functions.

They built a dynamic model embedding firm behaviour which allowed both for firm-specific (idiosyncratic) sources of change and for entry and exit. Their estimation algorithm involves a two-stage procedure to correctly estimate productivity.[11] The OP method uses investment decisions to retrieve information on a firm's unobservable productivity.

The model envisages that, at the beginning of every period, the firm makes three decisions:

(1) Should it continue to operate or exit the market, with the owners receiving a sell-off value (ϕ)?
(2) How many employees should it hire?
(3) How much should it invest?

The OP algorithm requires two assumptions to achieve consistency:

(1) There is only one unobserved state variable, productivity, that determines firm behaviour and follows a Markov process.[12]

---

[11] In what follows, we will use a standard Cobb–Douglas productivity function, as in Equation 3.1, for consistency with the rest of the text. Olley and Pakes (1996a) assume a productivity function slightly different, including the age of a firm but not considering intermediate inputs. For more information, please refer to the original paper.

[12] That is $\omega_{it} = E(\omega_{it+1}|\omega_{it}) + \varepsilon_{it+1}$, where ε_{it+1} represents the innovation in the ω process which is unexpected by the firm. Moreover, it is assumed to be uncorrelated with capital in period $t + 1$.

(2) Conditional on the values of all the observed state variables, investments are increasing in productivity.

Labour is perfectly flexible and does not have any dynamic implications. Firm i chooses l_{it} in t without considering past labour dimensions.[13] Capital k_{it} is a dynamic input determined by the investment decision in $t - 1$. Capital accumulation is then given by the following:

$$k_{it+1} = (1 - \delta)k_{it} + i_{it}, \tag{3.6}$$

where δ is the annual depreciation rate of capital and i_t is the level of investment in t.

In the original paper, the authors show that investments are a function of current levels of productivity – known by the firm – and capital:

$$i_{it} = i_t(\omega_{it}, k_{it}). \tag{3.7}$$

Thereafter, we can reverse the preceding equation in order to explicate productivity by exploiting the monotonic increasing property of investments:

$$\omega_{it} = h_t(i_{it}, k_{it}), \text{ where } h_t(\cdot) = i_t^{-1}(\cdot). \tag{3.8}$$

The production function then becomes

$$y_{it} = \beta_0 + \beta_k k_{it} + \beta_l l_{it} + \beta_m m_{it} + h_t(i_{it}, k_{it}) + u_{it}^q. \tag{3.9}$$

Now, by defining the auxiliary function $\varphi(i_{it}, k_{it}) = \beta_0 + \beta_k k_{it} + h_t(i_{it}, k_{it})$ and plugging it into Equation 3.9, we get the following:

$$y_{it} = \beta_l l_{it} + \beta_m m_{it} + \varphi(i_{it}, k_{it}) + u_{it}^q, \tag{3.10}$$

where $\varphi(i_{it}, k_{it})$ is approximated by a higher-order polynomial in i_{it} and k_{it}.[14] Equation 3.10 can be then estimated parametrically with a simple OLS procedure, resulting in consistent estimations for $\hat{\beta_l}$, $\hat{\beta_m}$, $\hat{\varphi}$, and represents the first step of the OP algorithm.

Afterwards, the OP method exploits firm dynamics in order to disentangle the effect of capital on firm productivity. The authors

---

[13] Labour markets are assumed to be perfectly competitive, that is, there are no firing costs or labour adjustment costs.

[14] A function $f(v)$ can be approximated by a polynomial in v
$f(v) = \rho_0 + \rho_1 + \cdots + \rho_G v^G.$

define an indicator for firm survival that take a non-null value only if today's productivity is larger or equal to its past values, namely

$$\chi_{it+1} = 1 \text{ if } \omega_{it+1} \geq \omega_{it}. \tag{3.11}$$

We can now derive the predicted value of $\varphi(i_{it}, k_{it})$ using firm's expectations conditional to survival:

$$E(y_{it+1} - \beta_l l_{it+1} - \beta_m m_{it+1} | K_{it+1}, \chi_{it+1} = 1)$$
$$= \beta_0 + \beta_k k_{it+1} + E(\omega_{it+1} | K_{it+1}, \chi_{it+1} = 1). \tag{3.12}$$

The second stage of the estimation algorithm can then be derived as follows:

$$y_{it+1} - \beta_l l_{it+1} - \beta_m m_{it+1}$$
$$= \beta_0 + \beta_k k_{it+1} + E(\omega_{it+1} | \omega_{it}, \chi_{it+1} + \varepsilon_{it+1} + u_{it}^q \tag{3.13}$$
$$= \beta_0 + \beta_k k_{it+1} + g(P_{it}, \varphi_t - \beta_k k_{it+1}) + \varepsilon_{it+1} + u_{it}^q.$$

where $E(\omega_{it+1} + \varphi(i_{it}, k_{it}) = g(P_{it}, \varphi_t - \beta_k k_{it})$ follows from the law of motion for the productivity shocks and P_{it} is the probability of survival of firm i in the next period. Substituting in Equation 3.13 $\hat{\beta}_l$ and $\hat{\beta}_m$ obtained from the first stage estimation and approximating $g(P_{it}, \varphi_t - \beta_k k_{it})$ with a higher-order polynomial expansion, we obtain the final equation for the second step:

$$y_{it+1} - \beta_l l_{it+1} - \beta_m m_{it+1}$$
$$= \beta_0 + \beta_k k_{it+1} + g(\hat{P}_{it}, \hat{\varphi}_t - \hat{\beta}_k k_{it}) + \varepsilon_{it+1} + u_{it}^q. \tag{3.14}$$

Equation 3.14 can be estimated with a non-linear least squares procedure.

The Levinshon and Petrin (2003) Approach

Levinshon and Petrin (2003) ("LP" from now on) questioned whether investments needed to be strictly increasing for identification, which is the critical assumption of the Olley and Pakes algorithm. Using a database of Chilean firms, they showed that roughly half of the observations had no investments, and so for those firms it is not possible to estimate TFP through the OP methodology. They concluded that a large chunk of the data available to researchers could not be used to estimate TFP. Levinshon and Petrin (2003) use the same procedure as Olley and Pakes, but propose intermediate inputs as the instrumental variable, rather than investments. They show that data on intermediate inputs (energy costs, for example) are more accessible and in general positive for every firm, allowing for a more consistent estimation. Following the OP methodology, they define the intermediate input's demand function as

$$m_{it} = m_t(\omega_{it}, k_{it}), \tag{3.15}$$

where m_{it} is assumed to be a variable, non-dynamic input, exactly like labour.

Then, assuming monotonicity, it is possible to invert this function and back out productivity as a function of intermediates and capital:

$$\omega_{it} = s_t(m_{it}, k_{it}), \text{ where } s_t(\cdot) = m_t^{-1}(\cdot). \tag{3.16}$$

The production function can be expressed as follows:

$$y_{it} = \beta_k k_{it} + \beta_l l_{it} + \beta_m m_{it} + s(m_{it}, k_{it}) + u_{it}^q. \tag{3.17}$$

By defining the auxiliary function $\phi(m_{it}, k_{it}) = \beta_0 + \beta_k k_t + \beta_m m_t + s_t(m_{it}, k_{it})$, it is possible to estimate the first-stage equation:

$$y_{it} = \beta_l l_{it} + \phi(m_{it}, k_{it}) + u_{it}^q. \tag{3.18}$$

Finally, $\hat{\beta}_k$ and $\hat{\beta}_m$ can be estimated in a second stage:

$$y_{it} - \beta_l l_{it} = \beta_0 + \beta_k k_{it} + \beta_m m_{it} + E(\omega_{it}|\omega_{it-1}) + u_{it}^q. \tag{3.19}$$

Since there might be a correlation between intermediate inputs and the error term, the LP method uses an additional moment to identify the coefficient for materials: $E[(\epsilon_{it} + u_{it}^q)m_{it-1}] = 0$ or $E[\epsilon_{it} m_{it-1}] = 0$.

The main difference here is that LP do not incorporate the survival probability in the second stage because the efficiency gains of doing so presented by OP were too small.

The Ackerberg et al. (2015) Correction

Ackerberg et al. (2015) ("ACF" from now on) criticised both the OP and LP methodology. They provided an extensive discussion on the assumptions underlying both algorithms, proving the existence of a collinearity problem in the first-stage (parametric) estimation. By analysing the data generation process (DGP) of the labour input, ACF showed that it is possible to demonstrate that labour depends on the same variables as materials input (the LP framework) or investments (the OP framework).

To overcome this issue, they proposed a revised version of the original OP methodology. The labour coefficient is no longer estimated in the first stage. Instead, this stage is used only to remove the unobservable and unpredictable error. They also incorporated labour market rigidities in the model by assuming that materials are chosen at the same time (or even after) the labour choice. In formula, this means

$$m_{it} = f_t(\omega_{it}, k_{it}, l_{it}). \tag{3.20}$$

Hence, the production function becomes

$$y_{it} = \beta_k k_{it} + \beta_l l_{it} + f_t^{-1}(m_{it}, k_{it}, l_{it}) + \epsilon_{it}, \tag{3.21}$$

and it is clear that β_l cannot be estimated in the first stage.[15] In the first stage, it is then possible to estimate the following aggregated term:

$$\Phi_t(m_{it}, k_{it}, l_{it}) = \beta_k k_{it} + \beta_l l_{it} + f_t^{-1}(m_{it}, k_{it}, l_{it}), \tag{3.22}$$

which represents the *predictable* part of firm's output. To perform the second-stage estimation, they add a further moment condition:

$$\frac{1}{N}\frac{1}{T}\sum_i\sum_t \hat{\xi}_{it}(\beta_1, \beta_2) l_{it-1} = 0. \tag{3.23}$$

The Wooldridge (2009) Approach

Wooldridge argued that the complex two-step procedure proposed by OP, later revised by LP and ACF, can easily be implemented in a single estimation using a generalised method of moments (GMM) framework. This has advantages:

- It overcomes the collinearity problem discussed by ACF.
- It efficiently obtains robust standard errors.
- By specifying a two-contemporaneous-equations model, the GMM estimator takes advantage of the cross-equation correlation to enhance efficiency, and the optimal weighting matrix efficiently accounts for serial correlation and heteroskedasticity.

[15] They do not include m_{it} directly in the production function as it cannot be instrumented by m_{it-1} (Bond and Söderbom, 2005).

- The framework lets us test the identification assumptions underlying the model.
- The procedure is able to account for the identification issues raised by ACF.

More specifically, Wooldridge assumed that the idiosyncratic shocks are independent from the exogenous regressors and that productivity is correlated to the first lags of the production inputs.[16] His second assumption yields the following moment conditions:

$$E(e_{it}|l_{it}, m_{it}, k_{it}, l_{it-1}, m_{it-1}, k_{it-1}, \ldots, l_{i1}, m_{i1}, k_{i1}) = 0,$$
$$\text{with } t = 1, 2, \ldots, T \quad (3.24)$$

$$E(v_{it}|l_{it}, l_{it-1}, m_{it-1}, k_{it-1}, \ldots, l_{i1}, m_{i1}, k_{i1})$$
$$= E(v_{it}|v_{it-1}) = f[g(k_{it-1}, m_{it-1})]. \quad (3.25)$$

The two equations system can then be specified as follows:

$$\begin{cases} y_{it} = \alpha + \beta_l l_{it} + \beta_k k_{it} + g(k_{it}, m_{it}) + e_{it}, \text{ with } t = 1, 2, \ldots, T \\ y_{it} = \alpha + \beta_l l_{it} + \beta_k k_{it} + f[g(k_{it-1}, m_{it-1})] + u_{it}, \\ \qquad\qquad\qquad\qquad\qquad\qquad\qquad\qquad \text{with } t = 2, 3, \ldots, T, \end{cases} \quad (3.26)$$

where $u_{it} = a_{it} + e_{it}$ and a_{it} represent an innovation shock.

This system of equations means we can perform a one-step estimation that is more efficient than the two-step semi-parametric algorithm of OP, LP and ACF.

Given the two orthogonality conditions of the two equations, we can use contemporaneous capital, any lagged inputs and any function of them as instruments. To estimate the two equations, Wooldridge used third-degree polynomials, as proposed by LP. More generally, $g(k, m)$ contains all polynomials of order three or less. We can write

$$g(k_{it}, m_{it}) = \lambda_0 + c(k_{it}, m_{it})\lambda \quad (3.27)$$

for a $1 \times Q$ vector of functions $c(k_{it}, m_{it})$. Wooldridge then assumes that $c(k_{it}, m_{it})$ contains at least k_{it} and m_{it} separately since a linear

---

[16] Wooldridge (2009) shows that these assumptions can be relaxed conditioning only on the first lag.

version of $g(k, m)$ should be allowed as a special case. Moreover, $f(\cdot)$ can be approximated by a polynomial in v:

$$f(v) = \rho_0 + \rho_1 + \cdots + \rho_G v^G. \qquad (3.28)$$

The system of equations then becomes

$$\begin{cases} y_{it} = \alpha_0 + \beta_l l_{it} + \beta_k k_{it} + c_{it}\lambda + e_{it}, \ with \ t = 1, 2, \ldots, T \\ y_{it} = \eta_0 + \beta_l l_{it} + \beta_k k_{it} + \rho_1(c_{it}\lambda) + \cdots + \rho_G(c_{it}\lambda)^G + u_{it}, \ with \\ \qquad\qquad\qquad\qquad\qquad\qquad\qquad\qquad t = 2, 3, \ldots, T, \end{cases}$$
$$(3.29)$$

where α_0 and η_0 are the new intercepts. The most straightforward choice for IVs is $z_{it1} = (1, l_{it}, k_{it}, c_{it}^0)$ for the first equation and $z_{it2} = (1, k_{it}, l_{it-1}, c_{it-1}, q_{it-1})$ with c_{it}^0 being c_{it} without capital and q_{it-1} a set of non-linear function of c_{it-1}. GMM estimation of Equation 3.29 is now straightforward.

3.4 From Theory to Practice

In this section, we discuss how to estimate TFP using a common statistical software for applied microeconomic analysis: Stata. More specifically, we will introduce a new Stata module that means you can straightforwardly apply all the methodologies explained in Section 3.3.

Stata Implementation

The Stata module that measures TFP at firm level is *prodest*. Written by Gabriele Rovigatti and Vincenzo Mollisi, it is extremely flexible and implements all methodologies using control functions with a simple interface. Further reference can be found in the methodological paper Mollisi and Rovigatti (2018).

The general syntax of the command is as follows:

```
prodest depvar, free(-) proxy(-) state(-) method(-)[acf valueadded].
```

- *depvar* indicates the dependent variable in the production function. As we have seen, it can be either total revenues or value added. In the latter case, the *valueadded* option (indicated in the syntax by brackets) must be specified at the end of the command syntax.

- *free(–)* allows to specify the endogenous input variables that are assumed to change freely without any dynamic implication. In OP, LP and Wooldridge, this denotes the labour input.
- *state(–)* allows one to specify which variable cannot be estimated in the (parametric) first stage and should be rather derived by using a control function. In OP, LP and Wooldridge, it is generally capital.
- *proxy(–)* allows the user to specify which instrument is used to proxy the state variable. In OP, it is generally investments; in LP and Wooldridge, it is intermediate inputs.
- *method(–)* allows one to specify the estimation algorithm to use. The command *method(op)*, *method(lp)* or *method(wrdg)* tells the program to run the Olley and Pakes (1996a), the Levinshon and Petrin (2003) or the Wooldridge (2009) routine, respectively. Moreover, it is possible to enforce the Ackerberg et al. (2015) correction by specifying the *acf* option at the end of the command line, once the OP or LP algorithm is chosen as estimation method.

A number of additional, more technical options are available in the syntax, and we refer the reader to the original paper.

A Practical Example

In Table 3.1, we have calculated the coefficients of the estimations on a firm-level dataset obtained using the methodologies described earlier. The specific commands we used to estimate the coefficients are the following:

- The Olley and Pakes (1996a) approach:

```
prodest ln_r_va , free(ln_l) state(ln_r_k)
proxy(ln_r_investments) method(op) id(mark) t(year) level(99)
reps(50) valueadded
```

- The Levinshon and Petrin (2003) approach:

```
prodest ln_r_va , free(ln_l) state(ln_r_k)
proxy(ln_r_m) method(lp) id(mark) t(year) level(99) reps(50)
valueadded
```

- The Olley and Pakes (1996a) approach with the Ackerberg et al. (2015) correction:

```
prodest ln_r_va , free(ln_l) state(ln_r_k)
proxy(ln_r_investments) method(op) id(mark) t(year) level(99)
reps(50) valueadded acf
```

Table 3.1. *TFP estimates: an overview.*

Variables	(1) OLS	(2) OP	(3) LP	(4) ACF_OP	(5) ACF_LP	(6) WRDG
Labour	0.525***	0.446***	0.482***	0.496***	0.530***	0.550***
	(0.038)	(0.059)	(0.035)	(0.059)	(0.023)	(0.023)
Capital	0.504***	0.262	0.658***	0.537***	0.519***	0.568***
	(0.031)	(0.161)	(0.169)	(0.058)	(0.020)	(0.147)
Observations	1,439	812	1,439	812	1,439	1,439

Standard errors in parentheses. Significance levels are: *** $p < 0.01$, ** $p < 0.05$, * $p < 0.1$.

Note: Data shown refer to firms operating in the Italian food and beverage sector. As data on investments are not available within our dataset, we obtain them by inverting Equation 2.3 and assuming a depreciation rate of 2.5%.

- The Levinshon and Petrin (2003) approach with the Ackerberg et al. (2015) correction:

```
prodest ln_r_va , free(ln_l) state(ln_r_k)
proxy(ln_r_m) method(lp) id(mark) t(year) level(99) reps(50)
valueadded acf
```

- The Wooldridge (2009) approach:

```
prodest ln_r_va , free(ln_l) state(ln_r_k)
proxy(ln_r_m) method(wrdg) id(mark) t(year) level(99) reps(50)
valueadded
```

Retrieving TFP Estimates

When we execute the procedure in the first part of Section 3.4, we obtain the estimated coefficients of the production function, the factor productivities such as those reported in Table 3.1. We can then compute the firm-level productivity measure – TFP – that we have been seeking. This is quite easy to do, because Stata automatically stores the results of the production function estimation performed under *prodest*. This mean that we can retrieve TFP as the residual difference between actual and predicted output, as in Equation 3.4. We can use the *predict* command embedded in the routine:

```
predict newvar, residuals
```

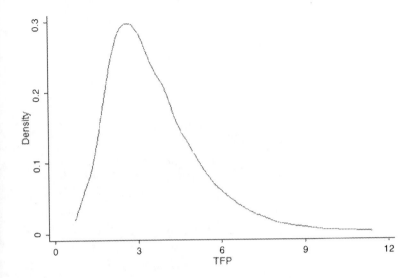

Figure 3.1 TFP distribution.

Source: Authors' calculation.

Note: The figure plots the kernel-density distribution of firm-level TFP, as retrieved from the coefficients reported in Table 3.1, column 6. After the estimation, the first and 99th percentiles of the distribution have been eliminated to control for outliers.

The command automatically creates a new variable (*newvar*). It is the difference between the observed value of the dependent variable and the fitted one. Clearly, since we ran our estimation routine on log-linear variables, if we want to retrieve the level of firm-level TFP (as per the original A term of technological progress in the production function), we have to calculate the exponential value of our *newvar*:

```
gen TFP\index{Total Factor Productivity} = exp(newvar)
```

We can then verify the heterogeneity in the distribution of firm-level TFP, by plotting it, as shown in Figure 3.1.

Now that we finally have retrieved a valid proxy of firm-level TFP, we can correlate productivity with other firm-level characteristics, for example size or export activities, or perform more structural analysis. We can even use information at the firm level to decompose productivity indicators in a growth accounting exercise, or use the estimated coefficients of the production function to study market efficiency. We will do all of these things throughout the rest of this book.

4 | *Measuring Market Efficiency*

Aggregate productivity growth, one of the key drivers of economic growth, can be interpreted as a weighted average of firm productivity as shown in Equation 2.9. Any change of aggregate productivity over time may be the outcome of individual producers becoming more productive or also of compositional changes between firms. There will be changes in market share among surviving firms (we might expect more productive firms to become larger, for example), but also the entry of new producers and the exit of old ones.

Empirical studies have shown that compositional changes cause changes in aggregate productivity (Foster et al., 2001; Bartelsman et al., 2013). These findings have spurred the development of methods of **productivity decomposition** that break down aggregate productivity changes into components: productivity shifts within incumbent firms, market share reallocation among the same firms, the entry of new producers and the exit of old ones.

We present in this chapter the empirical techniques used to measure market efficiency and its implications, starting with the so-called OP gap – a measure developed by Olley and Pakes (1996a) – and its dynamic version, recently proposed by Melitz and Polanec (2015). We will then discuss the productivity decomposition method proposed by Foster et al. (2006) and the techniques to measure allocative inefficiency developed by Hsieh and Klenow (2009) and Petrin and Sivadasan (2013).

Market inefficiency is also related to concentration and market power. When competition in a market is reduced, aggregate productivity growth may decrease, reducing consumer welfare. So, first we will discuss a sector-level index of concentration, the Hirschman–Herfindahl index, and its advantages and drawbacks. We will then analyse other proxies for the markups, which are – like productivity – are firm-specific.

First we will discuss why the simplest semi-parametric measure of market power at the firm level – the price-cost margin or Lerner index that we introduced in Chapter 2 – is insufficient to measure a firm's market power. Thereafter, we will present the most widely used – parametric – version of firm-level markup, developed by De Loecker and Warzynski (2012). Finally, we discuss the joint market imperfection index, recently proposed by Dobbelaere and Mairesse (2013).

4.1 Allocative Efficiency

Covariance Analysis: The OP Gap

In Section 3.3, we introduced Steven Olley and Ariel Pakes and their semi-parametric method for TFP estimation. In the same paper, they also introduced an innovative non-parametric measure of resource allocation. In their work, they defined aggregate productivity at the industry level as an output-weighted average:

$$p_t = \sum_{i=1}^{N_t} s_{it} p_{it}, \tag{4.1}$$

where p_t is the industry productivity at time t; s_{it} is firm's i market shares of output, always at time t (hence $\sum s_{it} = 1$); and p_{it} is firm-level productivity. They then decomposed aggregate productivity into two terms:

$$
\begin{aligned}
p_t &= \sum_{i=1}^{N_t} (\bar{s}_t + \Delta s_{it})(\bar{p}_t + \Delta p_{it}) \\
&= N_t \bar{s}_t \bar{p}_t + \sum_{i=1}^{N_t} \Delta s_{it} \Delta p_{it} \\
&= \bar{p}_t + \underbrace{\sum_{i=1}^{N_t} \Delta s_{it} \Delta p_{it}}_{\text{OP Gap}},
\end{aligned} \tag{4.2}
$$

where $\bar{s}_t$ and $\bar{p}_t$ are the unweighted average output share and productivity across the industry, and Δs_{it} and Δp_{it} are the firm-specific deviation from these averages, that is, $\Delta s_{it} = s_{it} - \bar{s}_t$ and $\Delta p_{it} = p_{it} - \bar{p}_t$.[1] The last term of Equation 4.2 is what we call the *OP gap*: the sample covariance between productivity and output.

Intuitively, the index is larger when firms more (or less) productive than the average ($\Delta p_{it} > 0$) also have a market share larger (or smaller) than the average ($\Delta s_{it} > 0$): in this case, both elements of the product are either both positive or both negative for firm i and thus contribute positively to the OP gap. If, instead, relatively more productive firms have a smaller-than-average market share (or vice versa), the product $\Delta s_{it} \Delta p_{it}$ becomes negative for that specific firm, reducing the OP gap.

Hence the OP gap allows us to analyse the allocative efficiency of the market in a simple and intuitive way: *the larger the covariance, the larger the share of output produced by the most productive firms.*

The OP gap is, by now, widely used as an indicator of resource allocation. In practice, output has frequently been substituted by shares of production inputs – or a mix of capital and labour – to study the allocation of resources. For example, one of the most-used combinations, relatively easy to calculate, uses labour productivity and labour share as elements.

Using input shares instead of output gives us a problem: you cannot control for changes in the composition of firm's production structure. If a firm, for example, decides to automate, and invests in machinery that requires fewer employees for the same output, the resultant OP gap calculation implies a worse allocative efficiency of labour.[2]

Dynamic OP Gap

The main limitation of the OP gap is that it is static. In each year, Equation 4.2 decomposes industry-aggregated productivity in two

---

[1] Note that $\bar{s}_t = \sum s_{it}/N_t = 1/N_t$.

[2] This issue can be solved by adding standard measures of capital intensity to the analysis.

terms only. Changes in the sample (firms entering and exiting, for example) inevitably lead to comparability problems when we want to compare the gap in two years. Melitz and Polanec (2015) proposed an extension to overcome this. They extend the original measure by dividing the industry aggregate productivity into three terms:

- The (weighted) average productivities of surviving firms (S)
- New entrants (E)
- Exiters (X)

Simply by differentiating the equations for two years, they get the productivity difference over time for each group. In terms of the original OP methodology:

$$
\begin{aligned}
\Delta p &= (p_{S(t+1)} - p_{S1}) + s_{E(t+1)}(p_{E(t+1)} - p_{S(t+1)}) + s_{X1}(p_{S1} - p_{X1}) \\
&= \Delta \bar{p}_S + \Delta cov_S + s_{E(t+1)}(p_{E(t+1)} - p_{S(t+1)}) + s_{X1}(p_{S1} - p_{X1}).
\end{aligned}
\tag{4.3}
$$

Foster Decomposition

Foster et al. (2006) developed a time-varying indicator of resource allocation starting from measures of individual firm TFP. Their approach, initially developed in Baily et al. (1992), relies on our ability to track productivity and share changes for each firm, distinguishing firms in a given year into those that stay in the market (C), those that enter (E) and those that exit (X).

Foster et al. (2006) also introduced a reference to average aggregate productivity and firm-specific deviations from it, and – as for the OP gap – they added a covariance term capturing underlying market adjustments. Their approach can be expressed as follows:

$$
\Delta \Omega_t = \underbrace{\sum_{i \in C} s_{i,t-k} \Delta \omega_{i,t}}_{\text{within}} + \underbrace{\sum_{i \in C} \Delta s_{i,t}(\omega_{i,t-k} - \Omega_{t-k})}_{\text{between}} + \underbrace{\sum_{i \in C} \Delta s_{i,t} \Delta \omega_{i,t}}_{\text{covariance}}
$$

$$
+ \underbrace{\sum_{i \in E} s_{i,t}(\omega_{i,t} - \Omega_{t-k}) - \sum_{i \in X} s_{i,t-k}(\omega_{i,t-k} - \Omega_{t-k})}_{\text{net entry}},
\tag{4.4}
$$

where Ω_t represents the average productivity at time t; $s_{i,t}$ and $\omega_{i,t}$ are firm i's market share and productivity at time t respectively, and Δ is now the standard time-difference operator between time t and $t - k$.[3]

The first line in Equation 4.4 separates the contribution to aggregate productivity of surviving (C) firms from the contribution from those entering (E) and exiting (X). The contribution of surviving firms is also split into within- and between-firm components, and the covariance between changes in market share and productivity for each firm. The interpretation of each component in the sum is as follows:

- The *within* term is the change in aggregate productivity attributable to the productivity growth within a firm $\Delta\omega_{i,t}$, given its initial market share $s_{i,t-k}$: a positive sign implies that firms, controlling for their size, are growing more productive over time.
- The *between* term accounts for the growth of market shares, keeping the productivity constant with respect to a benchmark: it captures the gains in aggregate productivity coming from the expanding market of high-productivity firms, or from low-productivity firms' shrinking shares.
- The *covariance* (or cross) term gives information about the underlying market adjustment in size and productivity: a positive sign would indicate that market shares and productivity are changing in the same direction. Firms able to increase (decrease) their productivity are also able to grow larger (smaller) in size, with positive effects for overall growth; a negative sign would show that productivity and market shares are moving in different directions – implying firms whose productivity is decreasing are growing larger and vice versa. This would reduce underlying productivity growth.
- The *net entry* term indicates the extent to which the market is able to select firms in accordance with their competitiveness: if the term is positive, it implies that firms with below-average productivity are forced to exit the market, while firms that are more productive than average are entering.

---

[3] Recall that in the expression of the OP gap, the operator Δ was instead used to measure the difference between productivity (or market share) of a firm i and the industry average, consistently with the "between" dimension across firms in a given year of the standard OP gap indicator, compared to the "within" dimension of a given firm over time captured by a Foster-type decomposition.

The Hsieh and Klenow (2009) Decomposition

In 2009, Hsieh and Klenow (2009) (HK) developed a new framework to analyse market inefficiencies. They introduced generic output and capital distortions in an otherwise standard model of monopolistic competition. This novel approach makes no attempt to disentangle these distortions, instead proving (and quantifying) their existence.

Hsieh and Klenow (2009) employ a standard Cobb–Douglas function of the form $Y = AK^{\beta_K} L^{\beta_L}$, which means they do not consider intermediate inputs. Their profit function is written as follows:

$$\pi_{si} = (1 - \tau_{Ysi})P_{si}Y_{si} - wL_{si} - (1 + \tau_{Ksi})RK_{si}, \qquad (4.5)$$

where π_{si}, Y_{si}, L_{si} and K_{si} represent firm i's profit, output, labour and capital, respectively, in industry s, while P, w and R are prices of output, labour and capital, respectively.

The two terms τ_Y and τ_K are their key contribution. The first represents distortions in the output market and negatively affects a firm's sales, while the latter embodies distortions in the capital market, which increases capital cost. Using these terms, they show that the marginal revenue product (MRP) of labour and capital – that is, the extra revenue generated when an additional worker or unit of capital is employed – can be written as follows:

$$MRPL_{si} = w\frac{1}{1 - \tau_{Ysi}} \qquad (4.6)$$

and

$$MRPK_{si} = R\frac{1 + \tau_{Ksi}}{1 - \tau_{Ysi}}. \qquad (4.7)$$

If we start from the assumption that output elasticity with respect to a specific input must equal its cost in a perfectly competitive market (in the case of the labour input, for example, the wage w), we can measure market distortion as the distance of the MRPs from input costs. To provide further evidence, they empirically measure market inefficiency using micro-data from firms in the US, China and India.

The approach developed by Hsieh and Klenow (2009) is based on a simple algorithm and is empirically flexible, and so it is broadly used. Popularity doesn't equate to a problem-free methodology. It requires some strong assumptions:

- On the demand side, every producer must face an isoelastic residual demand curve.
- On the supply side, producers must have marginal cost curves that are invariant to quantity.
- Those marginal cost curves must have negative unit elasticity with respect to total factor productivity, measured with respect to output quantity.

In their critique, Haltiwanger et al. (2018) use a novel micro-level dataset that provides information separately on firm prices and quantities in 11 product markets, and they find that the condition which the HK model rests upon does not hold in any of these markets. This matters: they additionally show that, when the conditions are not met, the HK approach implies MRP dispersion and so implies market inefficiency. But in this case, it may simply represent shifts in demand, or movements of the firm along its marginal cost curve. Therefore, they conclude, a researcher employing the HK method might infer misallocation when there is none. We will return to this discussion in Chapter 7 when we evaluate the role of labour markets in driving firm-level TFP.

4.2 Concentration and Markup at the Firm Level

From a theoretical point of view, the degree of competition in a market is closely connected with the notion of market power. Market power translates the ability of a firm to set and sustain prices above marginal cost – the welfare-maximising reference under perfect competition. We will now analyse a number of indicators that can be used to proxy market power, always assuming the underlying heterogeneity of firms' characteristics.

The Herfindahl–Hirschman Index

The Herfindahl-Hirschman index (HHI), better known as the Herfindahl index, is a statistical measure of concentration. The HHI is calculated by squaring the market share of each firm competing in the market and summing the results:

$$HHI = \sum_{i=1}^{N} ms_i^2, \qquad (4.8)$$

where N is the total number of firms operating and ms_i is firm i's market share. This is generally the firm's turnover over total market turnover. Alternative specifications use firm characteristics such as value added or employment. HHI is occasionally expressed as a percentage rather than a fraction.

The HHI approaches zero in the hypothetical case of perfect competition, in which many firms have small, virtually zero, market share. A single-firm monopoly gives a HHI of one.[4]

Price-Cost Margin

The price-cost margin (PCM) is considered to be the empirical application of the Lerner index that we encountered in Chapter 2. It is calculated using total revenues (or sales) as a proxy for prices. Variable costs – cost of labour, intermediates and services – are the marginal costs. Like the Lerner index, the PCM is defined as follows:

$$PCM_i = \frac{Total\ Revenues_i - Variable\ Costs_i}{Total\ Revenues_i}. \qquad (4.9)$$

In theory, it should equal zero in perfect competition and its largest value would be in monopoly (the maximum would be one in absence of variable costs).

The main empirical problem with this directly measured "accounting" version of the PCM is that we use a proxy of average costs, rather than marginal costs, to calculate it. If there are increasing (decreasing) returns to scale, PCM will be biased upwards (downwards). In the formula, efficiency gains generated by innovations or enhanced product quality, which translate to lower costs or higher prices, will be interpreted as as declining level of competition. Also, the measure assumes that capital is fixed over time, meaning that investments are not considered variable costs. This means that we can compare PCM within an industry, but cross-sectoral comparisons of PCM levels should be complemented with measures of capital intensity or technology.

---

[4] Note that if market share is expressed as a percentage, the HHI takes value 10,000 in monopoly.

Parametric Measures of PCM

To overcome these problems, De Loecker and Warzynski (2012) propose a parsimonious method for estimating firm markup based on the estimation of the production function that we discussed in Chapter 3. This approach, suitable for different price-setting models, strongly relies on the hypothesis that, in perfect competition, output elasticity of a production factor will be equal to its expenditure share in total revenue. In other words, any form of imperfect competition will create a distortion, a wedge between input revenue share and output elasticity.

They define firm i's markup at time t, μ, as follows:

$$\mu_{it} = \theta_{it}^q \left(\alpha_{it}^q\right)^{-1}, \tag{4.10}$$

where θ^q and α^q are input q output elasticities and expenditure shares, respectively. They estimate a production function, as in Equation 3.3, and measuring the input q's marginal productivity to find the input elasticity, the term that we have denoted as $\hat{\beta}^q$. Output elasticity is defined as follows:

$$\alpha_{it}^q = \frac{P_{it}^q q_{it}}{P_{it}^y y_{it}}, \tag{4.11}$$

with $P_{it}^q q_{it}$ being the nominal value of the input, and $P_{it}^y y_{it}$ being total revenues.[5] A more general problem of PCM measures is that they are typically unable to capture reallocation and selection effects. If efficient incumbents adopt more aggressive pricing strategies, their market share increases (*reallocation effect*). This may force inefficient firms to exit the market (*selection effect*). In this case, the market PCM may increase, suggesting that there was a reduction in competition.

---

[5] De Loecker and Warzynski (2012) note that we are implicitly allowing for measurement errors and for unanticipated shocks to production by using total revenues. Therefore, they split revenues into $y_{it} = q_{it} + \epsilon_{it}$, where ϵ_{it} includes unanticipated shocks to production and iid shocks, including measurement error – what we refer to as u_{it}^q in Chapter 3. They include the following correction in Equation 4.11:

$$\alpha_{it}^q = \frac{P_{it}^q q_{it}}{P_{it} \dfrac{y_{it}}{exp(\hat{\epsilon}_{it})}},$$

where $\hat{\epsilon}_{it}$ is retrieved from the estimation of the production function.

But, in fact, the opposite is true. We will provide a detailed discussion of these dynamics in Chapter 9.

Joint Market Imperfections

Sabien Dobbelaere and Jacques Mairesse introduced a new technique to determine and quantify market imperfections. As for De Loecker and Warzynski (2012), they start from the hypothesis that the output elasticities of inputs should equal their revenue share in perfect competition.

More formally, starting from the assumptions that there is imperfect competition in product markets, firms are price takers in input markets, and they maximise profits in the short run, they show that any difference between output elasticities and revenue share is due to market distortions. The extent of distortions in product and labour markets can thus be measured as the difference between output elasticity and revenue share of each production factor:

$$\psi_{it} = \frac{\theta_{it}^M}{\alpha_{it}^M} - \frac{\theta_{it}^L}{\alpha_{it}^L}, \tag{4.12}$$

where ψ represents the indicator of joint market imperfections.

This index provides a very straightforward way to assess the degree of competition of a given industry. Using it, and considering the within-industry *average* joint product and labour parameter, ψ, we can define two cases:

(1) $\psi = 0$: the industry is characterised by perfect competition in both product and labour market.
(2) $\psi \neq 0$: the industry is characterised by some degree of imperfect competition in one or both markets.

In the paper, the authors also provide an extensive analysis on how to determine the competition regime under which the industry is operating.

5 | Sources of Data

As discussed in Chapter 2, in recent years there has been a move away from the concept of representative firm, given the evidence that firms are strongly heterogeneous. The papers that established the theoretical underpinnings for this development were published in the 1990s and early 2000s, making it clear that firm heterogeneity had important implications in fields such as labour economics, international economics, industrial organisation and firm theory.

Economists who wanted to embed firm heterogeneity in empirical research had a problem: there was little quality firm-level data. A few early studies used micro-level data, but the data were usually not public and covered a single country, and sometimes only specific industries. Since firm-level data mainly come from accounts and surveys, the data for firms from different countries were rarely compatible. And so, until recently, data limitations made it almost impossible to conduct microeconomic cross-country research.

This problem was and partly remains particularly severe in the EU, as it hampers the possibility of conducting economic assessments covering the whole European Union. For this reason, European institutions have coordinated many efforts to assemble quality, comparable micro-level data across as many European countries as possible. Such data include both firm- and industry-level datasets. The EU funded projects aimed at developing and making these kind of datasets publicly available. Datasets sponsored by international institutions supplemented those owned by private corporations.

In this chapter, we will present the most relevant micro-level datasets, which are available and are being used both in the academia and in policy institutions. We will start assessing industry-level datasets such as that developed within the EU Klems project and the World Input Output Database (WIOD). Then we will discuss Orbis and its European version Amadeus, firm-level datasets developed by Bureau van Dijk. We will also briefly discuss the OECD's developed firm-level datasets, DynEmp and MultiProd. We will then move on to European Firms in a Global Economy (EFIGE), and finally we will present the Competitiveness Research Network (CompNet) dtatset. Table 5.1 summarises their content, coverage and availability.

5.1 EU Klems and WIOD

EU Klems and the World Input Output Database (WIOD) are two industry-level databases funded by the European Commission. EU Klems ran from 2003 to 2008; the WIOD ran from 2009 to 2012.

They slightly differ in their scope. EU Klems is a database on measures of economic growth, productivity, employment creation, capital formation and technological change at the industry level for all European Union member states from 1970 onwards. The objective was to help policy evaluation for economic growth and competitiveness. In particular, to understand the relationship between skill formation, technological progress and innovation on one hand, and productivity on the other. Productivity measures used growth accounting methods (Section 2.4). Input measures include categories of capital, labour, energy, material and service inputs.

The core of the WIOD is a set of harmonised supply and use tables, with data on international trade in goods and services. These two sets of data are integrated into sets of intercountry (world) input–output tables. The WIOD has a stronger focus on trade analysis and the impact of global value chains (GVCs) than EU Klems, which is particularly useful in assessing the standard dimensions of competitiveness and productivity. The WIOD can be integrated with industry and country-specific information on energy use and carbon dioxide emissions.

The first version of EU Klems was released in 2007 and updated in 2008 and 2011. The first release, which adopted the NACE Rev 2 classification,[1] was in 2012. The most recent version of the database was published in 2017, covering all EU-28 member states, several EU aggregates and the US. Most industries and countries are covered from 1995 to 2015. The data on output, employment, value added,

[1] NACE is the acronym used to designate the various statistical classifications of economic activities developed since 1970 in the European Union. The regulation establishing NACE Rev. 2 was adopted in December 2006, substantially increasing the detail of the classification.

Table 5.1. *Main sources of micro-level data.*

Name	Provider	Content	Level of aggregation	Countries	Time span	Last release	Availability
EU KLEMS	EU Commission	The EU KLEMS dataset is the result of a corresponding EU project which aimed at vreating a database on measures of economic growth, productivity, employment creation, capital formation and technological change at the industry level for all EU member countries from 1970 onwards. This dataset aimed at providing an input for EU policy evaluation in the realm of competitiveness and economic growth	Industry level	EU and US	1995–2015	September 2017 (revised July 2018)	www.eyklems.net
WIOD	EU Commission	The World Input–Output Database (WIOD) provides time-series of would input–output tables for 40 countries and a model for the rest of the world. These tables have been constructed on the basis of officially published input–output tables in conjunction with national accounts and international trade statistics. It also provides data on labour and capital inputs and pollution indicators at the industry level	Industry level	EU 28 countries and other 15 major economies	2000–2014	2016	www.wiod.org/home
Orbis	Bureau van Dijk	Orbis and its EU-version Amadeus are databases of comparable financial and business balance sheet information. They include standardised annual accounts, financial ratios, sectoral activities and ownership data. The dataset is suitable and widely used for research on competitiveness, economic integration, applied microeconomics, business cycles, economic geography and corporate finance	Firm level	Worldwide (43 countries for Amadeus)	1990–present	Weekly updates (each vintage includes Information on the previous 10 years)	Access can be acquired by purchase

	Provider	Description	Data type	Countries	Time period		Access
DynEmp	OECD	The OECD DynEmp project developed a cross-country database of micro-aggregated form-level data from administrative data sources, mainly national business registries. It aims at providing comparable data for international analysis of firm employment dynamics.	Micro-aggregated	OECD countries	1998–2013 (but varies across countries)	2019	The data are available for only internal OECD use
MultiProd	OECD	Similar to the DynEmp dataset, the OECD MultiProd project created a cross-country dataset of micro-aggregated firm-level data for international analysis of policies related to competitiveness and economic growth.	Micro-aggregated	OECD countries	2000–2012 (but varies across countries)	2016	The data are available for only internal OECD use
EFIGE	Bruegel	THe EFIGE dataset is the result of the EFIGE project (European Firms in a Global Economy), funded by the EU Commission. The data are based on a harmonised survey in seven European countries and they contain information on different aspects of firm performance, ownership, employment, innovation, international activities and competitiveness.	Firm level	7 European countries (Germany, UK, Austria, Hungary, France, Italy and Spain)	2010	Only one cross-section	https:// bruegel .org/ publications/ datasets/ efige/
ComNet	Competitiveness Research Network	The CompNet database is an outcome of the Competitiveness Research Network, firstly initiated by the ECB with the participation of national EU central banks and statistical institutes. It aims at providing a consistent framework for the analysis of competitiveness across EU countries. It is a micro-aggregated database of firm-level information source at the national level and contains several indicators of competitiveness.	Micro-aggregated	EU countries	2001–present	8th Vintage was published in September 2021. The dataset is updated at an annual pace.	www.comp-net.org

capital formation and prices are consistent with Eurostat industry-level data. Each country's data are organised around a basic file with information on productivity, output and value for 34 industries and eight aggregates, according to the NACE Rev 2 industry classification.

A capital input file contains additional information on investments and capital stocks for the same industries as the basic file. A labour input file includes additional information on several types of labour for more aggregate sectors.[2]

The most recent version of WIOD was released in 2016. It covers 43 countries and 56 sectors between 2000 and 2014. The sectors are classified according to the International Standard Industrial Classification revision 4 (ISIC rev 4)[3].

The main strength of EU Klems and WIOD is that they cover all EU member countries with relevant country aggregates. They also cover nearly all industries in these countries' economies. The universal coverage and full harmonisation across European countries make them particularly useful if we want to measure European-wide competitiveness. EU Klems focuses particularly on productivity dynamics, but WIOD is useful when we want to assess the role of GVCs and of energy consumption. These features make them particularly useful to policy institutions that want to learn about the drivers and development of productivity across Europe.

On the other hand, EU Klems and WIOD do not capture within-industry dynamics, as available at the firm level or with micro-aggregated datasets, as discussed later.

5.2 Orbis

Orbis is a large firm-level dataset published by Bureau Van Dijk, a publisher of business information owned by Moody's Analytics. It contains balance sheet and financial statement information on more than 360 million public and private firms from across the world. The database provides information on firms' domestic and foreign

[2] For a summary overview of the methodology and construction of the EU Klems database, please see Jäger (2017); van Ark and Jäger (2017) and its website: www.euklems.net.
[3] For an overview of WIOD, please see Timmer et al. (2015) and its website: www.wiod.org.

owners and subsidiaries. This allows to observe global connections between firms through their ownership. The European version of Orbis is called Amadeus.

Every year Bureau van Dijk provides a new release of the Orbis database. Each version includes the information about firms from previous releases but dropping firms that have not reported information for a certain period of time. This might lead to systematic biases if researchers use a single vintage to build their datasets. It is also important to use data across vintages to capture changes in the industrial classification of firms that are expanding.

Initially intended for corporate analysis, Orbis is now widely used for broader economic analysis of firm productivity. Orbis includes all information required for retrieving firm characteristics, such as for total factor productivity and markup estimation, meaning economists can use Orbis data to estimate firm-level productivity on samples from every region, and can combine it with other firm-level information covering nearly all aspects of the firm's financial position and corporate ownership.

Orbis is attractive for economic researchers and policy makers alike because of its broad country coverage, relative ease to use and because – unlike EU Klems and WIOD – it allows to conduct firm-level analysis.

On the other hand, Orbis is – at times severely – limited with regard to national industrial structures and accurate cross-country comparisons.[4] Orbis data are sourced from more than 160 government and commercial information providers. Financial and balance sheet information comes from business registers, governed by country-specific legal and administrative filing requirements, and coverage of small firms and financial variables varies due to different national business register filing requirements, and in general is inadequate. Researchers who want to improve cross-country comparability and within-country representativeness should re-weigh the observations or follow the processes developed and described by Kalemli-Ozcan et al. (2015).

Another limitation of Orbis is that it was created to assist financial and corporate analysis and covers almost exclusively firm balance

---

[4] An assessment of Orbis was done by Kalemli-Ozcan et al. (2015).

sheet information. This limits its usefulness for analysing other dimensions of firm performance, such as a firm's ability to export.

In addition, for certain types of firms a lot of relevant information is not available. This is particularly problematic for small firms from some countries, such as Germany (German law allows small firms to not report information that would be important for the study of firm dynamics). As a result, researchers must ensure that datasets based on Orbis data are internally consistent.

5.3 MultiProd and DynEmp

MultiProd and DynEmp are the names of two recent OECD projects to create firm-level-based datasets.[5] They are constructed by using the "micro-distributed approach", developed in the early 2000s by Bartelsman et al. (2004). This method is necessary to overcome confidentiality problems when collecting firm-level data. In addition, it also helps solve the issue of cross-country comparability of firm-level data originally collected within different administrative frameworks.

National data providers who use this decentralised method (also used by CompNet) collect counts, totals and other moments of the distribution of firm characteristics (employment, output, productivity, wages, age and so on) using a centrally written but locally executed computational program that is flexible and automated enough to run across different data sources in different countries. This methodology puts a lower burden on national statistical agencies and limits running costs while overcoming the confidentiality constraints of using national micro-level statistical databases. The result is a higher degree of harmonisation and comparability across countries and sectors and over time.

The MultiProd database provides information on productivity dynamics across a set of OECD member countries and over time.[6] The result is a harmonised cross-country micro-aggregated database on productivity patterns from confidential micro-level sources. It contributes to the analysis of productivity by offering new evidence based on firm-level data from production surveys and business registers. This enriches the policy debate on productivity by extending

---

[5] They were recently reviewed by Desnoyers-James et al. (2019).
[6] It is described and reviewed by Berlingieri et al. (2017).

the analysis beyond aggregate industry performance to the underlying developments within industries, such as productivity dispersion within industries. Data are comparable across countries, and so each country's performance measures can be assessed against common benchmarks.

The first full version of MultiProd was released in September 2015. A second round of data collection is currently under way. Twenty countries are covered by MultiProd: Australia, Austria, Belgium, Canada, Chile, Denmark, Finland, France, Germany, Hungary, Ireland, Italy, Japan, Luxembourg, the Netherlands, New Zealand, Norway, Portugal, Sweden and Switzerland. Time coverage varies by country. For most of them, the series begins in the early 2000s, with some going back to the mid-1990s. The end of the series varies by country between 2011 and 2015.

DynEmp is a parallel OECD project. It publishes a dataset similar to MultiProd, but more focused on employment dynamics. It starts from the assumption that measuring employment and its economic effects needs to take into account firm characteristics, size and evolution. Thanks to the micro-distributed approach, DynEmp data provide valuable support for analysing employment dynamics based on firm-level data sourced from business registers and social security data.

The first version was released in 2013. It covered 18 countries from 2000 to 2011. Updates were released in the following years, widening the scope of the database. The country and time coverage is now consistent with MultiProd. At time of writing, there is a new data collection round.[7]

MultiProd and DynEmp have been successful in providing high-quality microeconomic data that have been used for correspondingly high-quality research, which we will discuss later.

But there are also concerns:

- The databases are not publicly available. Only OECD economists can rely on them for their in-house research. This clearly limits their ability to support the policy debate around the drivers of productivity and employment dynamics.
- The inclusion of very different countries is potentially harmful for cross-country comparability (although a large coverage in terms of

---

[7] For an overview of DynEmp, see Criscuolo et al. (2014).

countries is certainly a positive achievement). While the majority
of the countries covered by both databases is made of European
countries, countries as different as Japan, Chile, Australia and New
Zealand are in the database. This may arise issues in terms of
comparability.

- Neither of the databases include information on a relevant dimension of firm performance, which is their ability to export. Therefore, one cannot use such datasets for trade analysis.

5.4 EFIGE

The EU-EFIGE/Bruegel-UniCredit dataset (known as the EFIGE
dataset) is a database collected by the EFIGE project. EFIGE stands
for European Firms in a Global Economy. Its goal is "internal
policies for external competitiveness", supported by the Directorate
General Research of the European Commission through its Seventh
Framework Programme and coordinated by Bruegel.[8]

This is a survey of almost 15,000 firms with 10 employees or more
across seven EU countries (Germany, France, Italy, Spain, United Kingdom, Austria and Hungary), capturing their international activities,
such as exports, foreign direct investment (FDI) and imports. Their
responses are combined with quantitative and qualitative information
on 150 items, including R&D and innovation, labour organisation,
financing and organisational activities and pricing behaviour, sourced
from the Amadeus dataset.

The data were collected in 2010, covering the crisis years from 2007
to 2009. Questions relating to the behaviour of firms at this time were
included in the survey.

EFIGE is a unique source of information on the international characteristics of European firms. It was designed specifically to capture
this, and provides data not available from other sources that, as we
have seen, typically rely on balance sheets and financial statements.
The dataset was built so that it could be easily combined with balance
sheet data. The information in the dataset means EFIGE is a unique
support to inform policy decisions in Europe.

---

[8] An overview of the project and the dataset is provided by Altomonte and
Aquilante (2012).

On the other hand, EFIGE suffers from the drawback of all survey data. It is very expensive to do a survey of this scale. For this reason, EFIGE was not repeated after the first wave of data. Nonetheless, even 10 years after its release, it is still widely used to assess the international dimension of European firms because it is still the best source for this kind of information.

5.5 The Competitiveness Research Network

The Competitiveness Research Network (CompNet) is a hub for research on competitiveness, productivity and market efficiency. It provides high-quality research results and policy advice, as well as innovative and freely available data.[9]

The Inception of CompNet

CompNet was established in 2012 by the European Central Bank in order to investigate competitiveness using an innovative and holistic approach. Research at the time had shown that the representative firm hypothesis was no longer valid. After the financial crisis, it was also clear that country competitiveness could no longer be assessed with a small set of aggregated indicators. The dynamic behaviour of the economy needed a more complex analysis than a simple accounting exercise of inflows and outflows.

CompNet was the answer to these newly discovered theoretical and methodological issues. Its goal was to provide a complete picture of the European economy by combining three types of data:

(1) Micro-analysis
(2) Macro-analysis
(3) The analysis of GVCs

The idea was that the interaction of these three complementary areas would lead to new research results and innovative policy advice.

In its early years, CompNet produced two novel databases embedding information crucial for new kind of research. Its first work-stream created a micro-aggregated firm-level database that applied

---

[9] More information and details on CompNet can be found on its website, www.comp-net.org, including its research, methodological reports and data.

the distributed micro-data approach developed in Bartelsman et al. (2004) to firm-level data provided by the national central banks or statistical offices participating on a voluntary basis. It created harmonised indicators, comparable across countries, by sending the same STATA program to all institutions to run on their data. This devolved approach protected the strict confidentiality of firm-level data, but exploited the richness of the information.

A second workstream collected the most innovative indicators, measuring economic performance and competitiveness at the country level in a single source that was freely available to researchers and policy makers. It included some indicators from the CompNet aggregated firm-level database.

CompNet members published more than 70 papers by combining new theoretical frameworks with this data.

The New Phase

CompNet became an independent research forum in 2016, embracing new member institutions and adopting a more structured management organisation hosted at the Halle Institute of Economic Research (IWH). This was a huge restructuring process, but resulted in more stability and financial independence.

The European Central Bank, still playing a leading role, was joined as a CompNet funding partner by the European Commission, the European Bank for Reconstruction and Development, the European Investment Bank, the European Stability Mechanism (ESM), two EU Productivity Boards – the German Council of Economic Advisers (SVR) and France Strategie – as well as the Tinbergen Institute.[10]

This reorganisation, as well as the participation to the project of an increasing number of National Statistical Institutes (NSI) allowed CompNet to add new data and countries every year as well as improving significantly the quality of the dataset. Last September, the network has published the eighth vintage of its dataset covering up to 2018–2019. CompNet now produces annual releases of cross-country comparable data, which cover some 20 European countries, including Switzerland, and several relevant dimensions of firm performance,

---

[10] More information on the internal structure and organisation is available at: www.comp-net.org.

including trade information. There is a lively CompNet community, bringing policy makers and researchers from Europe and elsewhere together at a variety of events (Conferences, workshops, podcasts) throughout the year.

The most important output of CompNet, of course, is its dataset. To emphasise its uniqueness, we will compare it to Orbis/Amadeus, the previously mentioned and widely used source of micro-level information on European firms:

- Unit of analysis: While Orbis directly provides firm-level information, CompNet data are aggregated at the sector level. The CompNet dataset, however, includes not only averages at the sector level, but all other moments of the firm distribution in each sector (median, curtosis, decile values and so on). This offers therefore a rather detailed information of the within-sector firm structure. In addition, the dataset includes the output of several hundred joint distributions, such as interaction between productivity and labour costs.
- Sector coverage: Orbis coverage is narrow and biased towards manufacturing and large firms in countries in which provision of employment information is not compulsory. In many cases, CompNet data providers complement balance sheet information with other sources to improve coverage.
- Cross-country comparability: The micro-distributed approach used by CompNet to collect its data makes it comparable across countries, and so more useful for cross-country studies than Orbis. Regarding trade, Orbis has very little information on firms' exporting activities, while CompNet developed a trade module and has an extensive picture of trade activities in Europe.
- Country coverage: CompNet covers some 20 EU countries out of 27, which makes up, for more than 80% of EU output and employment. The EU coverage by Orbis/Amadeus is much lower.
- Time coverage: This is limited to 10 years in each Orbis vintage, while CompNet's seventh vintage covers all countries from the early 2000s to 2017.[11]

---

[11] A complete assessment of CompNet data and a 360° comparison to Orbis and other datasets were made in the cross-country comparability report, published togheter with the sixth vintage dataset (CompNet, 2018).

For these reasons, and particularly for the simplicity to access and completeness of the firm data, CompNet possibly offers the best perspective to analyse the European economy in the scope of this book. This is the reason why in the next four chapters, we will use the CompNet dataset to empirically assess four hotly debated topics in the ongoing policy discussion in Europe: finance, labour, competition and trade.

6 | *Productivity and the Financial Environment*

6.1 Introduction

The economic literature has traditionally treated the productivity growth of firms and the financing conditions in which they operate entirely separately, mainly because, using macro data alone, it is not obvious how we can disentangle the relationship between the two variables. But it is critical that we understand this link: every firm's financing conditions are a key determinant of its investment decisions. The investment decisions made by the firms in an economy, in turn, are a structural driver of productivity and therefore economic growth.

The availability of micro data, in which both productivity and access to finance can be measured at the firm level, has stimulated this area of research.[1] Economists and policy makers now have a clearer picture of the relationship between a country's financial structure, firms' heterogeneous performance and aggregate economic growth. We can also use these data to evaluate firm productivity in response to a shock such as COVID-19. We will cover this in an appendix to this chapter.

In the micro literature, firms' financing conditions are crucial in determining their investment decisions: frictions in accessing external sources of finance, perhaps due to imperfect information or a lack of collateral, prevent firms from exploiting productive investment opportunities.

Country-specific variables also affect firm performance. The role of insolvency regimes, the efficiency of the banking industry and financial policies regarding capital markets all contribute to productivity growth.

So productivity and growth are affected by the financial environment as a whole. This environment is a combination of firms' financial

---

[1] For a recent review of this literature, see Heil (2017).

conditions (the demand side) and a country's quality of financing institutions (the supply side).

In what follows, we discuss in detail how financial frictions hamper firms' access to finance, how this negatively affects investment decisions and the impact on productivity growth. We will focus on the impact of so-called zombie firms: those that, thanks to soft budget constraints, manage to remain active despite low productivity. We will use CompNet data to document trends of these phenomena around Europe.

6.2 Literature Review

Financial Frictions

Financial frictions are the elements that prevent firms accessing external financial resources when not enough funding is available internally.[2]

Because firms need funding from some source if they want to invest, frictions will bias their investment decisions. Note that the same investment decision can be related to tangible or intangible capital (see Chapter 2 for the distinction), and these two types of capital might be associated with different financial constraints.[3] Those investments, tangible or intangible, might have been productive and growth enhancing. Therefore, financial frictions have the potential to damage the entire economy.

Given the productivity slowdown after the financial crisis, it is no surprise that economic policy institutions started devoting attention to the interaction between the financial environment and productivity. An IMF study (Duval et al., 2017) found that the combination of firm-level financial fragility and country-level tight credit conditions explains much of the international post-crisis productivity slowdown. Firms that entered the crisis with weak balance sheets or were operating in countries in which credit conditions tightened the most had the largest productivity losses during the crisis. The study also emphasises that, after the crisis, a decrease in investment in intangible

---

[2] For a review of this literature, please also view Ferrando et al. (2015), Heil (2017) and Merler (2018).

[3] Tangible capital per se is a form of collateral, while financing intangibles might be subject to higher frictions.

capital was an important channel through which the productivity growth of weaker firms has lagged that of more resilient firms.

Besley et al. (2020) provided a theoretical framework for us to study the impact of financial frictions on the post-crisis productivity slowdown. In their model, a firm's default probability is used as a measure of credit frictions. They use the framework to estimate how much of the post-crisis productivity slowdown in the UK can be attributed to financial frictions. The authors found the following:

- Credit frictions cause an output loss of around 28% per year on average for the UK.
- These losses are much larger for firms with fewer than 250 employees.
- Losses are overwhelmingly due to a lower overall capital stock rather than misallocation of credit potentially failing to reward the most productive firms.

The authors also found that these losses accounted for more than half of the decline in productivity between 2008 and 2009 in the UK. Confirming the preceding results, Chadha et al. (2017) argued that the UK financial sector, based on the provision of intermediate services, accelerated the post-crisis productivity slowdown.

Input misallocation has generally been an impediment to economic performance. Capital misallocation in particular happens when financial resources are not allocated efficiently to the firms that would use them most productively. Instead, some of those resources go to less efficient firms (see Section 4.1). Several studies have shown this is a primary channel for poor economic growth in both advanced and developing countries. Olley and Pakes (1996a) were the first to emphasise the role of capital reallocation as the primary factor leading to increased aggregate productivity growth following deregulation of the US telecommunications industry.

Barnett et al. (2014) focused on capital misallocation in the UK and argued that it might explain the aggregate productivity slowdown after the financial crisis. For Italy, Calligaris et al. (2017) found that capital misallocation helps explain Italy's low productivity growth in recent years: they calculate that Italian aggregate productivity would have been 18% higher had capital misallocation remained at its 1995 level. The authors argued that misallocation has grown mainly within sectors rather than between them, with steadier increases in high-tech sectors. This shows the problem of reallocating capital in sectors where technological change is more rapid. In another study of Italian firms, Manaresi and Pierri (2017) showed that the 2009 credit crunch resulted in a loss of about one quarter of Italian total factor productivity growth.

Capital misallocation is often a by-product of poor national financial policies. These policies include the following:

- Bad insolvency regimes. These make it costly for bad firms to leave the market, meaning they remain active.
- Poor incentives for mergers and acquisitions. Had more of these gone ahead, they would have made firms larger and more productive.
- Growth impediments to the financial sector as a whole. This leads to a banking system that underperforms combined with scarce use of the equity and alternative finance that could have been used to fund productive investment when debt financing was not available (or optimal).

Indeed, Gopinath et al. (2017) put forward capital misallocation as a reason for the pile-up of imbalances that emerged in southern Europe since the 1990s. The authors showed both empirically – using a panel (1999–2012) of firm-level data of Spanish manufacturing firms – and theoretically – using a model with firm heterogeneity, financial frictions and capital adjustment costs – that the decline in the real interest rate that is usually attributed to the euro convergence process has led to an increase in capital misallocation and lower productivity growth.

In this case, underdeveloped capital markets caused capital inflows to divert to less productive firms within industries. The authors examined the dispersion of the return to capital, as measured by the marginal revenue product of capital (MRPK), and the return to labour, as measured by the marginal revenue product of labour (MRPL).

As discussed in details in Section 4.1, this approach was developed by Hsieh and Klenow (2009), who suggested that an increase in the dispersion of a factor's return across firms within a sector might reflect barriers to the efficient allocation of resources. This would imply a loss in aggregate TFP.

The authors found an increase in the dispersion of MRPK across Spanish manufacturing firms from 1999 to 2012, with an acceleration after the crisis feeding into low productivity growth. The dispersion of MRPL does not show the same pattern. They rationalise these findings by developing a model with heterogeneous firms, borrowing constraints, and capital adjustment costs. The decline in the real interest rate since 1994 explains the dynamics in the manufacturing sector in Spain in those years: capital inflows, increase in capital misallocation across firms and a decline in sectoral TFP.

They also extended their empirical analysis to Italy, Portugal, France, Germany and Norway. The paper strikingly finds that the dynamics in Spain were replicated in Italy and Portugal. By contrast, there were no parallels in Germany, France and Norway, which authors attributed to the relative underdevelopment of financial markets in southern Europe. Therefore, effective policies should aim at reducing frictions in financial markets.

Additional evidence of the interplay between the relative level of financial frictions in southern Europe and capital misallocation was also investigated by di Mauro et al. (2018), who focused on the relationship between credit and productivity in three euro area countries: Germany, France and Italy. They found a strong core–periphery divide in the euro area, with credit allocated less efficiently by banks to firms in Italy than in France and Germany. This supports the argument that the financial sector in Italy is less efficient than in core euro area countries. In turn, this might explain Italy's slow aggregate productivity growth.

Zombie Firms

This debate leads us to ask whether loose monetary policy could be keeping unproductive or distressed firms in the market. These zombie firms are less productive (typically in the first decile of the productivity distribution), have higher levels of leverage and are often clustered in stressed industries or regions (McGowan et al., 2017).

Zombie firms reduce aggregate productivity because they suck in capital that they use sub-optimally. The best policy option would be for these firms to exit, and their resources could be reallocated to more productive competitors.

Clearly this would cause political problems. If zombie firms were forced to exit, unemployment would increase until more productive firms reabsorbed those workers – if they actually did employ them.

Most likely not all jobs would be re-absorbed, because technological change and automation are labour saving. And so policy makers have little incentive to eliminate the perpetual inefficiency of zombie firms.[4]

A horde of zombie firms would significantly reduce economic growth. Hence, we must understand the characteristics of these firms and why they exist. This is particularly relevant post-COVID, from at least two perspectives:

- In countries that already have a high number of zombie firms, the COVID shock might generate an unwelcome (for policy makers, at least) increase in the number of firm failures.
- The economic shock might increase the number of zombie firms in countries that, up to that point, had been less afflicted by them[5].

This horde of zombie firms might also hamper recovery growth rates in two ways:

- These firms have, on average, very low levels of productivity. Researchers have found that these firms are not innovative, and innovation is a major driver of productivity growth. They also have lower turnover and investment than non-zombies.
- The persistence of zombie firms prevents reallocation of resources (including credit) to the most productive firms in the economy. McGowan et al. (2017) used a harmonised cross-country firm-level dataset available at the OECD to show that a high concentration of capital in zombie firms within industries was associated with lower investment and employment growth among average non-zombie firms in the same industry. The result: less productivity-enhancing capital reallocation. And so we have a negative impact on the overall economy via lower investment and productivity.

CompNet data by Lopez-Garcia et al. (2018) confirmed these findings. For country-sector years in which the concentration of

---

[4] See in particular Acemoglu and Restrepo (2020) for first evidence of the role of automation on jobs.

[5] Gopinath et al. (2017) have suggested that the emergence of zombie firms might be due to imperfect monetary policy transmission channels. Similarly, Acharya et al. (2019) showed a resurgence of zombie lending by banks after the enforcement of the ECB's unconventional monetary policy during the financial crisis (see infra). Both conditions are likely to repeat, post-COVID.

distressed firms is higher, the average levels of investment and job creation were significantly lower. In addition, the authors also found a positive correlation between the share of distressed firms and the share of credit-constrained but healthy firms in the same sector. This demonstrates that zombie firms hold resources that could be reallocated to more efficient firms.

Finally, Andrews and Petroulakis (2017) found a strong correlation between capital misallocation and aggregate productivity growth in a panel of 11 European countries. In particular, there was a strong association between the share of capital sunk in zombie firms, and credit availability for healthy firms within the same sector. Distressed firms, it seems, were crowding out credit allocation to healthy enterprises.

If zombie firms are so bad for the economy, and so inefficient, why do they still exist? Andrews and Petroulakis (2017) connected the presence of zombie firms to the health of the banking sector. The authors argued that impaired banks may have an incentive to conceal non-performing loans to avoid losses on their balance sheets, and so they do not cut their losses on zombie firms. In this way, the banks are able to remain active in the market too. The research also found that, in countries where the insolvency framework is hostile to efficient restructuring processes, healthy banks made limited efforts to reduce the number of non-performing loans.

Schivardi et al. (2021) also studied the link between weak firms and under-capitalised banks in a panel dataset (2004–2013) of bank–firm relationships in Italy. They argued that weak banks were more likely to extend credit to distressed firms during the euro area crisis, when they were facing difficulties in raising capital to meet stricter capital requirements. This resulted in a serious misallocation of capital that increased the failure rate of healthy firms and reduced the failure rate of distressed firms. But the authors disagreed with previous findings that capital misallocation drove down aggregate productivity growth in Europe after the great recession.

Ongoing research at the ECB, part of which is summarised in Lopez-Garcia et al. (2018), is using CompNet data to perform a similar analysis. The hypothesis is that in those countries where capital adequacy ratios are on average lower, the leverage of distressed firms continued increasing after the crisis. The authors are also studying the impact of weak banks' institutional characteristics on firms' leverage.

Like Schivardi et al. (2021), they have found that, after the financial crisis, firms' leverage increased the most in countries in which banks are under-capitalised. By contrast, more capitalised banks lent relatively more to healthy firms before the crisis. They found that leverage growth is higher in distressed firms than in healthy ones across all countries covered by the CompNet dataset.

Acharya et al. (2019) argued that monetary policy in the euro area has caused zombie firms to reduce economic growth. They linked the persistence of zombie firms in European periphery countries with the recapitalisation of banks in those countries following the announcement of the ECB's Outright Monetary Transactions (OMT) program.

The authors showed that the OMT program led to an increase in the value of sovereign bonds issued by southern European countries, which indirectly recapitalised the banks in these countries due to their holdings of these bonds. But these funds did not lead to economic growth. Instead, the banks that remained relatively under-capitalised – even after the announcement of the OMT program – and continued financing low-productivity firms with which they had strong connections. Distressed firms used these funds to pile up cash reserves, snuffing out any benefits for real economic growth. The authors focused on industries with a relatively high share of zombie firms and found that healthy firms in those industries suffered as a result of this credit misallocation.

Box 6.1   The OMT program, access to finance and firm productivity

The OMT program in Europe was also assessed in the 2020 CompNet report (CompNet, 2020). The authors highlighted that there was a peak in the share of financially constrained firms in Europe in 2013 and linked it with the announcement of the OMT program by the European Central Bank. The OMT program was never actually implemented, but it provided a powerful weapon for the ECB to calm the financial markets at the peak of the sovereign debt crisis in Europe. It was specifically aimed at easing the financial market conditions of stressed debt countries, but it also represented a turning point for access to finance for euro area firms (Rostagno et al., 2019; Ferrando et al., 2021).

The report also shed light on where credit-constrained firms are located. Figure 6.1 shows that the share of financially constrained firms in Europe dropped from 2013 to 2016. This decrease was due to the

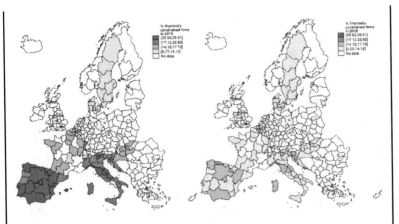

Figure 6.1 Proportion of financially constrained firms in NUTS2 regions in Europe by quintile, 2013 (left) and 2016 (right).
Source: CompNet Firm productivity Report – CompNet (2020)

announcement of the OMT, which led to an improvement in access to external finance. The report provides econometric evidence that the OMT announcement might have relaxed the problems in credit access and the negative link with productivity.

On the other hand, Figure 6.1 also shows that there is strong spatial autocorrelation in the distribution of the share of credit constrained firms in Europe. This means that the presence of financially constrained firms in one NUTS2 region is correlated with the presence of credit-constrained firms in neighbouring regions. Therefore, policies aimed at improving the business environment in one region might be influential to improve the business environment in neighbouring regions. The authors argue that the announcement of the OMT program was as example of this, and show that the OMT had a positive effect in decreasing the degree of spatial autocorrelation of credit-constrained firms in Europe.

6.3 Productivity and Financial Markets

Since its inception CompNet has studied the role of financial markets in productivity and growth. The early findings of CompNet research on finance are summarised in Ferrando et al. (2015). It provides descriptive evidence of the evolution of firms' financial position during the financial crisis and early recovery. Moreover, structural analyses are also performed to study the link between investments and productivity. The report reviews several indicators of the financial and financing conditions of firms, including firm performance, the structure of external funding and financial fragility and independence. Information available in the CompNet dataset allowed the authors to propose and compute two indicators of financial constraints, combining firm balance sheets with survey data.

The first indicator is based on information derived from a survey of firms – SAFE, which is conducted at the ECB – on financing constraints. It is then matched with their financial statements. The methodology is as follows:

(1) They estimated an equation designed to rank firms according to the probability that they were credit constrained, using previous results that the probability that firms face financial obstacles is a function of their financial situation, in particular financial leverage, financial pressure, profit margin, collateral and cash holdings.
(2) The estimated coefficients of this regression were used to compute a score, ranking firms from the least to the most financially constrained.
(3) They set a threshold using the exogenous averages of credit-constrained firms by country. Firms above the threshold were defined as credit constrained.

The second indicator of financial constraints is built based on information from balance sheets and profit and loss accounts. Both indicators of credit constraints provide an approximation of the share of firms that are credit and investment constrained in the economy.

Ferrando et al. (2015) also investigated how heterogeneity in the financial position of firms directly led to financing problems. The authors exploited the availability of balance sheet indicators in Comp-Net to provide an overview of how the financial structure of European firms has changed during and in the years after the financial crisis. They did this by analysing the financing gap, which is the difference between investment and cash flow over turnover, and so a measure of the extent of external resources needed to finance new investments. Lower or negative values, driven by large cash flows, imply that firms mostly finance new investments through internal resources, or they may be driven by low new investments in a given year.

The authors found on average a higher financing gap for firms in stressed countries, meaning that these firms relied more on external resources for investment reasons than enterprises in non-stressed economies. The financing gap increased in stressed economies and reduced in non-stressed countries after the crisis, but this might not signal a convergence in firms' access to external resources. In fact, firms across all countries faced a reduction in cash flows during the crisis which, not supported by the banking sector, meant that investment contracted.

What are the dynamics? In 2008, the crisis hit the cash flow of all firms at the same time, and so in all countries the financing gap decreased. Then, in non-stressed countries, easier financial conditions created an increase in the financing gap, while in stressed economies the financing gap was already high, and so banks were not able to support firms. In turn, this required investment to keep the financing gap stable.

This implies the contraction of investment was due to a lack of external financing in stressed countries during and after the crisis. This would be a supply-side argument, in line with the credit-crunch evidence: the decrease in investment was essentially due to a broken banking sector. However, Ferrando et al. (2015) also observed that collateral in stressed and non-stressed economies have moved together since the crisis. If higher collateral is a signal of higher probability of receiving a loan, then we would expect that, in stressed countries in which the share of distressed firms is higher, the average collateral would be higher than in non-stressed countries. Indeed, firms assessed as risky would need to put forward higher collateral to receive a loan.

To confirm the hypothesis that the supply-side argument is only part of the story, Ferrando et al. (2015) also looked at levels of debt ratio. If financially distressed firms in stressed economies had financing constraints, we should expect to see deleveraging after the financial crisis. They found that higher leverage levels in stressed economies fed into lower levels of investments after the crisis, and this mechanism acted as a drag on firms' productivity and profitability – consequently, on aggregate economic growth too.

To sum up, financing and financial constraints in stressed countries created low-profit investment, which exacerbated the negative effects of the crisis and the gap between these countries and those who coped better with the demand shock. A paper by Ferrando et al.

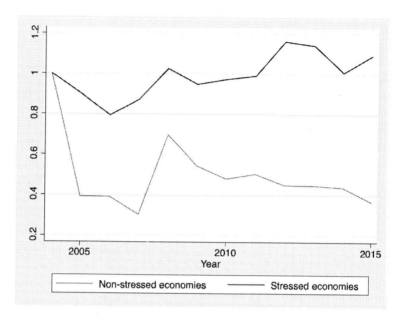

Figure 6.2 Share of credit-constrained firms, 2004 = 1.
Note: Authors' elaboration of CompNet sixth vintage data.

(2015) shows how country-level financial frictions fed poor economic performance through negative incentives to invest at the level of firms. Importantly, Ferrando et al. (2015) also provided econometric evidence that investment decreased after the crisis in countries that had been severely affected because of the low profitability of investment and the unhealthy status of the business and financial environment.

In the rest of this empirical chapter, we provide additional evidence on some of the patterns identified by previous research using updated CompNet data.

Figure 6.2 shows the credit-constraint indicator used by Ferrando et al. (2015) to capture the health of the business environment in Europe. We follow the same classification of countries as "stressed" and "non-stressed" economies as in Ferrando et al. (2015). Figure 6.2 shows how the share of credit-constrained firms evolved in these two groups of countries from 2004 to 2015, using the sixth vintage of CompNet data. The figure uses the full sample, covering the total economy.

The figure shows a persistent difference in the share of credit-constrained firms between stressed and non-stressed economies in Europe. Worryingly, the trends diverge. Non-stressed countries had a lower share of financially constrained firms in all years covered by the sample. For those countries, the share of firms encountering financing constraints significantly decreased in the pre-crisis period, following good monetary conditions in those years. Afterwards, the crisis seriously worsened the business environment across Europe, affecting countries in both groups. As a result, we see two spikes in the share of credit-constrained firms around 2008.

However, non-stressed countries managed to recover quickly, with a decreasing number of credit-constrained firms since 2010. In stressed economies, the share of credit-constrained firms carried on rising after the financial crisis. In 2015, the last year of the panel, the average share of credit constrained enterprises had increased in stressed economies. Worryingly, the poor post-crisis financial environment in stressed countries did not provide a sufficient impulse to improve access to external sources of financial resources for their firms.

Structural issues in stressed economies made their firms more vulnerable to overall macroeconomic shocks. But these divergent trends may also indicate that the gap in financial conditions between these two groups of countries has worsened over time.

Figure 6.3 shows the expected negative correlation between the share of credit-constrained firms and their investments on average in our sample. This implies that as the number of financially constrained firms in an economy increases, productive investment tends to decrease. Since the share of credit-constrained firms in an economy is a proxy for the health of its business and financial environment, the graph in Figure 6.3 shows that investments are fewer – and smaller – in financially stressed environments than in healthy ones.

Figure 6.4 shows the average share of credit-constrained firms by TFP decile in stressed and non-stressed economies. It illustrates the difference between the pre-crisis and the post-crisis periods in both groups of countries. As expected, the relevance of credit constraints is negatively correlated with firms' average productivity in both groups of countries.

The share of credit-constrained firms in low deciles of the TFP distribution is significantly higher in stressed economies than in non-stressed economies, though approximately the same at the top of the

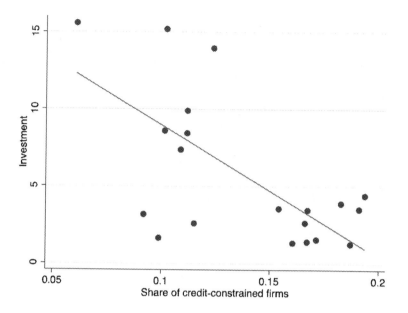

Figure 6.3 Correlation between the share of credit-constrained firms and their investment.

Note: Authors' elaboration of CompNet sixth vintage data.

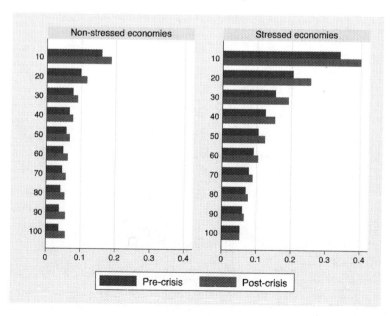

Figure 6.4 Share of credit-constrained firms by TFP decile.

Note: Authors' elaboration of CompNet sixth vintage data.

TFP distribution. Taking the non-stressed economies as a benchmark, this implies that in stressed economies there was already a problem of access to finance before the financial crisis.

In the post-crisis period, not surprisingly the share of firms facing financing constraints increased for both groups of countries. The increase is, however, much larger for stressed countries. Moreover, within this group of countries, the increase in credit constraints tends to be proportionally larger until at least the fourth decile of the productivity distribution. This is consistent with the idea that scarcely efficient firms slowed down the recovery in countries that underwent serious financial distress during the crisis, due as we have seen to capital misallocation.

To fully appreciate these stylised facts, we need a micro-level perspective. We cannot rely on aggregate macroeconomic figures, and so we need to provide some econometric evidence of the relationship between productivity and credit constraints.

TFP and Firms' Credit Constraints

We argued that the share of credit-constrained firms increased after the global financial crisis at low deciles of the TFP distribution, especially in financially distressed countries. Thanks to the CompNet dataset, we can assess whether the higher incidence of credit-constrained firms in a given sector, country and year is associated with different moments of the same sector's productivity distribution.

To that extent, we have run simple linear regressions of the form:

$$TFP_{s,c,t} = \alpha + \beta SAFE_{s,c,t} + \gamma_c + \sigma_s + \tau_t + \epsilon_{s,c,t}, \quad (6.1)$$

where $\tilde{TFP}_{s,c,t}$ is a specific moment (first decile or mean, for example) of the total factor productivity distribution in sector s of country c at year t, and $SAFE_{s,c,t}$ is the average index of credit-constrained firms in sector s of country c at year t. We complement our specification with γ_c, σ_s and τ_t country, sector and year fixed effects, respectively.

Table 6.1 shows the results of this empirical exercise. In columns (1)–(4), we see the relationship between financial constraints and different deciles of the TFP distribution. These results show that higher sector-level credit constraints are significantly associated to lower productivity for firms at low levels of the TFP distribution, while the

Table 6.1. *TFP and financial constraints at sector level.*

	(1) log TFP p10	(2) log TFP p50	(3) log TFP mean	(4) TFP p90	(5) log TFP p50	(6) log TFP p50	(7) log TFP p50
SAFE index	-0.639***	-0.336**	-0.240	-0.160	-0.484***	-0.501***	-0.245**
	(0.155)	(0.153)	(0.163)	(0.175)	(0.166)	(0.187)	(0.123)
Italy dummy					0.638***		
					(0.0570)		
Italy*SAFE index					-1.312***		
					(0.320)		
Netherlands dummy						-0.247***	
						(0.0538)	
Netherlands*SAFE index						1.121***	
						(0.292)	
Germany dummy							-1.295***
							(0.148)
Germany*SAFE index							-0.238
							(0.724)
Observations	4,973	4,990	4,990	4,973	4,991	4,991	4,991
R-squared	0.530	0.524	0.529	0.538	0.236	0.209	0.263
Sector FEs	Yes	Yes	Yes	Yes	Yes	Yes	Yes
Country FEs	Yes	Yes	Yes	Yes	No	No	No
Year FEs	Yes	Yes	Yes	Yes	Yes	Yes	Yes

CompNet's 20E sample.
Robust standard errors are in parentheses.
*** $p < 0.01$, ** $p < 0.05$, * $p < 0.1$.

effect is not statistically significant at the upper tail of the distribution. This is consistent with the idea that low-productivity firms tend to rely more on external finance, while high-productivity firms can use cash flows to finance their activities. Therefore, when financial constraints emerge, the firms at the low end of the TFP distribution are those suffering the most.

In addition, in columns (5)–(7) we assess whether this effect at the median of the TFP distribution is different across three relevant countries: Italy, Netherlands and Germany, affected differently by the financial crisis. In column (5), we can observe from the coefficient on the interaction term between each country dummy and the SAFE index that the impact of credit constraints on firm productivity is particularly negative in Italy, while it is positive in the Netherlands and not significant in Germany. This means that Italian firms on average relied more on external funds to finance their activities than Dutch firms, and as a result they suffered more when credit constraints emerged, as it may have happened after the global financial crisis. This is consistent with the picture in Figure 6.4.

This has important implications for speed of recovery following the COVID-19 crisis: the greatest impact of the pandemic in Europe was in countries such as Italy and Spain that rely to a great extent on external finance.

TFP and Other Financial Indicators

We can see the heterogeneous impact of financial variables across the productivity distribution when we look at other financial indicators.

Figure 6.5 shows the average levels of investment ratios at different moments of the TFP distribution in stressed and non-stressed economies. The investment ratio represents the growth rate of capital plus depreciation, divided by total assets.

We can see it has been persistently higher in non-stressed economies than in stressed economies. It has also increased steadily in healthy economies after the crisis both at the bottom and at the top of the TFP distribution, while it has stagnated in between.

In stressed economies, investment has recovered to some extent after the crisis, but the increase was sustained only by the firms at the top of the distribution. The recovery of the investment ratio was not as strong as in non-stressed countries.

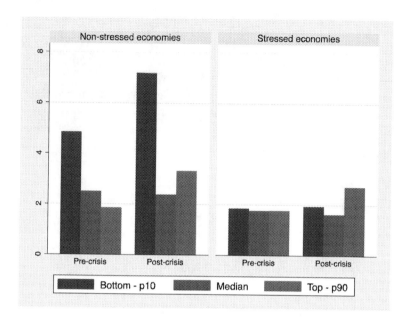

Figure 6.5 Investment at bottom, median and top of TFP distribution.
Note: Authors' elaboration of CompNet sixth vintage data.

Alongside the analysis of firm heterogeneity and financial frictions across European countries conducted by Ferrando et al. (2015), we also look at the pattern of debt ratio and return on assets (ROA) levels. If financially distressed firms in stressed economies had financing constraints, we should expect to observe deleveraging after the financial crisis.

In Figure 6.6, we compare the average level of leverage in stressed and non-stressed economies before and after the crisis at different deciles of the TFP distribution. The debt ratio increased in both stressed and non-stressed countries in the post-crisis period. This is consistent with a story of firms borrowing from banks in a period of financial hardship. We do not observe any deleveraging process in stressed economies; instead, we see a surge in debt ratios, once again driven by firms in the bottom deciles of the productivity distribution.

Finally, in Figure 6.7 we observe the trend in ROA. The graph shows that ROA, while on a decreasing trend since the global financial crisis in both groups of countries, is much higher in non-stressed economies

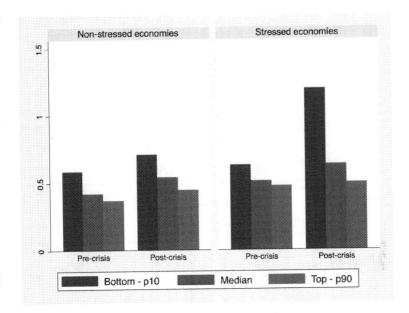

Figure 6.6 Leverage at bottom, median and top of TFP distribution.
Note: Authors' elaboration of CompNet sixth vintage data.

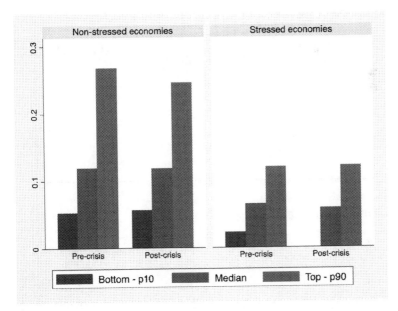

Figure 6.7 ROA at bottom, median and top of TFP distribution.
Note: Authors' elaboration of CompNet sixth vintage data.

than in stressed countries. This seems to suggest that a mutually reinforcing mechanism of low investment and low profitability of investment in these countries since the financial crisis. It is also important to notice that the average level of ROA is driven up by the most productive firms.

The main policy message is that a number of elements are needed in order to be able to assess whether a country financial structure is able to sustain its growth potential:

- The share of credit constrained firms within a country
- Their evolution over time
- Their relationship with investment and (different moments of) the productivity distribution

The evidence clearly implies that financial variables need to be carefully assessed in their micro dimension when we analyse economic growth, as their meaning is different for more or less productive firms. Firm-level analyses are essential if we want to capture the heterogeneity of these phenomena.

We conclude that to foster sustained economic growth, policy makers must develop a fully grounded financial context with a sound banking sector; one that is able to channel capital to highly productive firms and innovative entrepreneurs, while allowing low-productivity and severely financially constrained firms to go bankrupt, letting resources flow to the most efficient firms in the economy.

Importantly, we have also seen that these factors have a different impact on the dimensions of performance that we considered at different points in the productivity distribution of firms.

We have seen, in particular that, on average, leverage is disproportionately higher in low-productivity firms and, specifically, among these firms in financially distressed countries. Research into these zombie firms has flourished in recent years as international policy institutions have noted their role and lamented their persistence, in particular in southern European countries.

TFP and Zombie Firms

Zombie firms at the bottom of the productivity distribution, as we have seen, have acted as a drag on investment in stressed economies (Ferrando et al., 2015). As we observed in Figure 6.6, leverage growth in Europe has indeed been associated with low-productivity firms since the global financial crisis. Therefore, policy institutions should carefully assess precisely which firms are increasing their debt levels, because it will help them to predict whether those levels will be sustainable – especially in the post-COVID world. As the 2008–2009 financial crisis taught us, the sustainability of debt in the non-financial sector influences the stability of the financial sector too.

The CompNet dataset contains four ways of characterising a firm as a zombie:

(1) If it has paid interests higher than its operating profits in the previous three years.
(2) If its markup was lower than one.
(3) If it has reported three consecutive years of negative profits.
(4) If reporting negative profits for three consecutive years, and not being high-growth, where high-growth firms are those growing (in terms of sales) at a rate equal or larger than 3% per year.

We use the last definition in this book, but results are generally robust across the different definitions of a zombie firm.

First, we characterise the average zombie firm in Europe. Figure 6.8 shows the ratio of some indicators for zombie and non-zombie firms on average between 2004 and 2015. We continue using the same classification of countries as stressed and non-stressed economies. If the ratio is larger than one, then it means that on average zombie firms have a higher value for that indicator than healthy firms. If it is lower than one, then that measure is higher for healthy rather than distressed firms. Finally, if it is equal or close to one, then zombie and non-zombie firms are equal or very similar on average.

Figure 6.8 shows that, on average, distressed firms perform worse in stressed economies than in healthy ones. This is consistent with previous research and with our analysis: the persistence of these firms in the market in stressed countries might be at least a partial explanation of their bad aggregate economic performance.

The graph shows that zombie firms are on average half as competitive as healthy firms in both groups of countries. On average, they have fewer employees, are less productive, produce much smaller turnover and invest much less than healthy firms across countries. The only notable exception is that zombie firms seem to be closer to the investment benchmark in stressed countries. We take it as yet

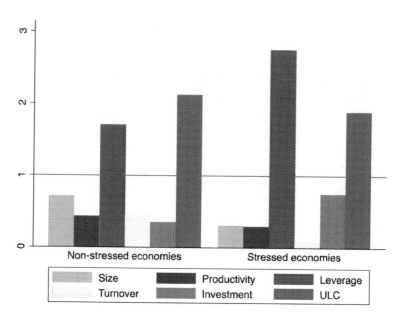

Figure 6.8 Characteristics of zombie vs. non-zombie firms.
Note: Authors' elaboration of CompNet sixth vintage dataset

another indication that investment levels of healthy firms in stressed economies are biased down by persisting frictions in the financial environment (including the large share of zombie firms).

From Figure 6.8, it also emerges that zombie firms have accumulated much higher average debt levels than healthy firms. This difference is even larger in stressed economies, in which on average zombie firms are nearly three times more leveraged than healthy ones.

Figure 6.9 zooms in to show the average share of zombie firms at different deciles of the productivity distribution in stressed and non-stressed countries.

The graph shows that, not surprisingly, the share of zombie firms is higher at low-productivity deciles than at the top of the productivity distribution. There is, therefore, across countries, a strong and negative association between firm productivity and the probability of them being financially unhealthy. In stressed economies, the share of zombie firms at the lowest deciles of the TFP distribution is higher on average between 2004 and 2015 than in countries that were less

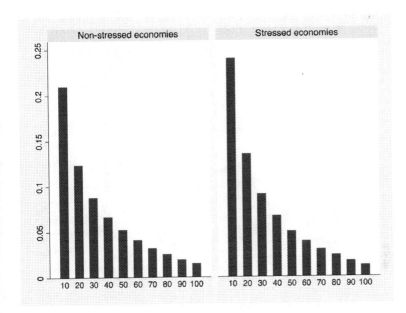

Figure 6.9 Share of zombie firms by TFP decile.

Note: Authors' elaboration of CompNet sixth vintage dataset

affected by the financial crisis. The share of distressed firms at the top of the distribution is similar across these two groups of countries.

Figure 6.10 breaks down the share of zombie firms in stressed and non-stressed economies at different points of the TFP distribution and over time (comparing the pre- and post-financial crisis positions). It shows that, before the crisis, stressed economies had, on average, fewer financially distressed firms at the each of the bottom, median and top of the productivity distribution than countries that suffered relatively less from the crisis.

After the crisis, however, the share of zombie firms in stressed countries at the bottom of the distribution increased by nearly 20%. It also increased in non-stressed economies, but the rise was much smaller. The share of distressed firms also increased at the median and at the top of the TFP distribution in stressed countries, although by a relatively smaller amount than at the lowest deciles. On the contrary, the same shares remained stable in non-stressed countries.

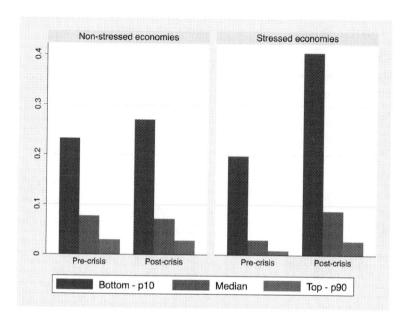

Figure 6.10 Share of zombie firms at bottom, median and top of TFP distribution, by period.

Note: Authors' elaboration of CompNet sixth vintage dataset.

This might be related to the particular nature of the 2008–2009 crisis, linked to the banking sector. Stressed countries were characterised by loose banking policies before the crisis, and hence an abundance of credit at favourable conditions to firms that didn't deserve it (recall the discussion on capital misallocation). The sudden stop in capital flows created a credit crunch, which in stressed countries created relatively more non-performing loans. Then, loose monetary conditions and the implicit recapitalisation of banking systems in stressed countries created favourable conditions for zombie firms (Acharya et al., 2019), as discussed.

Finally, looking explicitly at capital misallocation, Figures 6.11 and 6.12 show the correlation between the share of distressed firms and average investment and turnover, respectively, in stressed and non-stressed economies, controlling for cyclical conditions. Both correlations are negative (as we would expect), but less so in stressed countries. This is further evidence of a distortion in these countries' financial systems.

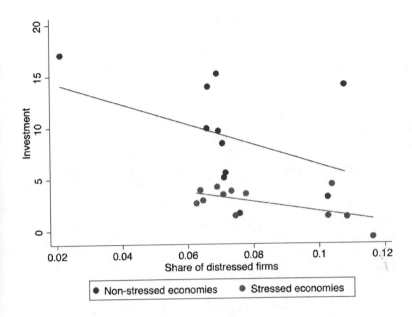

Figure 6.11 Share of zombie firms and investment, by country.

Note: Authors' elaboration of CompNet sixth vintage data.

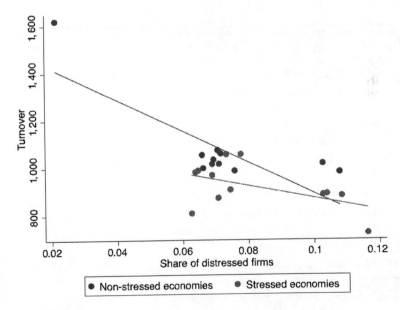

Figure 6.12 Share of zombie firms and turnover, by country.

Note: Authors' elaboration of CompNet sixth vintage data.

6.4 Conclusion

It is harder for growing firms in malfunctioning financial environments to access the external financial resources they need for productive investment. As a result, their productivity growth stagnates, creating low aggregate economic growth as well.

We also argued that firms in countries that underwent serious financial distress due to the financial crisis have persistently suffered from its consequences. The situation led to debts piling up, a contraction of investments and a strong decrease in firm profitability. Core European countries also suffered from the effects of the great recession, but they recovered more quickly.

This process also led (and is partially due) to an increase in the number of low-productivity zombie firms in periphery countries after the financial crisis. These firms would exit from the market if capital allocation were more efficient. Distressed firms have a negative impact on aggregate economic performance because they are not productive and hinder innovation, divert resources from the most productive enterprises within industries and invest less than healthy firms.

Zombie firms are associated with the existence of frictions within relatively underdeveloped financial markets in southern Europe, as well as with pre-existing connections between distressed firms and weak banks. This has allowed zombie firms to survive after the financial crisis. Unconventional expansive monetary policy in the euro area since 2012 may have also added further incentives for weak banks to extend credit to zombie firms.

This already persistent situation may get worse after COVID-19, as the same (financially) stressed countries, notably Italy and Spain, are also among those that have been most severely hit by the pandemic.

So it may be necessary to speed up the full development of capital and financial markets across Europe. In this perspective, completing the capital markets union in a short time would seem to be a desirable policy outcome. Hopefully, this would likely remove any remaining frictions that still prevent many countries from developing a financial structure able to efficiently allocate resources across firms.

In this context, it is also necessary to reduce the political economy problem that links weak banks and distressed firms, deepening credit misallocation. To this extent, the labour market support schemes put forward as a response to the COVID-19 emergency might also accelerate the restructuring of affected sectors, minimising (or at least masking) the associated political costs in each country.

If a unique set of financial policies is to be developed at the European level, then it needs to be structured so that it supports the growth of innovative, rather than distressed and unproductive, firms. This means that insolvency regimes should be reformed to make restructuring processes of poor-performance firms more efficient and less costly. In addition, adequate incentives to merger or acquire might foster the rise of stronger and larger firms at the top of the productivity distribution without damaging European competition policy (see Chapter 8 for a more detailed discussion on market power).

Finally, we need to get over the European bias towards debt financing. There is a negative cultural attitude to equity financing among entrepreneurs in parts of Europe, but we need stronger incentives for successful entrepreneurs to resort to equity over debt if we want to unlock Europe's growth potential. Even better, we need more integrated policies to create a real European market for alternative finance. As the experiences of the US and China teach us, this means encouraging venture capital investors who will enhance the potential of high-growth and innovative start-up firms.

Appendix 6.1: Zombiefication after COVID-19

The unprecedented crisis brought by the COVID-19 pandemic prompted huge government intervention to support firms. We have seen public credit guarantee schemes, debt moratoria, direct financial aid, central bank lending and purchase programs and a loosening of micro- and macro-prudential supervisory rules (Laeven et al., 2020).

But economists and others fret that these costly programs could generate zombie firms and zombie lending. We know from the Japanese crisis of the 1990s and the Global Financial Crisis that weak banks preserved their lending relationships by rolling over credits to unviable firms (either to avoid loan loss recognition or to preserve valuable relationships (Laeven et al., 2020), making it possible for those firms to artificially survive market competition. We can name this process "zombiefication".

Zombiefication reduces productivity growth (Hsieh and Klenow, 2009). Reversing it implies that unproductive firms will shrink and eventually exit from the market.

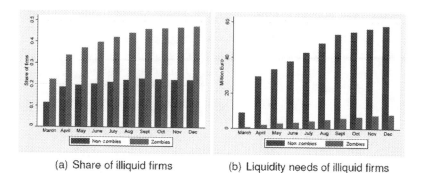

(a) Share of illiquid firms   (b) Liquidity needs of illiquid firms

Figure 6.13 Zombie and illiquid firms in Italy.
Source: Adapted from Schivardi et al. (2020)

Antoni et al. (2019) found that, in Germany, plants linked to banks with access to an asset purchasing programme (APP) are approximately 20% less likely to exit the market; aggregate entry and exit rates in regional markets with high APP exposures are also lower.

The authors argue that, by impeding the exit of firms from the market, APPs seem to have encouraged zombiefication. Similar evidence has been provided by Jiménez et al. (2014), that show that a loose (conventional) monetary policy in the euro area induced weak Spanish banks to inefficiently extend credit to unproductive firms in Spain.

This evidence casts doubts on the effectiveness of support schemes put in place by governments and by European institutions. The support provided by public institutions is of unprecedented size, but short-run support may ultimately slow down any recovery.

Schivardi et al. (2020) have argued that this is a second-order concern: the authors showed that in Italy the bulk of liquidity needs during the crisis came from firms that were financially sound before crisis, as the shock hit firms with an intensity that was independent of their financial conditions. Figure 6.13 shows the evidence provided by the author.

Similar evidence has been provided by Nurmi et al. (2020). They found that in Finland the congestion effect estimated as in Caballero et al. (2008) weakened the performance of non-zombies in the market – not because of misallocation of resources, but rather because of the higher number of firms in the market. This constrained the investment and growth opportunities for the best firms. They found that zombies were often not truly distressed, but rather firms that temporarily suffered from low revenues relative to interest payments. Roughly one-third of the zombie firms in their sample were growing firms, while two-thirds of them recover from the zombie status to become healthy firms again.

Zombiefication may still represent a huge threat for Europe's economy. But, as argued by Schivardi et al. (2020) and Laeven et al. (2020), the framework in which we are currently embedded is radically different from the past:

- The pandemic shock hit sectors that are otherwise healthy.
- Banks were more prepared for this crisis, with relatively more space to absorb losses.

Hence, in order not to let many solvent firms exit the market, governments should not hold back from providing credit to firms during the pandemic: the theoretical prediction of a congestion effect due to the larger share of zombie firms is still controversial, whereas the risk of displacing otherwise viable firms is large.

7 | *Productivity and the Labour Market*

7.1 Introduction

In a world of heterogeneous firms, aggregate economic performance is crucially connected with how the factors of production are allocated. We discussed the theory behind this in Chapter 4. And we concentrate here on the labour factor.

In traditional specifications of the production function, capital and labour are the two most important production factors of a firm. We discussed in Chapter 6 how an inefficient allocation of credit to firms feeds into bad investment decisions, distorted capital accumulation and poor economic performance in the aggregate. In this chapter, we turn to the role of labour misallocation, defined rather loosely as all situations where the factor labor is not fully exploited in its intrinsic productivity potential. This can come for instance from (i) unproductive firms employing too many people, (ii) productive people being in the wrong jobs, and alike. This has an impact on individual firm productivity as well as of course on its aggregation at sector and country level.

We will use variations of the productivity–decomposition formula developed by Foster et al. (2006), which we discussed in detail in Chapter 4. According to those types of decomposition, aggregate productivity growth is the result of a combination of factors:

(1) Productivity of individual firms (the within term)
(2) Size of firms (the between term)
(3) Changes in the market share of the least and most productive firms (the covariance term)
(4) Entry of innovative and productive firms
(5) Exit of inefficient firms (factors 4 and 5 combine as the net entry term)

As with capital misallocation, a distorted distribution of workers across the firms within industries prevents productivity growth. Both the between and covariance terms are affected: firms struggle to grow, and those that do grow are not necessarily the most productive.

As aggregate productivity is the *weighted* average of individual firm productivity, labour misallocation lowers aggregate productivity growth, essentially by hindering the shift of market share from inefficient to more productive firms. At the same time, the presence of inefficient firms in the market is a drag on overall economic growth, as we pointed out when discussing zombie firms.

Once again, the heterogeneous productivity of firms is at the heart of this phenomenon. Labour misallocation is relevant for economic growth only if firms differ in their productivity levels, and labour market institutions generate frictions that prevent the efficient allocation of workers across those firms.

In this chapter, we will reconnect the evidence on labour misallocation to the literature on firm heterogeneity. We will start by presenting the most relevant literature on labour misallocation and how firms take employment decisions. We will devote particular attention to labour misallocation in the EU, the role of different wage regimes, and the evolution of the labour share in the economy. We will link this to the empirical results of the CompNet labour module. Finally, we will use the CompNet dataset to analyse recent patterns of labour misallocation and firm growth dynamics in European countries, also taking into account the COVID-19 shock.

7.2 Literature Review

Labour Misallocation

A useful review of early studies of the process of resource reallocation was provided by Bartelsman and Doms (2000). In general, this research found that, in crisis and non-crisis periods alike, in both shrinking and growing industries, there was a continuous process of job creation and job destruction, with firms entering and exiting the market. This is direct evidence of resource reallocation that shapes aggregate growth.

Davis and Haltiwanger (1992) made an important contribution to this topic. They estimated the heterogeneity of establishment-level employment changes in the US from 1972 to 1986 by measuring gross job flows across plants. These could be the result of employment changes across firms, or because a firm had entered or left the market. This led to three streams of research into business dynamics that analysed the connection between job and worker reallocation, the heterogeneity of employment dynamics at firm level and the cyclical behaviour of the labour market.[1]

To our knowledge, the paper by Bartelsman et al. (2004) was the first empirical assessment of labour misallocation in a cross-country setting. The authors relied on a novel dataset covering two-digit industries in 24 countries. They reported evidence of a continuous process of creative destruction, with massive reallocation of resources across firms within industries and countries. In all markets, firms constantly entered and exited with many entrants failing, and successful ones expanding. This process directly affected aggregate productivity growth, because resources were reallocated away from less productive firms to more productive ones.

This study also shed light on the net entry component. Entry and exit rates were similar across advanced countries, but there was heterogeneity in the post-entry growth, which was higher in firms in the US than in Europe. In Europe, barriers to firm growth seemed more relevant than barriers to entry. Analogous results – particularly as concerns the smaller post-entry growth of successful entrants in the EU than in the US – were also obtained by a subsequent study of 10 OECD countries (Bartelsman et al., 2005).

Barriers to firm growth are a clear sign of poor business dynamism. It is commonly believed that the business environment has historically been less dynamic in the EU than in the US, but more recently there is also evidence that business dynamism has slowed down in the US too. Decker et al. (2014) in particular found evidence that business dynamism has been in retreat in the US since at least the beginning of the twenty-first century, with, for example, data suggesting a strong

---

[1] Equivalent research on the parallel role of capital misallocation across firms was initially less prevalent, due to the problem of extracting comprehensive data on firm capital from a balance sheet. In contrast, data on labour could be extracted from tax forms. From the 1990s onwards, new sources of firm-level balance sheet information gave rise to the research on capital misallocation that we discussed in the previous chapter.

decline in the share of US employment in dynamic young businesses. Hyatt and Spletzer (2015) found similar patterns, and argued that this might be due to a decline in the availability of short-term jobs.

Andrews et al. (2016) used firm-level evidence from 23 countries to explore the drivers of the productivity slowdown than characterises the post-crisis global environment (see Chapter 6). They find a divergent pattern of productivity across firms, with slow productivity growth for the "average" firm masking the fact that a small cadre of firms have been able to grow much faster. Between 2001 and 2013, average labour productivity at the global productivity frontier (the top 5% of most productive firms) grew at an average annual rate of 2.8% in the manufacturing sector, and 3.6% in the market services sector, while the corresponding growth rate of all other firms was around 0.5% in both sectors.

This is another feature of poor business dynamism, related to technology diffusion. Andrews et al. (2016) found that technologies developed at the global frontier are spreading faster across countries, but slower across firms within any economy. Many existing technologies were not exploited by a non-trivial share of firms in an economy. The authors also showed that there was more productivity divergence in sectors in which pro-competitive product market reforms had been least extensive, establishing a link between product market reforms (notably the incentives for technological adoption) and productivity.

There has also been research on how differences in economic performance across countries can be accounted for by differences in the efficiency of the reallocation process.[2] Hsieh and Klenow (2009) used firm-level manufacturing data to quantify the extent of misallocation in China and India and compare it to misallocation in the US for narrowly defined industries. They found that, once capital and labour were hypothetically reallocated to equalise marginal products to the extent observed in the US, manufacturing TFP gains in China should have been 30–50% larger. In India, the figure is 40–60%.

Bartelsman et al. (2013) developed a model for heterogeneous firms facing adjustment frictions and distortions, and used it to

---

[2] Inefficient institutions might generate frictions in the labour market, but also problems in product market search, financial frictions, barriers to entrepreneurship and so on.

investigate whether policy distortions across countries fed into labour misallocation. They were able to explain cross-country variations in aggregate economic performance and found that distortions that account for the differences in the labour reallocation process explained cross-country differences in aggregate economic performance.

A paper by Andrews and Cingano (2014) further strengthened this argument. They found that employment protection legislation, product market regulation and restrictions on foreign direct investments induced a worsening of allocative efficiency. In contrast, frictions in financial markets generated shifts in the productivity distribution. Finally, they found that stringent regulations were more disruptive to resource reallocation in high-tech sectors. This is also a feature of the cross-country study by Bartelsman et al. (2016), who explored the role of labour market institutions, as measured by the OECD's employment protection legislation (EPL). They found that, in high-EPL countries, high-technology sectors were smaller than the same sectors in low-EPL countries. This happened because firms in high-EPL countries benefitted less from the adoption of new technologies than firms in countries with less strict employment protection legislation. The conclusion was that rigid labour market structures prevented reallocation to more innovative firms in high-technology sectors.

The European Central Bank has also paid attention to the negative consequences of labour misallocation and a lack of allocative efficiency. Two ECB papers used the CompNet dataset to highlight the negative impact of labour misallocation in the euro area.

Gamberoni et al. (2018) conducted an analysis of the negative impact of corruption on misallocation dynamics and consequently on aggregate economic performance in nine countries in central and eastern Europe between 2003 and 2012. This effect is larger the smaller the country, the lower the degree of political stability and civil liberties and the weaker the quality of its institutions.

Gamberoni et al. (2016) focused on five euro-area countries – Belgium, France, Germany, Italy and Spain – between 2002 and 2012. They found that capital misallocation had increased in all countries except Germany, while labour misallocation remained stable. This development was largely driven by the service sector. The authors argued that this was caused by heightened uncertainty, restrictive banking credit standards, and high employment and product market legislation. The study also suggested that the 2008 global financial crisis had a cleansing effect, with a decrease in misallocation of both production inputs.[3]

Many of the studies reviewed here relied on the Hsieh and Klenow's (HK) measure of input misallocation, that is, the dispersion across firms (within a narrowly defined industry) in the marginal revenue product of labour or capital. This empirical framework has been criticised by some recent papers that argue that the within-industry dispersion in MRPL and MRPK is not the best measure of input misallocation, and that distortions might not be the only explanation of TFP dispersion within an industry.

Some papers, such as Bartelsman et al. (2013), have argued that the assumptions behind the Hsieh and Klenow (2009) framework are too restrictive. They preferred to use the Olley and Pakes (OP) gap, because it is less prone to mismeasurement. On the other hand, the OP gap does not consider time variation, and so does not account for entry and exit of firms.

Haltiwanger et al. (2018) also argued that HK's approach is strongly sensitive to model misspecification. In fact, their model relies on strong assumptions both on the demand and the supply side. The authors show that applying this framework when there is any deviation from these assumptions leads to the possibility that distortions in the data were not due to the allocative inefficiency argued by Hsieh and Klenow (2009). Rather, it may simply reflect demand shifts or movements of the firm along its marginal cost curve, possibly in profitable directions. Their conclusion: the HK's framework, while being a useful starting point to analyse inefficiencies, should be used with extreme care for the assessment of input misallocation.

The debate about the best measure for input misallocation is not settled. As we have seen, both the HK and OP gap measures have been used in recent literature on resource reallocation, despite their respective disadvantages. Perhaps this debate could lead to new

---

[3] The paper by Gopinath et al. (2017), discussed in Chapter 6, showed that capital misallocation has been the main driver of recent poor economic growth in southern Europe, because of its underdeveloped financial markets. The authors also investigated the role of labour misallocation to explain bad economic performance, but did not find convincing evidence, as in Gamberoni et al. (2016).

ways to measure misallocation. See Section 4.1 for a more detailed discussion of recent measures of allocative efficiency.

Reallocation and Wages during Recessions

Recessions may affect the process of resource reallocation for both labour and capital. Recessions could lead to the exit of less efficient firms; layoffs during downturns, and new job opportunities created during the recovery, might lead to an improved allocation of workers across surviving firms.

This ultimately improves aggregate productivity, and so is often known as the cleansing effect of a recession. Different mechanisms might reduce or strengthen the cleansing effect, but which of these mechanisms are policy-induced distortions, and therefore are country-specific, and which apply to all recessions?

Empirical research has taken advantage of the shock from the global financial crisis of 2008–2009 to measure its effects on productivity growth.

Krusell et al. (2017) developed a model of the cyclical properties of gross worker flows to show that reduced tightness in the labour market during recessions should decrease frictions in labour search. Therefore, labour misallocation should decrease in response to crises. The role of policy on firm incentives to protect workers during downturns was illustrated in the paper by Boeri and Brücker (2011). In their cross-country study of OECD countries, they showed that short-term jobs reduced job losses at the beginning of recessions.

Foster et al. (2016) assessed the patterns of labour misallocation in the US economy in crisis and non-crisis periods. They found that reallocation was less costly during downturns, evidence of a cleansing effect. Reallocation of labour input strongly enhanced productivity in downturns before the Great Recession on 2008 and 2009, and this effect was stronger than reallocation in non-crisis periods. The authors found, however, that reallocation during the Great Recession was less intense and less productivity enhancing than in previous US downturns. This is due to the fact that job creation fell by at least as much than the increase in job destruction, unlike previous recession episodes. The net result was a decrease in decreased overall reallocation. Foster et al. (2016) also found that the difference in exit and growth rates between high- and low-productivity firms declined when there were sharp contractions such as those generated by the Great Recession, ultimately leading to limited productivity-enhancing reallocation. Therefore, the effect depends on the magnitude and the nature of the shock. This might be important for the scale of reallocation after COVID-19 (see Appendix 7.2).

Bartelsman et al. (2018) complemented the analysis of Foster et al. (2016) by focusing on industries in the EU using the CompNet dataset. This was the first comprehensive assessment of capital and labour misallocation dynamics during economic downturns in EU countries. The authors also studied policy environments across EU countries to find out whether they generated different trends in resource reallocation during the crisis. They found that resource reallocation was productivity enhancing across all countries during the 2008–2009 Great Recession, but this effect was stronger in some countries than others. The authors attributed this difference, at least partially, to different national policies. In particular, stringent labour and product market regulation hampered the productivity-enhancing effect of reallocation during the Great Recession. Bartelsman et al. (2018) argued that this might be due to the sharp drop in exports after a collapse in trade in 2009, which hit large and productive firms relatively more than small firms, unlike what happened in other episodes. This supports evidence that large economic shocks (this time on the global trade) might hamper the cleansing effects of recessions.

Centralised wage bargaining prevents firms from offering their employees salaries in line with their productivity and therefore might amplify the labour misallocation problem. Therefore, others have examined the role of wage-bargaining regimes on economic dynamism and performance.

This argument was tested in a cross-country setting by di Mauro and Ronchi (2017), who investigated the European response after the Great Recession. They built a micro-distributed dataset linking data on wage bargaining institutions with information on firm characteristics provided by CompNet. The authors found that, consistent with standard assumptions, centralised wage bargaining was typically associated with wage rigidity, which prevented firms from adjusting wages quickly during the downturn. As a result, these institutions might have slowed the productivity adjustment after the crisis.

The Labour Share

Another line of research on labour markets and firm productivity examines the role of the labour share – the share of labour costs in GDP, or gross value added. The stability of the labour share is a foundation of standard macroeconomic models. But recent research has found that the labour share has been falling in the US (Elsby et al., 2013; Lawrence, 2015) and globally (Karabarbounis and Neiman, 2013) since at least the early 1980s. The secular decline of the labour share has been associated, at least in the US, with rising concentration and poor job dynamism, which by itself slows reallocation of resources.[4]

The cause of this secular decline has been intensively debated, with so far no consensus, but several candidate explanations. Karabarbounis and Neiman (2013) argued that the decrease in the relative price of investment goods, possibly due to advances in information technology, induced firms to shift away from labour and towards capital – therefore explaining at least half of the fall in the labour share since 1980 in most industries and countries.

Elsby et al. (2013) focused on the US and found that the decline of the labour share has been particularly concentrated in sectors that faced import competition from China. They argued that it may be due to the offshoring of labour-intensive parts of the production process. Therefore, the authors concluded, if globalisation continues the US labour share would decline even more, especially in sectors most susceptible to foreign competition.

In a similar vein, Boehm et al. (2017) found that multi-nationals accounted for 41% of aggregate manufacturing employment decline, lower than average employment growth rates. The authors estimated that 13% of the employment decline in US manufacturing between 1993 and 2011 was due to offshoring the labour-intensive components of the supply chain.

Kaymak and Schott (2018) highlighted the role of corporate tax rates in explaining the falling labour share in manufacturing sectors

---

[4] In Chapter 9, we analyse the role of the falling labour share with respect to the rising concentration of market power of firms. Here we discuss its implications for reallocation.

for OECD countries. They estimated that the decline in corporate tax rates was associated with 40% of the observed decline in the labour share.

Hopenhayn et al. (2018) showed that the decline in the labour share in the US can be explained by changes in population growth through firm entry rates. A decrease in population growth lowered firm entry rates, shifting the firm-age distribution towards old firms. An ageing firm distribution fully explained the concentration of employment in large firms and the decrease in the US labour share.

Another possible explanation for the secular decline of the labour share has to do with the spread of labour-saving technological change. Acemoglu and Restrepo (2017) analysed the effect of the increase in industrial robot usage between 1990 and 2007 on US local labour markets, and estimated large and robust negative effects of robots on employment and wages across commuting zones. In particular, they found that one more robot per thousand workers reduced the employment-to-population ratio by 0.2 percentage points, and wages by 0.42%.

Bonfiglioli et al. (2020) similarly found that robot adopters in the EU were larger, more productive and had a larger employment share of high-skill professions. They also found that that robot adoption occurs after periods of expansion in firm size, and is followed by improvements in productivity and labour demand shifts to high-skill professions. But Bonfiglioli et al. (2020) also found that, after adoption, the upward trend in employment reverses, suggesting that workers start to be displaced, in line with the evidence collected for the US. Productivity gains also do not translate into an equivalent fall in prices, meaning that the benefit is not entirely passed on to consumers.

7.3 Productivity and the Labour Market

Given the importance of resource reallocation to foster long-term growth and to accommodate the business cycle, it should be no surprise that governments and policy institutions in advanced countries put it at the centre of their policy-making process. For these reasons, CompNet has dedicated attention to the topic of resource reallocation since day one. The early findings of CompNet research on labour topics have been summarised in Fernández et al. (2017), while more

Table 7.1. *Average number of employees by size class.*

Size class	1st	2nd	3rd	4th	5th
Austria	4	14	34	124	861
Belgium	3	14	31	102	987
Croatia	3	13	30	104	730
Estonia	4	13	30	95	587
Finland	3	14	30	102	911
Germany	5	14	33	114	1,134
Italy	5	14	31	96	965
Lithuania	4	14	30	99	716
Malta	5	14	32	101	562
Portugal	3	13	30	97	814
Romania	3	13	30	103	765
Slovenia	3	13	31	107	764
Spain	4	14	30	94	1,892
Average	4	14	31	103	899

Source: CompNet Labour Module – Fernández et al. (2017).
Note: Size classes are defined according to the number of employees:

- 1: 1–9 employees
- 2: 10–19 employees
- 3: 20–49 employees
- 4: 50–250 employees
- 5: 250+ employees

recent findings were reviewed in the cross-country report released with the sixth vintage dataset (Lopez-Garcia et al., 2018).

The Labour Module of the CompNet dataset has studied employment dynamics within European firms. In particular, it tracks firms over time in order to analyse their strategies of expansion compared to their economic conditions. Table 7.1 shows the average firm size in each class.

During the Great Recession, the share of shrinking firms sharply increased in countries under stress, while firm growth slowed down in non-stressed countries. In stressed countries, the construction sector suffered the most, while in non-stressed countries manufacturing and services related to transportation and storage were mainly affected, possibly as a result of the trade collapse.

More recently, the network has devoted its attention to the relationship between wage growth, productivity growth and future inflation. This is particularly relevant for policy makers in central banks. Preliminary findings show that productivity and wage growth tend not to be connected, in particular in firms at low deciles of the productivity distribution. The same applies to productivity and wage dispersion. The argument to be further investigated is that low wage growth in the aggregate is driven by the dynamics in the low end of the distribution.

Secondly, CompNet is working to disentangle the role of high-growth firms in Europe. Preliminary results show that these firms are responsible for most job creation and job destruction, and overall in sectors with a higher share of high-growth firms more jobs are created than destroyed. One of Europe's biggest problems has been the creation of new jobs, so the study of high-growth firms is critical for European policy makers.

CompNet has also analysed firm performance as related to the education level of its workforce (CompNet, 2020). Firms with a more educated labour force tend to be more productive, and firms that face a shortage of educated workers react by expanding the number of workers they employ. Hence a greater shortage of high-educated workers is associated with larger firm size, which suggests a specialisation in labour-intensive production processes. On the other hand, a greater shortage of high-skilled workers is associated with lower total factor productivity.

CompNet data can be used to analyse patterns of labour misallocation in Europe. As mentioned in Chapter 4, CompNet has several measures of labour misallocation. In Figure 7.1, we show the benefit of having harmonised micro-level measures for cross-country comparisons. It shows strong differences across countries in misallocation dynamics, which might be due to country-specific policy distortions, as suggested by prior research. These charts also compare the two measures of labour misallocation that we have discussed so far – the OP gap and Hsieh and Klenow's dispersion of MRPL. Patterns within country across the two measures are only partly converging, if we exclude a few countries.

In Figures 7.2 and 7.3, we use the Hsieh–Klenow's measure of labour misallocation to analyse the average level of labour misallocation by TFP decile in three European countries for which the two misallocation measures provide close results: France, Hungary and

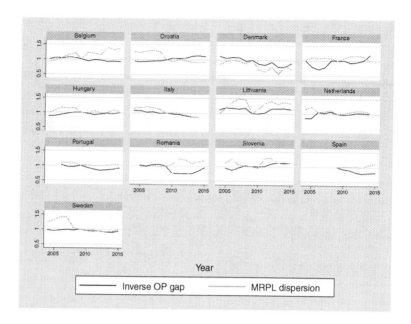

Figure 7.1 Evolution of labour misallocation, 2009 = 1.
Note: Authors' elaboration of CompNet sixth vintage data.

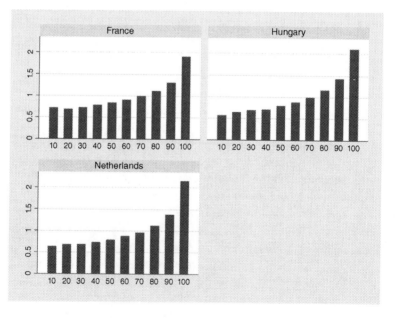

Figure 7.2 Labour misallocation by TFP decile.
Note: Authors' elaboration of CompNet sixth vintage data.

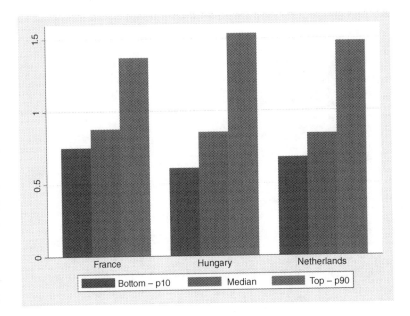

Figure 7.3 Labour misallocation at bottom, median and top of TFP distribution.

Note: Authors' elaboration of CompNet sixth vintage data.

the Netherlands. In all three, the HK index of labour misallocation is higher at the top deciles of the productivity distribution.

We can go deeper and check the extent to which labour misallocation may have changed after the global financial crisis, distinguishing segments of the TFP distribution.

In Figure 7.4, we show average levels of labour misallocation by different deciles of the productivity distribution in France, Hungary and the Netherlands before the crisis and in the recovery period. We also highlight the median levels during the Great Recession, to detect whether any cleansing effect was working – in other words, whether the crisis caused a decrease in labour misallocation.

The results are inconclusive. Possibly some cleansing effect took place in France and the Netherlands, then reversed. In Hungary, this pattern was less clear.

Finally, it is worth mentioning that the literature analysing patterns of labour misallocation in Europe using the HK index has highlighted

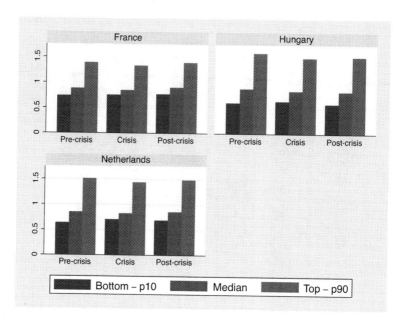

Figure 7.4 Labour misallocation at bottom, median and top of TFP distribution.

Note: Authors' elaboration of CompNet sixth vintage data.

that poor allocation of labour is associated with undesirable macro-economic performance, visible when adopting a firm- or micro-level perspective. In particular, Gamberoni et al. (2016, 2018) have found a negative association between levels of allocative efficiency in 2002 and subsequent growth rates of input misallocation, signalling that there was some convergence in the levels of input misallocation in European countries since at least 2002. This effect was stronger for capital misallocation than for labour misallocation. This is consistent with the idea that labour is more complex to substitute as an input in the production process.

These two papers also found that input misallocation dynamics were positively associated with real turnover growth, supporting evidence that allocative efficiency decreases during booms and increases during busts. The graph in Figure 7.5 shows that there is a positive association between real turnover and labour misallocation at the sector level, after controlling for country and year fixed effects.

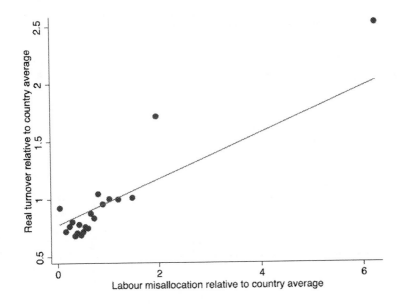

Figure 7.5 Correlation between labour misallocation and median real turnover.

Note: Authors' elaboration of CompNet sixth vintage dataset.

Therefore, in sectors with higher MRPL dispersion, real turnover is on average higher.

Tracking Firms over Time: The CompNet Transition Matrix

The CompNet transition matrices let researchers study the share and characteristics of firms with different growth performances over a three-year window. Conditional on surviving the three-year time period under study, firms are classified into five quintiles based on firm number of employees for year t and $t - 3$, respectively. Transition matrices track the evolution of firms in a given country/macro sector over three years; it is possible to study firm (employment) size dynamics using the movement of firms across these quintiles.

For example, we could analyse the share of firms that move from size quintile 1 in $t - 3$ to size quintile 5 in t. In addition, the transition matrices provide statistics on firm characteristics at time $t - 3$ and t,

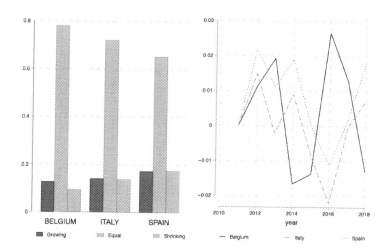

Figure 7.6 Average share of firms by status (left) and growth rate of firms remaining in the same quintile (right).

Source: Authors' calculation using data from CompNet's eighth vintage. Shrinking firms are firms whose position in the size distribution declines, and growing firms increase their position in the size distribution, while equal firms remain on the same position (sample comprising firms with at least 20 employees)

so that it is possible to analyse firm features in detail before and after they grow or shrink.[5]

The left-hand panel of Figure 7.6 plots the average (across the whole time span) share of firms in each status. In the selected economies, most firms (60–75%) do not change their position: this indicates that firms in those economies are more likely not to change their position in the employment size distribution. This phenomenon is more evident in Belgium than in the other economies, possibly indicating some limits to firm dynamics in that country. On the other hand, the right-hand panel of Figure 7.6 plots the growth rate of the share of firms that do not change quintile. There is volatility, but the patterns appear to be stable, with no evident trends.

---

[5] Please note that the design of the matrices means that the share of firms growing and shrinking needs to be exactly equal. Any divergence is due to randomly assigning firms with exactly equal employment levels to quintiles, such that the number of firms in each quintile is exactly the same.

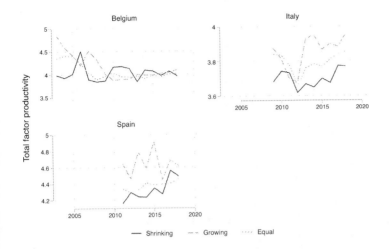

Figure 7.7 Average firm productivity by growth performance in selected European countries.

Source: Authors' calculation using data from CompNet's eighth vintage. Shrinking firms are firms whose position in the size distribution declines, and growing firms increase their position in the size distribution, while equal firms remain on the same position (sample comprising firms with at least 20 employees)

Figure 7.7 uses data from CompNet's eighth vintage to study the ex ante productivity performance of firms with different (employment) growth trajectories over time. In Italy and Spain, firms improving their position in the employment distribution have higher average ex ante productivity levels than other firms. There does not seem to be heterogeneity in ex ante productivity levels of growing firms in Belgium.

Wage Bargaining and TFP

We can also examine the relationship between wage bargaining institutions and TFP development. To do this, we merge two firm-level based datasets: the Wage Dynamics Network, which contains information on wage bargaining, and CompNet's sixth vintage, which includes productivity indicators for several European countries. The resulting

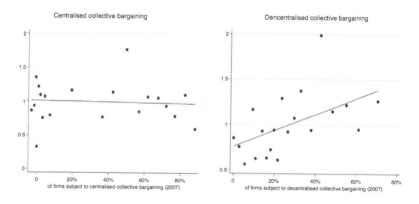

Figure 7.8 Collective bargaining and TFP across countries.
Source: TFP measure comes from CompNet's sixth vintage of data; collective bargaining shares are calculated on the basis of WDN first wave. TFP is normalised by country-year TFP mean

dataset shows two main differences between central and eastern Europe (CEE) and other countries for wage bargaining institutions.[6]

Pooling all countries (CEE and non-CEE), Figure 7.8 (right-hand panel) shows that average TFP – normalised by country-year TFP mean in each country and macro-sector in 2007 – is strongly correlated with the share of firms with decentralised contracts, after controlling for country and sector fixed effects. There is no correlation when considering firms that use centralised collective contracts (Figure 7.8, left-hand panel).

If we use a regression analysis, keeping fixed the 2007 level of decentralisation in each country and macro-sector observation, we can be more precise about the impact of collective bargaining on the response of firms after the Global Financial Crisis (GFC), and on their productivity afterwards. This means we can evaluate the performance of the pre-crisis collective bargaining structures, avoiding endogeneity issues due to changes in industrial relations as a response to the financial crisis. The independent variable is the percentage of firms

[6] A detailed analysis of these findings is provided in Aglio and di Mauro (2020).

Table 7.2. *Wage bargaining and TFP.*

	Non-CEE countries TFP	CEE countries TFP
ML	0.82*** (0.18)	
FL		0.14 (0.61)
ML*crisis	0.36** (0.17)	
FL*crisis		−0.14 (0.61)
Constant	137*** (45.01)	27.19 (63.54)
Observations	489	462
R-squared	0.23	0.68

Reproduced from Aglio and di Mauro (2020). OLS regressions include dummies for country, macrosector, year, and size effects, as well as controlling for crisis period. Clustered standard errors at sector and year level in parentheses. *** $p < 0.01$; ** $p < 0.05$; * $p < 0.1$.

subject to decentralised collective agreements in 2007, just before the beginning of the GFC, which is considered as an exogenous shock.

Wage bargaining decentralisation (ML and FL, respectively for non-CEE and CEE) has a different impact on TFP in the two regions (see Table 7.2):

- In the non-CEE countries, decentralisation correlates positively with productivity. There is a stronger effect after the outbreak of the crisis.
- In CEE countries, there is no significant result.

As far as the channels through which this relation exists, decentralisation (multi-level collective bargaining) in the non-CEE region is negatively correlated with the unit labour cost (ULC), which means that firm competitiveness improved with decentralisation, as labour costs were kept in line with productivity. There is no significant effect in CEE countries.

7.4 Conclusion

We have focused on labour allocation as another factor that helps explain aggregate economic growth through its effects on productivity. The effect of labour misallocation is potentially large in all countries for which we have data.

Evidence has been obtained thanks to the increasing availability of disaggregated data. The development of good-quality firm-level datasets, both in Europe and in the US, has helped consolidate economic analysis, allowing policy makers to appreciate the importance of allocative efficiency as a driver of aggregate economic performance.

So there is an increasing awareness of the need to promote policies and institutions (both in labour and financial markets) that foster a more efficient allocation of resources across firms. Clearly it is not only important to foster within-firm productivity growth using innovation policies, but to promote reallocation of resources, in particular labour, to the most productive firms within sectors and countries. This would create sustained economic growth.

But any policy fostering reallocation of workers needs jobs to churn in the first place. Only if workers lose jobs in unproductive firms can they find alternative occupation in more productive firms. This is a politically painful process. By definition, it creates winners and losers, and low-skilled workers displaced from low productive firms cannot instantly acquire the human capital that makes them attractive to innovative, high-productivity firms. It follows that policies promoting labour reallocation should be accompanied by active labour market policies to reduce the displacement costs of workers, or specific policies aimed at reducing potential wage disparity.

For example, a recent study by Dustmann et al. (2020) found that the introduction of a minimum wage in Germany in 2015 not only reduced inequality through higher wages on average, but also did not reduce employment or increase unemployment. The policy was also able to generate a reallocation process of workers from smaller to larger and more productive firms that boosted aggregate productivity. In particular, small firms could not afford to increase their workers' salary in line with the standards set by the new policy, and consequently had to exit from the market or increase their size.

Increasing the minimum wage is thus a policy which could have positive reallocation effects for the economy. But if small firms are forced out of business as a result, the same policy might also reduce competition and lead to less choice for consumers.

These findings are useful at a time when policy makers, after COVID-19, try to find new tools to make reallocation to the most productive firms easier and quicker. They are also relevant now that the European Commission is discussing a minimum wage across the EU.

Appendix 7.1. Labour Reallocation Post-COVID

At the beginning of the COVID-19 crisis, many countries, with the goal of preventing unemployment, introduced job retention schemes. According to OECD (2020), these actions across countries supported more than 50 million jobs during 2020, 10 times as many as those supported during the global financial crisis of 2008–2009 (Figure 7.9).

In many countries, these schemes are short-time work (STW) schemes, such as the German Kurzarbeit, the French Activité partielle or the Italian Cassa Integrazione Guadagni. These schemes allow

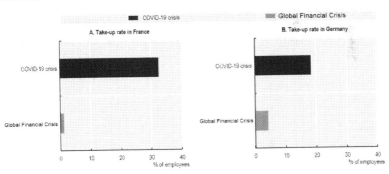

Figure 7.9 Job retention during COVID-19 vs. the Global Financial Crisis, France and Germany.

Source: OECD (2020).Take-up rates refer to actual use and are calculated as a percentage of dependent employees

firms to reduce the working hours for each worker. The State pays the difference between what they earn while working short-time and their usual wage.

In other countries, these schemes can take the form of wage subsidy schemes. These subsidise hours worked, but can also be used to top up the earnings of workers on reduced hours.

A crucial aspect of job retention schemes is that employees keep their contracts and wages with their employer even if their work is suspended. This has three good consequences:

- Firms with less money coming in do not need to pay their workers in full, and so do not run out of cash.
- Workers retain their wage, and so their purchasing power, avoiding a pro-cyclical consumption demand shock.
- Firms can quickly increase operations once economic activity recovers, without having to go through the process of hiring and training new workers.

On the downside:

- These schemes, if protracted and widespread, can become expensive.
- As countries recover, policy must strike the right balance between supporting viable jobs and firms and subsidising jobs that would normally disappear.

Economic research on job retention schemes shows that low-productivity firms tend to be over-represented as beneficiaries. These schemes, are preventing the movement of workers from low-productivity firms to other (potentially more productive) firms, stifling the efficient reallocation of labour. This has detrimental effects on productivity. For example, Giupponi and Landais (2018), looking at short-time work schemes in Italy after the Global Financial Crisis, found that STW had a significant negative impact on overall TFP in each local labour market, with a one-percentage-point increase in the fraction of workers treated by STW translating into a 2% decrease in TFP growth.

On the other hand, for TFP growth, it is important that workers move towards the right jobs in order to trigger a virtuous circle ending up in increased productivity. Aggregate productivity growth is made up by two components. The first is within-firm productivity growth, which depends on the way existing firms utilize the resources at their disposal – labour, physical capital and intangibles such as organizational knowledge and management practices. The second is a between-firm component that reflects the gains achieved by reallocation of economic activity that affect utilization of resources within a sector. This can create productivity growth through "cleansing" processes, that is, the exit from the market of unproductive firms and the reallocation of their resources (labour and capital): job reallocation affects productivity growth mainly through this channel. Syverson and di Mauro (2020) argue that throughout the pandemic, this channel will be triggered by the exit from the market of small firms, whereas credit provided to zombie firms may hamper the productivity-enhancing labour reallocation process.

8 | *Productivity in a Borderless World*

8.1 Introduction

Much of international economics is dedicated to investigating how much (and why) economic growth and international trade are linked (Frankel and Romer, 1999). It is notoriously difficult to estimate the causal impact of trade on growth, because countries whose income is higher for reasons unrelated to trade also tend to trade more. As a result, a lot of research has attempted to disentangle this relationship (Altomonte et al., 2018a).

Since the early 2000s, research on international trade has two additional features:

- A focus on firms. Traditionally, trade theory has relied on aggregate measures, at the country or country-industry level. It is increasingly clear that, in most countries, a few productive firms generate a large part of economic activity, including export sales and foreign direct investment (Mayer and Ottaviano, 2007). This heterogeneity in firm performance has been embedded in trade models, starting with Bernard et al. (2003) and Melitz (2003).
- Globalisation changed international trade. The fragmentation of production into GVCs changed the way we look at trade (see Amador and di Mauro, 2015, for a comprehensive analysis). GVCs broke production processes into narrower activities and tasks. Different steps of the production process are now located in different countries. As a result, since the 1990s international trade has involved much more movement of inputs and intermediate goods across borders.

This has upset traditional concepts of trade. Macroeconomic figures such as a country's exports had a different meaning: the inputs used to produce a product may be counted more than once in the total during the production process (Koopman et al., 2014). But GVCs also changed the way firms were involved in international activities. Traditionally, economists viewed firms as serving their own domestic market, and perhaps becoming an exporter. Today, they need to understand the degree to which they are also integrated in GVCs (see Altomonte et al., 2014, for an analysis across European countries).

In this chapter, we will review how trade theory has evolved over time, with particular attention to the models of international trade that embed firm heterogeneity. We focus on the link between internalisation and performance of firms, and also the response of multi-national firms to macroeconomic shocks. We will then present the CompNet trade module, and use data from it to analyse recent trends of internationalisation of European firms.

8.2 Literature Review

Trade Theory

Traditional theories of international trade explain the flow of goods between countries in terms of comparative advantage, defined as the difference in the opportunity costs to produce goods across countries and industries. In these theories, there are two sources of comparative advantage:

(1) Ricardian comparative advantage. This is the difference in countries' productivity across and within industries.[1]
(2) Cross-country differences in relative factor endowments. This follows the work of Eli Heckscher and Bertil Ohlin (Heckscher and Ohlin, 1933).

Whether driven by productivity or factor endowments, traditional trade models refer to the international exchange of one good for another, in other words *inter-industry* trade. These models hence predict that labour-abundant countries such as India would exchange labour-intensive products – apparel, for example – for capital-intensive products – let's say, cars – from skill-abundant countries such as Germany.

---

[1] This concept was developed by the British economist David Ricardo at the beginning of the nineteenth century (Ricardo, 1817).

These models imply that there would be more inter-industry trade if there was a larger disparity in comparative advantage. This is hard to reconcile with the fact that a vast share of international trade takes place between relatively similar trading partners, most notably within the same industries.[2] For example, Germany exchanges cars with the US, and Germany's trade with the US is relatively higher than that with India.

An explanation for this is known as "new trade theory". It was developed by Paul Krugman, Elhanan Helpman and William Ethier (Helpman and Krugman, 1975; Krugman, 1979, 1980, 1991), among others. This theory focuses on consumer preference for variety and horizontal product differentiation, which drives international trade. In these models, economies of scale lead symmetric firms to specialise in distinct varieties of the same product, creating two-way trade within industries between countries, or *intra-industry* trade.

In new trade theory, the number of horizontal varieties countries produce is determined by their size, with trade volumes predicted to rise with the similarity of trading partners' sizes. Consumers benefit from different varieties of the same product (they can buy an imported sports car vs. a sedan) and so they gain from trade. Therefore, trade produces a direct increase in consumer welfare.

New trade theory can explain the trade flows that characterise industrialised countries, but it still relies on the concept of a representative firm. In these models each firm is usually the unique producer of a specific variety, with firms otherwise identical in terms of production and export equilibrium levels.[3] This feature is hard to reconcile with the evidence of our eyes: obviously, firms differ in size and export ability.

To solve this problem, the new trade theory of Krugman and others has been integrated with features of firm heterogeneity, developing a class of theoretical models known as "new new trade theory". These models, after Melitz (2003), emphasise the importance of heterogeneity in productivity, and the role of reallocation across firms as a result of trade liberalisation.

---

[2] This was for example pointed out by Grubel and Lloyd (1975).

[3] The resulting market structure is monopolistic competition, with free entry and exit and positive markups over marginal costs, constant across all firms.

The Melitz framework in particular embeds supply-side firm hetero-geneity in Krugman's model of trade under monopolistic competition and increasing returns. This is a dynamic industry model that can explain why trade induces reallocation of resources among firms in an industry, while on the demand side preserves the feature that trade increases consumer utility through product differentiation and variety.

The model predicts that after economic integration only the most productive firms in a sector will engage in trade.[4] Firms with medium productivity choose to serve only the domestic market, while the least productive firms are forced to exit the market, because they are exposed to trade. The selection effect generated by trade therefore results in a reallocation of resources from low-productivity firms to their high-productivity peers, leading to an increase in aggregate pro-ductivity growth. Therefore, the model predicts that trade stimulates long-run growth.

So, in the Melitz framework, trade and economic integration produces high-productivity winners and low-productivity losers:

- Productive firms are efficient enough to sustain the cost of exporting, and will therefore gain market share.
- Low-productivity firms will not be able to sustain the cost necessary to start exporting and will be forced out of their main domestic market due to increased competition from abroad.
- Aggregate productivity, and therefore long-term growth, increases because resources are allocated more efficiently.
- Consumers benefit from lower prices and more choice.

This is, at least in theory, beneficial to the economy as a whole.

The presence of selection and reallocation effects is a novel char-acteristic introduced by Melitz (2003) in trade models, and a direct consequence of firm heterogeneity. Hence, the best tools to understand how these effects work in the context of the Melitz model are the decompositions of productivity developed by Olley and Pakes (1996a) and Foster et al. (2006), discussed in Chapter 4.

In the Melitz model, an increase in trade openness should produce greater reallocation and selection effects, average productivity levels

---

[4] This is due to the fact that the model firms that decide to start exporting pay a sunk fixed cost. Only the firms whose productivity level is above a certain cutoff threshold will be able to sustain that cost.

increase and aggregate economic performance increases as well thanks to the increase in trade integration. In both Olley and Pakes (1996a) and Foster et al. (2006) decompositions, this is a positive sign in the covariance term. Within the Foster et al. framework, the beneficial effects of trade predicted by the Melitz model also appear through an increase in the between term and a positive net entry effect, with new firms more productive than those which exit from the market due to trade openness.

Note that, while the effect of trade on the covariance and between term is uncontroversial, the role of the net-entry effect is more nuanced. In a recent study of Slovenian firms, Melitz and Polanec (2015) put forward a new version of the OP decomposition to account for some measurement biases associated with entry and exit that afflicted previous decompositions. They found that the bias was significant for Slovenian firms, accounting for approximately 10% of aggregate productivity growth.

Melitz (2003) used the same formulation as Krugman (1980) on the demand side, but the constant of elasticity (CES) utility function they use yields, in equilibrium, a constant markup over marginal cost for all firms in a given industry. Once more, this contradicts empirical evidence (see Chapter 7) that there is a large dispersion of market power across firms, another dimension of heterogeneity.

Melitz and Ottaviano (2008) built on the Melitz model by developing a setting with a quasi-linear demand system with product differentiation that incorporates endogenous markups. The model implies that trade benefits the economy through variety, selection and reallocation effects resulting from the assumption of firm heterogeneity and monopolistic competition with differentiated goods.

Quasi-linear demand adds a new factor: as trade increases, the market gets larger, leading to a change in demand elasticity. This was constant in the Melitz model. In particular, import competition in the domestic product market increases residual demand-price elasticities for all firms at a given demand level, leading to a downward shift in the distribution of markups across all firms. Firms with higher costs (lower productivity) would not survive this reduction in markup, inducing a selection effect in which, as in Melitz (2003), only the most efficient firms survive. Although the survivors have, in principle, lower marginal costs and higher markups, Melitz and Ottaviano (2008) show that the competition effect reduces the average markup.

Therefore, productivity gains (selection effect), lower markups (pro-competitive effect) and increased product variety in the model lead to welfare gains from trade.

Berthou et al. (2019) investigated the effects of flows of international trade on aggregate productivity. They showed that bilateral and unilateral export liberalisation increase aggregate productivity and consumers' welfare, while unilateral import liberalisation can act in both directions. Both reforms increase average firm productivity by increasing minimum productivity among active firms. Export expansion activates reallocation to the most productive firms, while import penetration does the opposite.

According to both their theoretical framework and empirical findings, globalisation enhances aggregate productivity by selecting productive firms and through reallocation across firms. But they also point out that, once input misallocation is embedded in their model, trade benefits are less clear. Efficient institutions and a well-functioning market amplify the productivity gains of import competition and decrease those from export expansion.

Trade and Firm Performance

Thanks to the increasing availability of quality firm-level data, several recent studies connect empirical findings on trade openness and firm performance with the theory in heterogeneity-enriched trade models. Bernard et al. (2007) were one of the first to document, for the US, the very large difference in the degree to which firms participate in international markets, both across and within sectors. Results also highlighted that exporters are concentrated among the most productive and largest firms in the economy.

In Europe, Mayer and Ottaviano (2007) similarly showed that most export activities are concentrated in a few firms in any sector or country. These firms were bigger, generated higher value added, paid higher wages, employed more capital per worker and more skilled workers and were more productive. For these reasons, the authors coined characterised the firms involved in international activities through export or foreign direct investments as the "happy few".[5]

---

[5] This notion of a "happy few" is relevant to many economic phenomena, as we discussed in the Introduction.

The authors found that there was an even more concentrated group of "superstar" firms that were responsible for a large proportion of trade activity. Specifically, the largest top 10% of exporters in Germany or France accounted for 90% of German or French exports – in France 1,000 exporters represented almost 70% of the country's total exports – and there was a similar concentration in the US where 2,200 firms (the top 1% of exporters, most of which were multinational firms) accounted for more than 80% of total US trade.

Mayer and Ottaviano (2007) argued that aggregate trade figures are driven by changes in two margins. The "intensive margin" represents the average value of export and other trade activities undertaken by each firm. The "extensive margin" refers to the number of firms actually involved in international trade. The latter would be visible only when we examine firm-level data, not data from aggregate trade figures.

This is important for policy. Changes in aggregate trade volumes can be a change in either margin, or a change in both, but the effect of these marginal changes on the underlying market structure is not the same. In particular, there is consensus today that a change in the number of exporting firms (extensive margin) is more important than a change in the average export volume of each firm (intensive margin) as a route to create trade and economic growth. This is because of the concentration of exporting activity in a few high-performance firms: what we define as competitiveness for a country also depends on the number of firms in it that are competitive enough to engage in international activities. It follows that policy should try to make this number larger.

We still must be clear on the direction of causality between firm performance and trade. Both theory and empirical evidence (De Loecker, 2007, 2011, for example) imply that the emergence of a larger cadre of productive firms in the economy leads to higher exports, not the other way round. In other words, the provision of export subsidies, or a package of export promotion activities, would likely increase exports along the intensive margin but not necessary translate into higher productivity for the firms that are doing the exporting (Martincus and Carballo, 2010).

In some contexts, especially in developing economies, some learning by exporting is possible. This was the finding of Van Biesebroeck (2005) for a group of sub-Saharan countries. Atkin et al. (2017)

conducted a randomised experiment among rug producers in Egypt to disentangle the beneficial impact of exogenously induced trade exposure on firm performance. They found that firms in the treatment (exporting) group not only increased their profits, but they also improved the quality of their product. This finding suggests that exporting increases technical efficiency and, therefore, in some circumstances there would be a learning-by-exporting effect.

Firm Response to Trade and Other Macroeconomic Shocks

Following the Global Financial Crisis of 2008–2009, empirical research has studied the impact of macroeconomic shocks on the underlying dimensions of firm heterogeneity.

For instance, Békés et al. (2011) studied a representative sample from 2010 of 15,000 European firms that had been surveyed in 2008 and 2009 to obtain information on their internationalisation activities.[6] The authors found that the crisis had hit firms hard: on average, they reported a 12% decline in sales and reduced employment by 6%.

These numbers conceal wide heterogeneity across countries and industries in how firms responded to the crisis. The report found that exporters were hit harder than non-exporters by the trade collapse. Exporting firms had higher declines in sales, although structural differences across countries might partially explain this result. They also find that the firms involved in more sophisticated trade linkages – that is, those involved in GVCs – suffered from the trade collapse less than pure exporters. The position of a firm in the chain was another significant factor that helped determine their ability of to respond to the crisis.

The message of the report was that, while international trade can occasionally propagate global downturns, some trade linkages – such as those resulting from the process of European integration – can mitigate the negative effects of global crises. These linkages enable

---

[6] As already discussed in Chapter 5, the European Firms in the Global Economy (EFIGE) dataset is a harmonised cross-country dataset containing quantitative as well as qualitative information on about 150 variables, It is a representative sample of 15,000 manufacturing firms surveyed in 2010 in Austria, France, Germany, Hungary, Italy, Spain and the UK.

firms to respond more flexibly to demand shocks and to reduce the propagation of those shocks to other sectors of the economy. During the 2009 trade shock, the position of a firm was nevertheless important: firms that dominated their production chain in terms of technology and ownership, employing a high-skilled workforce, for example, fared better.

Altomonte et al. (2011a) explored the role of GVCs in explaining the magnitude of the trade collapse by using transaction-level trade data from France matched with ownership data for dates between 2007 and 2009. They found that trade in intermediates was the main driver of the trade collapse, but different ways of organising the supply chain created different dynamic responses: trade that originated within multinational groups (related-party trade) reacted faster to the negative demand shock, but also recovered faster in the months that followed between independent firm's (arm's-length trade).

The authors argued that when firms adjusted inventories, amplifying fluctuations of trade with respect to GDP, this created a "bullwhip effect" as the adjustment of production and stocks to the new expected levels of output magnified the negative demand shock along the supply chain. Increased related-party trade could be explained by better handling of inventories within multinational groups, thanks to a more efficient and synchronised circulation of information, and better management of stocks that resulted, within the group.

Another prominent line of research follows the link between international trade and exchange rate movements. This was exclusively macroeconomic research until recently. But, given the variation in firms' international activities, it's no surprise that recent micro-founded research has shown that including the productivity distribution in the export equation drastically affects the average elasticity estimate of the exchange rate: the unobserved bias is reduced, and the exchange rate elasticity of exports is lower in sectors in which the dispersion of firm productivity is higher (Demian and di Mauro, 2015).

The authors also found that exports appeared to react far more to appreciations than depreciations, and exchange rate movements mattered more when they were large.

Berthou and di Mauro (2015) showed that the measured reaction of aggregate exports to relative price movements was largely determined by the reaction of the most productive and largest firms. Berthou and Dhyne (2018) used CompNet data to show that heterogeneous productivity levels were driving this response. They estimated the exchange rate elasticity for each country in their panel. It ranged from about −0.5 to −0.8, meaning that a 10% appreciation of the real effective exchange rate was predicted to reduce exports of the average firm by 5–8%. These estimates hide heterogeneity across firms characterised by different TFP levels within sectors and countries. Indeed, the elasticity for the low-productivity firms within each given sector, country and year was three to eight times higher than for the high-productivity firms in the same sector, country and year, depending on the elasticity measure adopted.

This implies that the least productive European firms tended to be more vulnerable to movements in the real effective exchange rate (REER) than the most productive firms, because the exports of productive firms are much less sensitive to changes in the REER. Since export elasticity relative to the REER is inversely correlated with size and productivity, the authors argued that European countries with relatively high density of low-productivity firms would be more vulnerable to real effective exchange rate variations than countries with a small density of low-productivity firms. This has implications for the transmission mechanism of monetary policy – yet another reason for European policymakers to incentivise the growth of high-productivity firms in each country and sector, and to incentivise unproductive firms to exit.

Other research examines how firms organise internally and how that influences their response to exogenous shocks. Caliendo et al. (2015) introduced the concept of "layers" of employees to explain a firm's organisation. Each layer corresponds to a group of employees with similar characteristics in terms of wages, knowledge and tasks performed. For instance, the layer of top managers is smaller (and has higher wages) because of its higher level of knowledge than the layer of blue-collar employees.

The authors populated their model of internal organization with a dataset of employer–employee relations from France. They showed that firms modify their layers of employees as they grow larger. Firms expand by either adding new layers, or keeping the existing structure. The authors found that when firms expanded by adding layers, they decreased wages in the existing layers. Average wages increased when firms grew without adding new layers of employees.

Friedrich (2015) used administrative employer–employee data and firm-level trade data from Denmark to argue that firm hierarchies are yet another channel through which trade shocks might feed into wage inequality. He built a dataset of firm-level trade shocks and used a boycott of Danish exports in 2006 as a natural experiment to corroborate his theory that within-firm wage dispersion could be as relevant a source of inequality as between-firms dispersion. He found that the trade shock had increased within-firm wage inequality by 2% in the 10–50 wage gap, and by 4.7% in the 90–50 wage gap.

Sforza (2020) used similar employer–employee and trade data from Portugal to compare firm response to two different kinds of shock: a credit shock – the Global Financial Crisis – and China's entry into the World Trade Organisation (WTO) as a trade shock. Firms reacted differently to these shocks. They responded to the Global Financial Crisis with a larger reduction in high-skilled than low-skilled workers, while wages were not affected. On the other hand, the China shock induced a full reorganisation of firm hierarchies, with a reduction in employment at all levels. These two studies suggest that the internal organisation of firms is yet another key channel of the transmission of shocks to the real economy.

Global Value Chains (GVCs)

Finally, a number of studies have recognised that exporting is not the only internationalisation activity in which firms engage. The United Nations Conference on Trade and Development (UNCTAD, 2013) estimated that about 80% of global trade (in terms of gross exports) is linked to the international production networks of multi-national firms, either as intra-firm trade (trade within the affiliates of the same multi-national company), through outsourcing activities (which include, among others, contract manufacturing, licensing and franchising), or through arm's-length transactions involving at least one affiliate of a multi-national company as a counterpart. That is, only 20% of trade flows worldwide takes place between individual, stand-alone firms.

This is the result of the emergence of global value chains (GVCs): the breakup of production processes into discrete activities and tasks, combined with the international dispersion of these activities and tasks across countries.[7]

Since the 1990s, following the Uruguay Round of the General Agreement on Tariffs and Trade (GATT) talks and the worldwide reduction in tariffs that followed, plus advances in information and communication technology (ICT) and reduction of transport costs from containerisation, different production steps have relocated globally to exploit comparative advantages – a process that Baldwin (2016) calls the "Great Convergence".

Trade increasingly involved multiple flows of inputs and semi-finished products across borders, and grew twice as fast as GDP from the middle of the 1990s until 2008. As a result, the share of total trade flows (imports and exports) in world GDP, one of many proxies of participation in GVCs, rose from around 30% in the 1990s to around 55% in 2010. The Global Financial Crisis caused only a dent, quickly reabsorbed, in this trend. After 2010, the growth rate stabilised.

Part of this effect, as measured in international trade statistics, is a result of double counting in gross trade figures:

- Think about an input x, which is produced in country A.
- This import is exported to country B.
- There it is assembled with other components in a semi-finished product, which we call y.
- This product is exported to country C.
- In C, it is used in the final product z.
- This final product is then exported to country D for final consumption.

In this example, the value of x has contributed three times to global (gross) export flows, while only once to global GDP, in the value added of country A. Double counting driven by GVCs is estimated to account for about 25% of gross trade flows (Koopman et al., 2014).

And so gross export figures have become less informative, especially because we are interested in the contribution that exports make to

---

[7] For an introduction to GVCs, please refer to Amador and di Mauro (2015) and the joint work of the OECD and the World Bank at: www.oecd.org/sti/ind/global-value-chains.htm.

domestic GDP growth. Economists have developed a number of ways to decompose each trade flow into its value-added components, for example by counting domestic and foreign value added separately (Koopman et al., 2014; Wang et al., 2017; World Bank, 2020).

Using these methods, we can create datasets that quantify the interconnections of the world input–output structure and its implications for competitiveness, such as WIOD, discussed in Chapter 5. The emergence of these data has boosted research on how the participation of a firm in GVCs, or whether it is upstream or downstream in them, affects its performance.[8]

These studies find that firms involved in complex GVCs behave differently from purely exporting firms, just as exporters differ from domestic firms. We must be mindful, then, of each firm's involvement in international trade if we want to explain patterns of trade dynamics for countries and sectors. This is particularly important in the EU, because the process of European integration promotes the participation of firms in regional and global value chains.

Altomonte et al. (2014), for example, developed a framework to study the link among innovation, productivity and internationalisation using EFIGE data. In their results, innovation boosted aggregate productivity growth by increasing the individual firm's productivity (the within component explored in Chapter 4). They found that large and very productive firms leveraged both their innovation and internationalisation activities, but they also found causality from innovation to internationalisation. This suggests that export promotion on its own is unlikely to lead to sustainable internationalisation. On one hand, the emergence of GVCs is such that internationalisation goes beyond simply exporting; on the other hand, in the medium and long run, internationalisation is likely driven by innovation.

But GVCs are a global phenomenon. It is important to study firm-to-firm connections elsewhere, and especially in developing economies, because trade can be a catalyst for development in these countries. For example, Bernard et al. (2018) studied the individual matches between exporters and importers in Colombia and examined their microeconomic relationship. This allowed them to study in depth the firm-level costs of trade. The authors found that, despite reductions in tariffs and

---

[8] See the contributions of Antràs and Chor (2013), Del Prete and Rungi (2017) and Alfaro et al. (2019).

other barriers thanks to trade negotiations and technological progress, there was evidence that firms faced important non-price barriers to trade, harming global integration.

Finally, Antràs (2020) gave an overview of the research on the key concepts related to GVCs and discussed their future evolution. He argued that the feared escalation of trade tensions between the US and other countries was unlikely to affect the geography of global production much, certainly compared to technologies such as digital platforms, blockchain, automation and artificial intelligence (AI). This is because the effect of new technologies will be structural for the world economy, while trade tensions are a function of a (varying) political cycle.

In principle, technology might have a different effect on the international fragmentation of production. Advances in robotics might be an alternative to offshoring for firms in developed economies, leading to some reshoring of labour-intensive tasks that could be automated – and a reduction in GVC participation as a result. But preliminary evidence from the World Bank (2020) showed that automation by firms in developed countries tended to decrease their costs and enhance their productivity, increasing their demand for intermediate inputs and their GVC participation. And digital technologies such as communication platforms, blockchain verification and automated translation have encouraged GVC participation by reducing the cost of communication while improving its quality, and also by improving the quality of matching between suppliers and producers.

The main impact of new technologies on GVCs, then, is not their intensity, but the consequences for redistribution. Automation typically complements skilled labour while substituting for unskilled labour, which accelerates a trend in many advanced economies, as we will see later. Baldwin (2020) points out that the possibility of simpler and more efficient forms of human interaction at a distance (a trend boosted by the COVID-19 shock) is likely to extend globalisation's displacement of workers, previously mostly restricted to the low-skilled, to any medium- and high-skilled workers whose tasks can be performed at distance.

Globalisation and Social Consequences

The increase in the participation of firms in GVCs has had important structural effects on the world economy. An important area of research in international trade focuses on the negative and unintended consequences of globalisation on society.

Autor et al. (2013) measured and assessed the "China shock" – the shock to the world economy after China joined the WTO in 2001. China's share of world manufacturing exports to grew from less than 5% in 2000 to almost 20% by 2010. As a result, in many industries, local production was replaced by Chinese imports.

Autor et al. (2013) measured the impact of rising competition from China on US local labour markets between 1990 and 2007. Their methodology, which became widely used in international economics, exploited variation in exposure to import competition from China from differences in specialisation in US markets. As imports from China could be endogenous to local demand conditions, the authors argued that this was a technological supply shock, and it was therefore exogenous to the import country. As a result, they instrumented US imports using Chinese imports by other high-income countries. They found that US labour markets in sectors more exposed to Chinese competition had lower labour force participation, and lower wages. This effect accounted for most of declining employment in US manufacturing industries between 1990 and 2007.[9]

In other papers, Autor et al. (2014) showed that earnings losses were larger for individuals with low wages, low tenure and low attachment to the labour force. Import shocks imposed high labour adjustment costs that were unevenly distributed among workers, with the losers being those with low skill levels and the worst conditions of employment in the pre-shock period. Autor et al. (2019) also explained how trade shocks have large and permanent societal consequences, because they reduced employment and earnings of only some young adult males, lowering the marriage rate and fertility. Finally, Autor et al. (2016) found strong evidence that congressional districts exposed to larger increases in import penetration disproportionately removed moderate representatives from office in the 2000s, polarising US politics.

[9] Caliendo et al. (2019) developed a general equilibrium model to quantify the negative impact of the China shock on the US labour market. According to their model, it resulted in a loss of more than 500,000 blue-collar jobs, about 16% of the overall decline in US manufacturing industry in the early 2000s.

There were similar impacts in western Europe. Bloom et al. (2015) showed that the China shock led to lower employment and wages across European firms – but that increasing imports from China also created positive technological change. In particular, they found that innovation increased in firms operating in sectors affected the most by the shock. The shock also led to a reallocation effect, increasing market shares for more innovative firms. These effects together accounted for about 14% of European technological upgrading in the early 2000s. Colantone et al. (2019) demonstrated a decrease in mental health for workers in the UK induced by competitive pressure from low-wage countries, while (Colantone and Stanig, 2018a,b) have been able to causally link the China shock to Brexit and the rise of nationalism across the EU.

8.3 Productivity and Trade

Firm-level information has been increasingly relevant for the analysis of trade flows, and the implications for society. Policymakers have also called for new empirical evidence using granular data on the internationalisation activity of firms.[10] For this reason, trade information has been a part of CompNet since day one, unlike EFIGE, in which data on the international activities of firms are cross-sectional, or ORBIS, in which the data are mostly missing. This makes CompNet a critical tool for trade analysis, because it allows analysts to combine information on firm internationalisation with the evolution of other firm-level characteristics.[11] By combining census data with trade flows, CompNet highlights the linkages between productivity and export performance as the result of the decision of firms to select into foreign markets, and the reallocation of resources across firms. Table 8.1 shows the relative importance of exporting firms in national economies, in terms of total employment, wages, production and turnover.

We can clearly see the relevance of exporting firms on the local economy, as we would expect, because these firms tend to be among

---

[10] Mario Draghi, *Structural Reforms, Inflation and Monetary Policy*, speech to the ECB Forum on Central Banking, Sintra, 22 May 2015, available at www.ecb.europa.eu/press/key/date/2015/html/sp150522.en.html.

[11] For more technical and detailed information regarding the trade dimension of the CompNet database, please refer to the trade methodological paper: Berthou et al. (2015).

Table 8.1. *Export intensity (at the country level).*

	Employment		Labour costs		Value added		Turnover	
	2006	2010	2006	2010	2006	2010	2006	2010
Belgium	0.81	0.80	0.84	0.82	0.85	0.85	0.90	0.88
Estonia	0.80	0.82	0.83	0.84	0.85	0.88	0.87	0.93
Finland	0.84	0.80	0.86	0.84	0.91	0.89	0.93	0.90
France	0.75	0.75	0.80	0.79	0.81	0.80	0.85	0.85
Hungary	0.64	0.70	0.74	0.78	0.78	0.80	0.88	0.90
Italy	0.82	0.84	0.85	0.86	0.86	0.88	0.87	0.89
Lithuania	0.66	0.69	0.71	0.76	0.76	0.81	0.82	0.88
Poland	0.79	0.79	0.82	0.82	0.85	0.83	0.86	0.86
Portugal	0.72	0.74	0.75	0.77	0.78	0.80	0.84	0.85
Romania	0.48	0.54	0.56	0.64	0.55	0.68	0.66	0.74
Slovakia	0.90	0.90	0.91	0.92	0.95	0.93	0.94	0.94
Slovenia	0.86	0.88	0.89	0.91	0.91	0.93	0.94	0.95
Average	0.74	0.75	0.77	0.79	0.80	0.82	0.85	0.86

Source: CompNet Trade Module – Berthou et al. (2015).
Notes: Selected European countries. Average share of total (national) employment, labour costs, value added and turnover accounted for by exporting firms in each country.

the largest in each economy. It is also striking to see the Pareto rule applies: exporters are around 20% of all firms in a given economy, but they account (on average) for 80% of the economic activity, as variously measured.

Measurements of exporters' productivity premiums also provide support for contemporary trade theory. Since Melitz (2003), it is conventional wisdom that exporting firms have, on average, higher productivity due to the high productivity bar required to operate profitably in global markets. Berthou et al. (2015) showed that exporters are on average 20% more productive than non-exporters in Europe.[12] Figure 8.1 shows the size of productivity premia, and their evolution with respect to a TFP index, comparing exporters and non-exporters.

---

[12] Interestingly, they also found that permanent exporters are more productive than new exporters, implying that productivity is an important determinant not only of entry, but also survival in the international market.

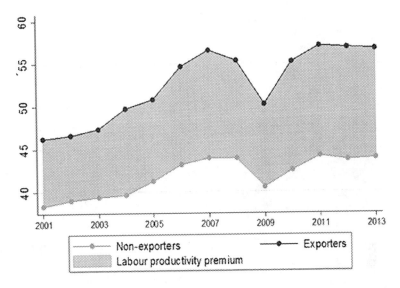

Figure 8.1 Productivity premia.

Source: European firms after the crisis – CompNet (2016). Average evolution of TFP index for non-exporters and exporters across EU countries

The export premium, however, hides a very strong heterogeneity in performance within the population of exporters. Again, consistently with previous results, aggregate exports are extremely concentrated, with the 10 largest exporting firms in each country representing more than 20% of total exports, as shown in Figure 8.2.[13]

In the CompNet (2020) report, the researchers of the network focus on trade margins and productivity developments in CEE and non-CEE countries. Figure 8.3 shows that exports increased on average by approximately 20% between 2010 and 2016, but this figure was entirely driven by growth in exports in CEE countries. In other countries in Europe, they declined slightly.

The authors decomposed these data to reveal whether the trend was driven by the extensive or the intensive margin. Figure 8.4 shows that intensive margin increased substantially in CEE countries between 2010 and 2016, but only slightly in non-CEE countries. This means that, between 2010 and 2016, firms that were already exporting from

[13] Berthou et al. (2015) gives more detail on exporters in European countries.

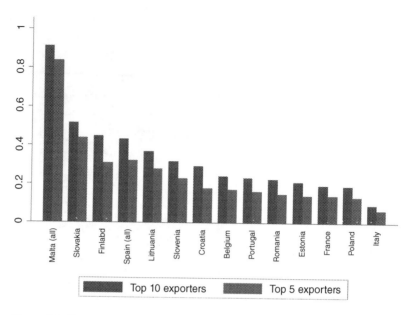

Figure 8.2 Export concentration.

Source: CompNet Trade Module – Berthou et al. (2015). Export share of the 10 largest exporting firms in the country

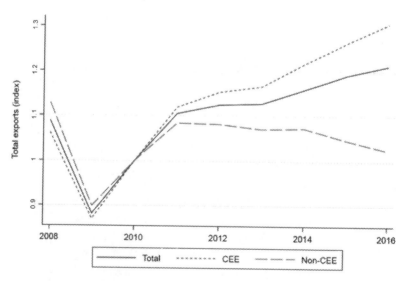

Figure 8.3 Index of export dynamics in average CEE and non-CEE EU countries, 2008–2016, 2010 = 1.

Source: CompNet (2020)

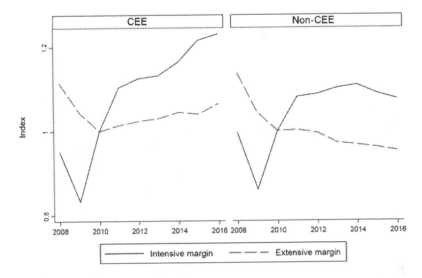

Figure 8.4 Index of intensive and extensive margins of export dynamics in average CEE and non-CEE EU countries, 2008–2016, 2010 = 1.
Source: CompNet (2020)

CEE countries increased their export activities by a lot, while the number of exporting firms also increased slightly. In other countries in Europe, the number of exporters declined slightly. This information is shown in Figure 8.3.

CompNet data also allowed the authors to investigate whether intra-EU or extra-EU exports drove this development. Figure 8.5 shows that the difference in export activity of CEE and non-CEE countries is the same for intra- and extra-EU trade. The overall trend in Figure 8.3 might, however, be partially due to declining exports from firms in non-CEE countries to countries outside the EU.

Finally, the authors showed that the diverging pattern in export activity was also reflected in divergent productivity performance between CEE and non-CEE countries (Figure 8.6). The data suggest that CEE countries were rapidly catching up with non-CEE countries.

We can use the most recent CompNet dataset for policy-relevant analysis on the relationship between trade and productivity in EU countries.

Figure 8.7 shows six relevant premia – along different dimensions of firm performance – of exporting firms relative to non-exporters in the

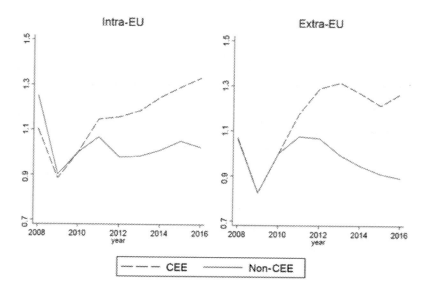

Figure 8.5 Intra-EU and extra-EU export dynamics for European firms, 2006–2016 (2010 = 1).

Source: CompNet (2020)

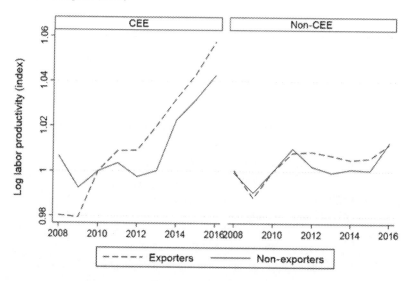

Figure 8.6 Index of labour productivity dynamics in CEE and non-CEE EU countries, 2008–2016, 2010 = 1.

Source: CompNet (2020)

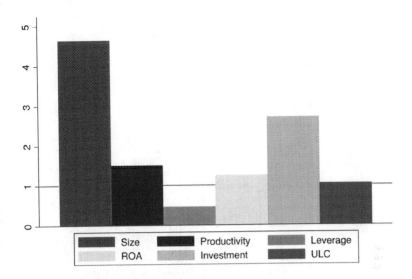

Figure 8.7 Characteristics of exporters vs. non-exporters.

Source: Authors' elaboration of CompNet sixth vintage data. Ratios of exporters vs. non-exporters characteristics

manufacturing sector in Europe, between 2004 and 2015. For each performance indicator, a value of 1 means that exporting and non-exporting firms were, on average, equal, while a value greater than one implies a premium for exporting firms.

Figure 8.7 shows that exporters were between four and five times larger, and approximately 50% more productive, than non-exporters. The results are broadly in line with previous research. The data also suggest that exporting firms performed better financially than non-exporters: they were less leveraged, invested almost three times more and had a slightly better ROA. Although not shown here, exporting firms had (deflated) sales approximately 12 times higher than domestic firms, although they did not seem to be more competitive than non-exporting firms as measured by their average unit labour cost (ULC).

At first glance, the ULC result seems counter-intuitive: often indicators that track competitiveness at the country level rely on the assumption that labour costs should decrease. Here, exporting firms are almost 50% more productive than non-exporters, but have a similar ULC. The reason is that exported goods are often of higher quality,

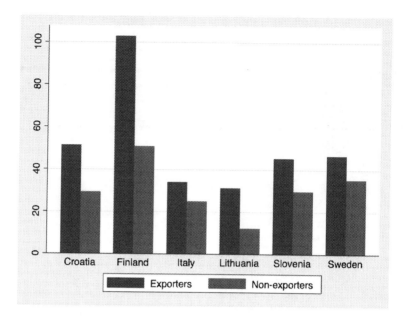

Figure 8.8 Average TFP by firm type.

Source: Authors' elaboration of CompNet sixth vintage data. TFP index for exporters and non-exporters across countries

and hence incur higher costs *at the firm level*. Data in CompNet (2020) show that exporting firms invest more on intangible assets, and offer higher wages because they typically retain workers with higher skills. Perhaps we should be sceptical of country-level indicators of competitiveness calculated using ULC measures, as discussed in Altomonte et al. (2012).

But while exporters are *on average* more productive than non-exporters, most empirical research has highlighted the large differences between countries. In Figure 8.8, we zoom in on these differences. It shows the average level of TFP for exporters and non-exporters in the manufacturing sector in six European countries between 2004 and 2015.

While exporters are more productive than non-exporters in all countries, the graph shows that there is cross-country heterogeneity both in the productivity level of both types of firm.

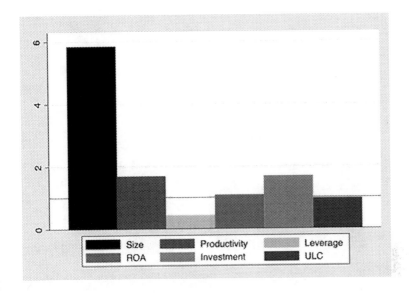

Figure 8.9 Characteristics of GVC vs non-GVC firms.
Source: Authors' elaboration of CompNet sixth vintage data

Performance and Participation in GVCs

CompNet data also provide information on firm internationalisation activities. It is possible to identify firms that both import and export, otherwise known as two-way traders. These firms are typically part of GVCs. Figures 8.9 and 8.10 are similar to Figures 8.7 and 8.8, respectively. The former show the premia for firms involved in two-way trade, relative to firms not involved. The latter show cross-country productivity differences between these two types of firms.

Figure 8.9 shows that firms involved in GVCs generally perform much better than those which are not, again consistent with what we know from previous research. They are on average almost six times larger, and approximately 75% more productive. They are less leveraged, have a higher ROA and invest about 75% more than firms that are not involved in GVCs.

Figure 8.10 shows the average productivity levels for five European countries for firms involved in GVCs, and those which are not.

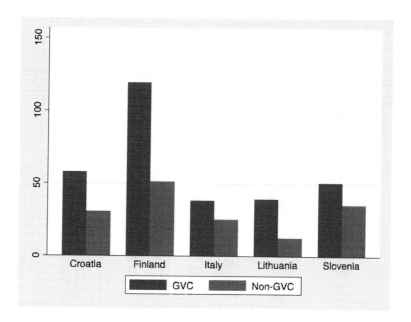

Figure 8.10 Average TFP by a firm's involvement in GVCs.
Source: Authors' elaboration of CompNet sixth vintage data

In addition to the usual cross-country differences, the graph shows that, in the same country, firms involved in GVCs are on average more productive than those that are not. The difference in average productivity levels is smallest in Italy.

CompNet data show that the differences between firms that are part of GVCs and those that are not are much larger than the equivalent differences between exporting and non-exporting firms. These results reinforce the argument that, for each firm, we need to take into account all its internationalisation activities, not solely its export status, when evaluating competitiveness.

In Figure 8.11, we look at the evolution of TFP, distinguishing between exporters and non-exporters. Not surprisingly, in all countries, with the exception of Croatia, exporting firms have been more productive than domestic firms.

Similarly, we can use CompNet data to analyse how three premia (employment, TFP and sales) have been associated with internationalisation and evolved over time, for both exporting firms and for

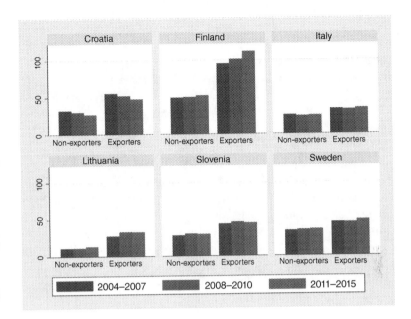

Figure 8.11 Average TFP by firm export status.
Source: Authors' elaboration of CompNet sixth vintage data

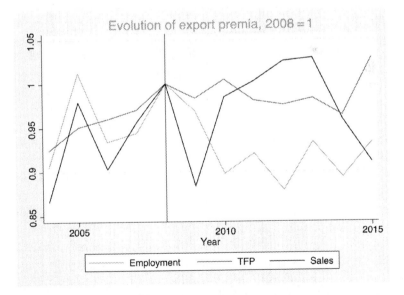

Figure 8.12 Evolution of export premia, 2008 = 1.
Source: Authors' elaboration of CompNet sixth vintage data

firms involved in GVCs. Figure 8.12 shows the evolution of premia associated with being an exporter between 2004 and 2015 in the countries in our sample. The values are indexed by their 2008 value to show the reaction of these premia to the 2009 trade shock.

Again, confirming previous research, all premia of exporting firms dropped in 2009. The sales premium of exporting firms fell by approximately 12% and the employment premium by 6%. By 2010, the sales premium was back to pre-crisis levels, but not the employment premium, which did not recover. Again, we conclude that workers have been indirectly affected by the trade shock through this permanent employment reduction among exporting firms. This backs up Békés et al. (2011), who found that exporting firms laid off unskilled workers after the trade collapse, and are generally consistent with research on long-run labour market effects from trade shocks. The average productivity premium of exporters also slightly dropped in 2009, by approximately 2%, and remained stable in the following years.

Figure 8.13 replicates this for firms involved in GVCs relative to those that are not. The effects of the 2009 trade shock on GVC-related premia are smaller than those on export-related premia. Following the crisis, firms involved in GVCs slightly reduced employment relative to firms not involved in GVCs, but the reduction in this premium was absorbed by 2015. Similarly, the sales premium decreased between 2008 and 2009, although by a smaller amount than the equivalent export premium. Finally, TFP increased after the crisis for firms involved in GVCs relative to those firms which are not, unlike the productivity premium of exporters. This supports the argument that firms participating in production chains reacted more flexibly than those involved in traditional trade activities, and so did not suffer as much from demand shocks.

Figures 8.7 and 8.9 show how firms' internationalisation (proxied by their exporter status or their participation in GVCs) made them more successful in several dimensions of performance. It also helps explain what makes countries successful at globalisation. By contrast, Figure 8.12 shows some of the already discussed negative consequences of internationalisation. Exporting firms become more vulnerable to shocks affecting global trade, and may make the impact on an economy of an international crisis worse. This is exactly what happened after the Global Financial Crisis.

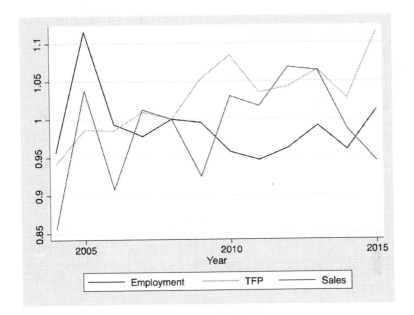

Figure 8.13 Evolution of GVC premia, 2008 = 1.
Source: Authors' elaboration of CompNet sixth vintage data

On the contrary, a structured participation in GVCs on top of simple export activity seems to allow firms to weather global trade shocks better, as with European firms participating in GVCs (Figure 8.13). This is internationalisation driven by a process of economic integration, such as that in the EU.

We can perform robust empirical regressions using the data represented in Figure 8.9 to discover whether firms integrated in GVCs also perform better in today's globalised economy. In doing so, we can also assess whether the variation in GVC premia after the Global Financial Crisis is statistically significant. To do so, we use sector-level CompNet data to run the following type of regression:

$$PerformancePremium_{s,c,t} = \alpha + \beta \, GVCs, c, t\gamma_c + \sigma_s + \tau_t + \epsilon_{s,c,t}, \tag{8.1}$$

where $PerformancePremium_{s,c,t}$ is one of three firm performance indicators (TFP, employment and sales) in sector s of country c at year t, and $GVC_{s,c,t}$ is the share of firms integrated in GVCs in

Table 8.2. *Performance premia and participation in GVCs at the sector level.*

	(1) TFP pr.	(2) Empl. pr.	(3) Sales pr.	(4) TFP pr.	(5) Empl. pr.	(6) Sales pr.
Integration in GVC	1.940**	4.579***	23.88***	1.689**	3.643**	23.76***
	(0.759)	(1.633)	(7.079)	(0.745)	(1.665)	(6.779)
Dummy crisis				−0.636	−2.721*	2.619
				(0.445)	(1.436)	(7.246)
Crisis*GVC				1.108	4.167*	−6.267
Observations	1,211	1,172	1,147	1,211	1,172	1,147
R-squared	0.337	0.330	0.255	0.335	0.327	0.248
Sector FEs	Yes	Yes	Yes	Yes	Yes	Yes
Country FEs	Yes	Yes	Yes	Yes	Yes	Yes
Year FEs	Yes	Yes	Yes	No	No	No

Note: Robust standard errors are in parentheses.
* $p < 0.10$, ** $p < 0.05$, *** $p < 0.01$.

sector s of country c at year t. γ_c, σ_s and τ_t are country, sector and year fixed effects, respectively. In other specifications, we include a dummy variable equal to 1 in years most affected by the crisis and the interaction between such variables and the share of firms integrated in GVCs in the sector.

Table 8.2 reports the results. Columns (1)–(3) show that TFP, employment and sales are on average higher in sectors with relatively more firms participating in GVCs. However, columns (4)–(6) show that the crisis did not exert a significant effect on TFP and sales at the sector level, but it had a small but significant impact in reducing employment. The coefficient on the interaction term in column (5) shows that the contraction of employment was smaller in sectors with more firms integrated in GVCs.

Export Margins and Productivity

CompNet data can illustrate the extensive and the intensive margins in various European countries. To illustrate the importance of the extensive margin, Figures 8.14–8.16, in particular, focus on the share of exporting firms at different deciles of the productivity distribution.

Figure 8.14 shows the share of exporters at each decile of the TFP distribution on average in CEE and non-CEE countries between 2004

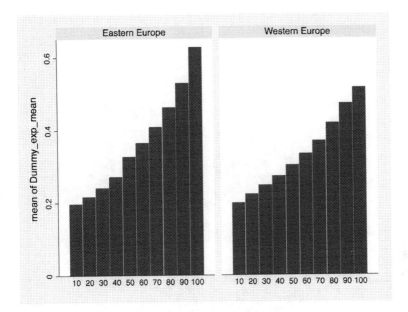

Figure 8.14 Share of exporters by TFP decile and region.
Source: Authors' elaboration of CompNet sixth vintage dataset

and 2015. While the share of exporters at low deciles of the distribution is approximately equal in both groups, in CEE countries there are on average relatively more exporters at the top of the distribution than in the others. This may be because high-performance firms in CEE countries were involved in German-led production chains.

In Figure 8.15, we have analysed whether the extensive margin was damaged by the demand shock between 2008 and 2010, again at different deciles of the productivity distribution. The effect of the crisis was mixed. The share of exporters increased both at the bottom and the top of the distribution during the crisis, while it decreased at the median. Finally, the share of exporters in top deciles increased more than in bottom deciles after the crisis, showing that high-performance firms were able to respond more flexibly to demand shocks.

Finally, in Figure 8.16 we ask whether there is cross-country heterogeneity in the share of exporters at the bottom, median and top of the TFP distribution, and if the share of exporters changed differently within countries. The graphs show that in some countries the extensive margin was more damaged than in other countries during

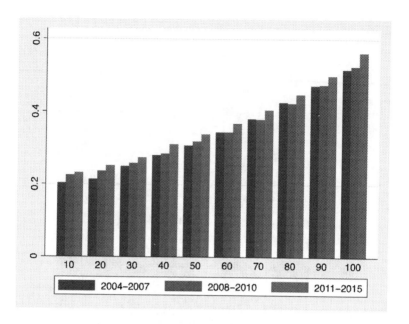

Figure 8.15 Share of exporters by TFP decile.
Source: Authors' elaboration of CompNet sixth vintage data

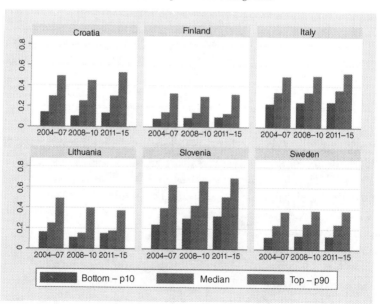

Figure 8.16 Share of exporters at bottom, median and top of TFP distribution, by period.
Source: Authors' elaboration of CompNet sixth vintage data

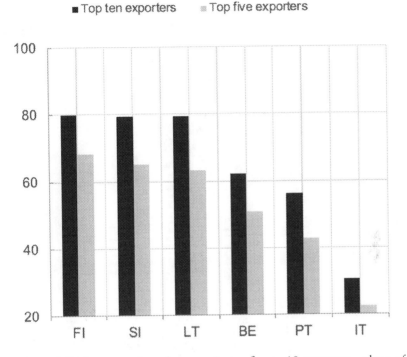

Figure 8.17 Concentration of exports in top five or 10 exporters – share of total exports.

Source: Authors' elaboration of CompNet fifth vintage dataset

the trade collapse. Between 2008 and 2010, the share of exporters decreased slightly, and uniformly across the TFP distribution, in Croatia, Finland and Lithuania. On the other hand, it remained stable in Italy, Sweden and Slovenia.

Turning to the intensive margin of adjustment of export flows, Lopez-Garcia et al. (2018) showed that the unprecedented drop in exports in 2009 in the euro area was driven by the intensive margin of few firms, consistent with our results. They found that in most countries the top 10 exporters accounted for more than 50% of the export drop. One notable exception was Italy, where exporters were smaller than in other countries of the euro area.

Figures 8.17 and 8.18 show the importance of this result. It shows the concentration of exports in the top 10 and top five exporters in available European countries using CompNet's preliminary seventh

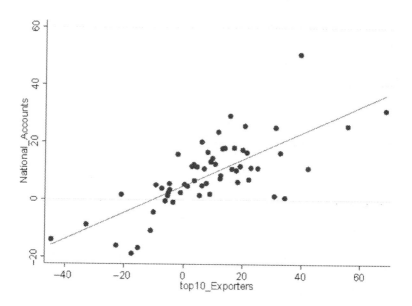

Figure 8.18 Correlation of export growth of top 10 exporters and aggregate export growth – annual growth rate.

Source: Authors' elaboration of CompNet fifth vintage data

vintage data, as well as the correlation between the exports of the top 10 exporters and Eurostat's aggregate figures. Except for Italy, and as the research into the happy few firms argued, in all countries there was a huge concentration of exports in the top 10, and even top five exporters. The high correlation between aggregate trade figures and the export figures of top exporters within each country implies that policymakers can predict aggregate trade figures by predicting those of a few firms in each country.

8.4 Conclusion

In this chapter, we discussed trade theory from early models to the new new trade models that use firm heterogeneity, as well as the evidence for positive welfare effects of trade on economic growth and some negative consequences for societies. Also, we examined the relevant characteristics of today's wave of globalisation, notably the spread of GVCs.

We exploited the increasing availability of good-quality firm-level datasets, and most notably CompNet, to provide evidence of several stylised facts:

(1) There is substantial variation both across and within industries in firms' ability to export.

(2) There seems to be a link between firms' presence in foreign markets and productivity.

(3) There are premia for firms engaging in internationalisation activities compared to those serving only the local market, and these premia increase with the complexity of the internationalisation activity. This implies that firms participating in GVCs are more productive than exporting firms in general, which in turn are more productive than firms serving only their local market. Premia for exporting firms decreased in response to the 2009 trade collapse, while those for firms involved in more sophisticated trade linkages reacted less negatively and sometimes even positively to the demand shock.

(4) Adopting a firm-level perspective helps explain several apparent paradoxes in aggregate figures, such as the relation between exporting activity and unit labour costs.

(5) There is causality from firm innovation to internationalisation. This implies that innovation policies would be a major driver of trade and economic growth.

(6) Few firms are able to export, and exporting is thus very concentrated in virtually all countries. Policymakers may be able to analyse and forecast nearly all aggregate trade figures by predicting a few firms' export value.

(7) Responses to exchange rate movements are heterogeneous across firms. Export elasticity to REER movements is inversely correlated with size and productivity, and therefore exports by larger and more productive firms are less sensitive to exchange rate movements.

This highlights the need for European policymakers to preserve the trade liberalisation of the past 20 years by supporting trade agreements under discussion at the time of writing (for example, with Japan and Latin American countries, as well as with the post-Brexit UK). They will be necessary to further reduce trade costs, both price and non-price. This may be difficult: as anger against globalisation increases, trade wars become a real threat.

There is also evidence of a large gap between the winners and losers from globalisation. For this reason, it is important for policymakers in Europe to promote an inclusive model of globalisation. To do this, they must nurture the most competitive firms in each industry. Promoting intra-industry competition and innovation would help increase the number of exporters and multinational firms, which in turn contribute most to aggregate economic growth. Policymakers will need to mobilise public and private resources to help firms investing in R&D activities, and so innovation policies will become even more important.

We must also promote firm growth. This means identifying and sustaining the potential superstar firms of tomorrow in the industries with the highest growth potential. Size matters for firm internationalisation. We need policies that encourage a reallocation of market share from low-productivity to innovative and efficient firms within sectors. Policymakers should encourage the mergers and acquisitions that can achieve this in all European countries.

Finally, traditional trade activities are no longer sufficient for firms to thrive. European firms need to be connected to GVCs to fully exploit the potential of globalisation. Policymakers need to remove barriers to the increase of foreign direct investment.

Appendix 8.1: GVCs after COVID-19

The disruption of GVCs was a negative side effect of the COVID-19 pandemic (Baldwin, 2020), particularly because of the impact on firm productivity (Syverson and di Mauro, 2020). In Europe, participation in GVCs is high, particularly in CEE countries.

Using WIOD input–output tables we can simulate a hypothetical restriction of trade on final and intermediate goods outside Europe and investigate how it would shrink the overall participation in GVCs by firms in each European region – and therefore affect their productivity. This is indicative of the extent to which GVC participation by EU firms is predominantly relevant inside the EU economy, or truly global.

To measure EU firm integration in GVCs, we use a GVC participation index developed by Koopman et al. (2014), which takes into account two factors:

- The extent to which exporters depend on foreign suppliers for intermediate inputs (the share of foreign value added in exports).
- The share of domestic value added contained in foreign exports to third countries.

The two components represent the GVC-related export value. We compute the index by dividing the sum of the components by the total value of gross exports in each country i and sector j pair. To do so, we can use the existing STATA routine *ICIO* that draws from the WIOD input–output tables[14]:

icio, exporter(country, sector) importer(country, sector);

The overall GVC participation index is obtained by not specifying any importer country, to account for the rest of the world. The resulting overall GVC participation of European firms is just over 40%, but varies greatly across countries: Malta, Luxembourg, Belgium and a number of eastern European countries are above the average, whereas Greece, Spain, France and Germany are below.

We also separate the portion of extra-EU import value added in each country–sector pair, as calculated via Belotti et al. (2020). By excluding this, we obtain an indicator of GVC participation which considers only GVCs within the EU. Obviously, this is a lower bound – we exclude countries such as China and the US that are central hubs in GVCs – but the within-EU indicator can be indicative of the economic impact of a disruption in the supply chains for the EU internal market.

Figure 8.19 proxies the two impacts (overall and within-EU) at sector level. Two groups of sectors are particularly affected: the most internationalised manufacturing sectors such as basic metals, rubber, chemical products and so on); and a few high value-added service sectors such as computer programming and engineering.

---

[14] See Belotti et al. (2020) for a comprehensive analysis of this toolkit.

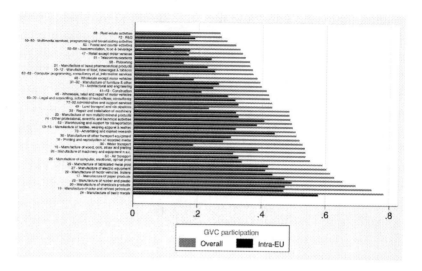

Figure 8.19 GVC participation in the EU excluding extra-EU countries, by sector.

Source: WIOD I-O tabes. The share of participation is computed as an average of the NACE 2 sectors' GVC share (2014); adapted from Altomonte et al. (2020)

Another important dimension of the GVC participation is regional, as territorial diversity in the extent to which firms participate in GVCs might create regional disparities following shocks. It is not easy to measure the degree of embeddedness in GVCs at the EU regional level, because all the relevant measures of trade flows are collected at the country and sector level.

To proxy it, we follow the methodology of Autor et al. (2013) and weight GVC participation at the sector level by the relative importance of each sector at regional level in the EU (using Eurostat structural business statistics data on the regional distribution of economic activities). The weight is normalised for employment in region *i* so that we do not give more importance to regions in which employment is larger.

Since the shock involves restriction of trade in EU regions, following Belotti et al. (2020) we separate the GVC-related trade into two components: domestic value added absorbed outside the EU, and the

Figure 8.20 Overall GVC participation (left) vs. GVC participation non-EU related (right) at NUTS-2 level (weighted by labour share).
Source: Adapted from Altomonte et al. (2020)

extra-EU import value added, which is the content of export originated outside the EU. Taking the average of these two components,
we obtain a measure of exposure to the GVC disruptions at the
country-sector level; by weighting it with the regional weights, we
obtain an index of regional exposure.

For the first component of this index, the STATA code is the same
as earlier; for the extra-EU import value added, we need the following
syntax to specify the country of origin of the selected trade flow:

icio, importer(country, sector) origin(all) output(va).

Figure 8.20 (left-hand panel) reports the regional overall exposure
to GVC. The right-hand panel represents the share of exposure due
to extra-EU-GVC-related activities. The darker regions are relatively
most affected by GVC disruptions, both overall (in line with their
overall GVC participation; left-hand panel) and with respect to extra-
EU trade (right-hand panel).

There are clusters of regions that are remarkably integrated in GVC
across different countries, for example most of the regions in which we
find CEE countries, Ireland or the Netherlands. The panel on the right,

however, shows that a shock to non-EU GVC participation would have a much more concentrated impact. Overall:

- Most regions in the EU core, notably in Germany, Italy, France and Spain, would be affected more severely by a GVC shock.
- Greek regions – and to a lesser extent Irish ones – are particularly affected because their GVC participation is mostly extra-EU.
- Most CEE regions are not exposed to extra-EU GVCs, since international participation for such regions is almost exclusively within Europe.

9 | *Productivity and Competitive Pressure*

9.1 Introduction

According to the European Commission's definition, competition is the condition which puts businesses under constant pressure to offer the best possible range of goods at the best possible prices. Where there is competition, and a firm sets prices that are too high, consumers have the choice to buy elsewhere. On the flip side, market power is the ability of a firm (or group of firms) to raise and maintain that price above what it would be if there was competition.

In a free-market economy, business is a competitive game on a level playing field, with consumers as the beneficiaries. Competitive markets also drive innovation, because firms are forced to invest to offer the best products at the lowest price so that they can remain in the market. In this case, competition is a necessary condition to create productivity growth.

But firms have incentives to limit competition by colluding, or to obtain advantages from a dominant position in the market. At times, these strategies might bring potential benefits to consumers (for example, in the case of R&D, or better distribution of products), in general anti-competitive practices hamper an equal distribution of gains in the market economy, as excessive market power becomes concentrated in a handful of firms.

Hence the role of competition policy. It is one of the most important tools to help policymakers strike a proper balance between the market, the state and citizens. In recent decades in OECD countries, governments have created specialised competition policy authorities, in some cases independent of political power. In Europe, competition policy has been delegated to the European Commission as an exclusive competence, so that today the network of the Directorate General Competition in Brussels, working with the national competition authorities in member states, is arguably one of the most important policy areas under the direct control of European institutions. In the US, competition policy is implemented by the Federal Trade Commission and the Antitrust Division of the Department of Justice.

To preserve well-functioning product markets, authorities such as the European Commission must prevent or correct anti-competitive behaviour. To achieve this, in the EU, the Directorate-General (DG) for Competition monitors the following:

- Agreements between firms that restrict competition in the single market. This means cartels or other unfair arrangements in which firms agree to avoid competing with each other, or try to set their own rules, which are always forbidden.
- Abuse of a dominant position. This is where a dominant firm tries to squeeze its competitors out of the market or control them with over-stringent contracts. Both are forbidden when the dominant position generates an abusive behaviour detrimental for consumers.
- Mergers and other formal agreements. Arrangements whereby firms join forces permanently or temporarily are legitimate provided that they expand markets and benefit consumers. They are not when they generate potentially abusive dominant positions.
- Efforts to open markets up to competition. Areas such as transport, energy, postal services and telecommunications are natural monopolies, closed to competition or state-run monopolies. Liberalisation can open access to the sector without giving an unfair advantage to the incumbents.
- Financial support (state aid) for firms from EU governments. This is allowed only if it does not distort fair and effective competition between firms in EU countries or harm the economy.
- Cooperation with national competition authorities in EU countries. They are responsible for enforcing aspects of EU competition law in operations that do not have a European scale, to ensure that EU competition law is applied in the same way across the EU.

Ensuring that these objectives are reached in an economy that is continuously transforming is a complex job with few simple answers. Thomas Philippon, a French economist based in the US effectively summarises the most relevant recent economic literature dealing with this topic. Philippon (2019) starts from the observation that, due to the emergence of large corporations operating in the technology industry (Facebook, Amazon, Apple, Google), concentration and profits have increased in the US, and this suggests that a decline in competition has been occurring in the US for at least 20 years.

His argument, therefore, is that the US no longer deserves its reputation as the home of free-market economics. This opinion is not unanimously shared. For example, De Loecker et al. (2020) look at markups of prices over marginal costs. While they find an overall upward trend across countries, they attribute the rise in markups to a within-industry redistribution of market shares from low- to high-markup firms, while the median firm's markup has not changed. We have already discussed that markups and productivity are positively correlated, so this would seem to suggest that concentration has mostly been the result of a redistribution of market share to the most efficient firms. Autor et al. (2020) look at the fall of labour's share of GDP in the US, and argue that as globalisation or technological change pushes sales to the most productive firms in each industry, product market concentration will rise as industries become increasingly dominated by superstar firms with high markups and a low labour share of value added. Hence, once again, the increase in concentration is the (unwanted) result of good competitive forces.

Despite reaching different conclusions, all these papers derive their insights from a careful analysis of firm-level data, and their arguments are all that there is a redistribution of economic activity across heterogeneous firms. In this chapter, we will review the recent economic research on market power that exploits firm-level information. We start by providing an overall assessment of the status of competition in the US and Europe. We discuss the connections between market power and trade, and the welfare effects of diminishing competition, the debate on market power, some conceptual frameworks and measurement issues. We then move to our own analysis, providing some descriptive evidence of market power in European countries, exploiting (as usual) CompNet data.

9.2 Literature Review

Competition Policy in the EU and US

De Loecker and Eeckhout (2017, 2020) tracked the evolution of US market power since the 1950s to show that market power has increased both within and across economic sectors in recent years. In doing so, they first analysed markups, a measure of whether firms can price their products above marginal cost (see Chapter 2 for a technical definition and discussion). They found that while average markups were approximately stable from 1955 to 1980, they have risen steadily since the 1980s, from 21% above cost to 61% above cost.

The authors also studied the evolution of firm profitability, because markups alone are not sufficient to provide a complete picture of market power. If markups were high because of high fixed costs, this would imply that a firm charges prices above marginal costs to cover fixed costs. In fact, they found that average profit rates in the US increased from close to 1% in 1980 up to around 8% in 2016, following a pattern similar to markups. Firms charging higher markups also had higher profits. They therefore argued that markups and profit increases were correlated: markups increased, and this led to increasing profits.[1]

More importantly, the distribution of markups has changed. While the median is constant, the average increase in markups has been driven by the rise at the higher percentiles of the distribution. Firms at the high end of the markup distribution have increased their average markups in the US since the 1980s. This occurred during a reallocation of economic activity: few large firms have high and increasing markups and profits, while the majority were stable and losing market share. This suggests that we need to focus on firm dynamics if we want to see the macroeconomic picture painted by the rise of market power and the forces of competition.

De Loecker and Eeckhout (2018) documented a global trend of declining competition and increase in market power, equivalent to the pattern in the US. Exploiting firm-level balance sheets across countries, they reported a rise in markups between 1980 and 2000, stable markups from 2000 to 2010, and a further rise afterwards. Overall, global markups increased in this period by less than in the US – from 1.1 in 1980 to 1.6 in 2016.

---

[1] See the paper by Melitz and Ottaviano (2008) reviewed in Chapter 8 for a theoretical framework linking markups, productivity and profits at the firm level.

This is consistent with Philippon (2019), which buttresses the argument that competition is in retreat in the US by comparing it to the EU. Measuring markups by taking into account the balance of cost of goods sold against other fixed-cost components of sales and administrative expenditure, markups have not risen in the EU, but have risen in the US.

Recent research at the European Central Bank by McAdam et al. (2019) strengthens the argument that any rise in market power seems to be an issue in the US, but not in Europe. The authors used both macroeconomic and firm-level microeconomic data to show that concentration has not increased in recent decades in the four largest countries of the euro area. The study found, in particular, that concentration ratios remained stable in the last 10 years in these countries while, in terms of markups, market power had been declining in the euro area since the late 1990s and early 2000s. This has largely been driven by declining market power in the manufacturing sector, highlighting heterogeneity across industries.

Several contributions have highlighted that market power has been increasing around the world, with the rise sharper in the US than in the EU. According to Philippon (2019), the reason is political, not technological: poorer competition policy in the US than in the EU in recent decades. In particular, European competition policy is the responsibility of the European Commission, not central governments. This makes it less prone to lobbying by large firms. In the US, lobbying and campaign contributions have made it possible for special interest groups to obtain weak antitrust enforcement, leading to rising market power and declining competition.

Market Power and Trade Theory

A long-held view in economic theory – supported by both history and data – is that the absence of competition hurt consumers and workers, because it led to higher prices. This mechanism is embedded in the model of firm heterogeneity and trade developed by Melitz and Ottaviano (2008), already discussed in the empirical chapter on productivity and trade (Chapter 8). In that framework, one of the benefits deriving from deeper economic integration and higher exposure to trade is that consumers get lower prices due to the competition from foreign firms that are allowed to operate in markets that are open to trade. This adds to the benefits of global trade that were introduced in the Melitz model (Melitz, 2003) (Chapter 8).

De Loecker et al. (2016) investigated how markups reacted to trade liberalisation. They used Indian firm-level data and India's trade liberalisation episodes to study how prices, markups and marginal costs responded to higher exposure to trade. In line with the theoretical results of Melitz and Ottaviano (2008), they found that trade liberalisation lowered factory-gate prices and that reductions in output tariffs have had the expected pro-competitive effects. They also found, however, that price falls were small relative to the decline in marginal costs, which fell predominantly because of input tariff liberalisation. There was incomplete cost pass-through to prices because firms raised markups in response to lower marginal cost. Therefore, the reform, while beneficial overall, benefitted producers relatively more than consumers.

Caselli and Schiavo (2020) explored the similar relationship between markups and international trade at the firm level using a large sample of French manufacturing firms between 1995 and 2007. In particular, they investigated the effect on markups of increasing import competition from China, and the way in which exporting interacted with this effect. As international trade theory would predict, results showed robust evidence that firms in competition with Chinese imports decreased their markups. Firms that became exporters experienced a smaller reduction in their price-cost margins, and results showed that firms facing tougher competition from China were more likely to start exporting to avoid such competitive pressures.

The link between trade and market power was further explored in a paper by Morlacco (2019), who developed a model with monopolistic competition and heterogeneous firms to estimate a measure of a firms' relative market power in foreign input markets using standard production and trade data. Using firm-level data on French manufacturing firms from 1996 to 2007, she provides evidence that the buying power of individual importers was large, with potential implications for the aggregate economy. This implies that, if global trade increases market power of large firms, competition in advanced economies might continue to decline.

Market Power, Investment and the Role of Intangibles

One of the key policy arguments related to the increase in market power across countries (whether this comes from a lack of competition, as in Philippon, 2019, or the natural result of competitive forces, as in De Loecker and Eeckhout, 2017, or Autor et al., 2020) is that this increase might lead to lower investment by incumbent firms, and reduce productivity growth as a result.

Midrigan et al. (2016) argued that the secular decline of competition in the US might explain the macroeconomic puzzle of very low interest rates, but weak corporate investment. They found that the investment gap was driven by firms in less competitive industries and, absent the decline in competition, the US would have recovered much more quickly from the Global Financial Crisis in 2008. Gutiérrez and Philippon (2016) also find that investment in the US has been low relative to measures of profitability – such as Tobin's q – in the past 30 years. They tested four hypotheses for this trend: a rise in financial frictions, changes in the nature of investment (due to both increase in intangible assets in firm balance sheet and globalisation-driven foreign direct investment), increased short-termism in management and a decline in competition. They argued that poor corporate investment rates were mainly driven by firms in more concentrated industries, while the increasing share of intangible assets and the corporate ownership structure explained the rest. In their framework, financial frictions did not play a role.

Gutiérrez and Philippon (2017) addressed the issue of causality more directly using natural experiments and an instrumental variable approach to link poor competition and weak investment rates. The natural experiments involved two measures of increased import competition from China, while the instrumental variable was a measure of excess entry in the 1990s. They showed that the amount of entry in the market in the 1990s was associated with diminished competition a decade later. Instrumenting industry concentration using excess entry, they found that investment rates were driven down by higher concentration.

Similar findings were reported in Covarrubias et al. (2019), who found that the nature of concentration in the US has changed during the last 20 years. In the 1990s, the rise in concentration was driven by the higher productivity of leaders that increased investment in intangible assets. In the 2000s, however, concentration was associated with lower investment, higher prices and lower productivity.

Akcigit and Ates (2021) contributed to this empirical debate by outlining a novel micro-founded macro model and US data, providing a theoretical framework of endogenous markups, innovation and competition in which it would be possible to understand the mechanisms that create the empirical findings. They conducted a quantitative investigation of alternative mechanisms that could have led to these dynamics, with new insights on the rise of patenting concentration, finding regularities:

- Market concentration has risen.
- Average markups have increased.
- The profit share of GDP has increased.
- The labour share of output has gone down.
- The rise in market concentration and the fall in labour share are positively associated.
- Productivity dispersion of firms has risen and the labour productivity gap between frontier and laggard firms has widened.
- The firm entry rate has declined.
- The share of young firms in economic activity has declined.
- Job reallocation has slowed down.
- The dispersion of firm growth has decreased.

They explored the theoretical predictions of this framework, shaped by two interacting forces: a composition effect that determines market concentration, and an incentive effect that determines how firms respond to a given concentration in the economy. The results highlighted that a decline in knowledge diffusion between frontier and laggard firms, driven by technological factors, could have been a significant driver of empirical trends in the data.

Evolution of market power is less clear-cut in the EU. In a 2010 report for the Directorate-General for Economic and Financial Affairs of the European Commission, Altomonte et al. (2010) constructed a dataset of firm-level indicators to assess competitive conditions in the single market and highlight whether the potential of the market was being fully exploited. The report focused on firms operating in a group of manufacturing and services sectors in eight EU member states (Belgium, France, Germany, Italy, Poland, Romania, Spain and Sweden) between 1999 and 2007. They found a striking positive and pro-competitive effect from the single market.

Other studies with different metrics, however, have found increasing concentration in EU industries. Bajgar et al. (2019), using the OECD MultiProd data for the EU (see Chapter 5), showed that between 2001 and 2012 the average industry across 10 European economies saw a two- or three-percentage-point increase in the share of the 10% of largest firms in industry sales. Using Orbis data, they also documented a four- to eight-percentage-point increase in industry concentration in Europe and North America between 2000 and 2014 for the average industry. Over the period, about three of four (two-digit) industries in each region saw their concentration increase.

The bottom line is that this increase in market power, especially in the US, could have been responsible for weak corporate investment from the 2000s onwards and, consequently, low productivity growth. The overall conclusion of these studies is that the decrease in competition in the US led to a fall in non-residential business capital of between 5% and 10% by 2016. This implies that excessive market power creates inefficiencies and reduces output today – and might also cut future growth by reducing investment.

The relationship between market power and investment may also be affected by intangible assets (Syverson, 2019). Research has found that the increasing importance of intangible assets such as software and IT systems is partly responsible for low business dynamism, rising market concentration and rising profits. Since, the argument goes, intangibles are scalable and have synergies, firms that invest in them successfully gain a competitive advantage, breaking away from competition (Haskel and Westlake, 2018; Autor et al., 2020; Akcigit and Ates, 2021).

Crouzet and Eberly (2019), among others, have argued that rising investment in intangibles might be linked to market concentration directly through two mechanisms, with causality going in both directions:

- Increased concentration, driven by declining competition, reduces the incentives of firms to invest. This might be correlated with growth in intangible intensity.

- If a company invests in intangibles to produce a better product at lower cost, it will gain market share. Both concentration and intangible intensity increase. In this case, the rise in concentration is part of a mechanism which enhances welfare.

Altomonte et al. (2018b) used French firm-level data to explore the link between increasing market power and financial frictions. They developed and tested empirically a model with imperfect financial markets, firm heterogeneity and variable demand elasticity able to link heterogeneous financial constraints, intangible investment and firm-level markups. Using a quasi-experimental variation in financial constraints across French firms around the years of the financial crisis, they showed that a positive and arguably exogenous shock to liquidity led to a significant increase in the amount of intangible assets held by firms. Higher intangibles in turn led to higher markups over marginal costs. Importantly, however, they found that the latter effect was mediated by financial constraints: firms with ex ante better access to finance increased their markups more following the liquidity shock – in other words, they have higher pass-through elasticity to markups.

A third strand of research links the rise in market power to the fall in the labour share, in particular of manufacturing jobs in advanced countries. De Loecker et al. (2020) showed how a rise in markups implies a decrease in the labour share, as the firm's optimisation decision leaning towards high markups would lead to lower expenditure on inputs such as labour. Therefore, there would be a negative association between markups and the labour share. The authors argued that, due to the reallocation of market share to large firms with very high markups, these firms are responsible for the decline in the labour share. In fact, these firms tend to be capital intensive, and so have low labour shares.

This is consistent with the findings of Autor et al. (2020). They were among the first authors to put forward the so-called superstar effect, that a few very large firms in each sector that have high productivity and markup levels drive aggregate economic activity. This phenomenon can only be tested, of course, using firm-level data. The authors examined the role that superstar firms played in the reduction in the US labour share. They argued that globalisation and technological change disproportionately benefitted superstar firms because they are capital intensive, not labour intensive. As this process results in a reallocation of market share to these firms, they become large enough to explain the fall of the aggregate labour share on their own – yet additional evidence of the relevance of granularity in economic processes.

This implies that the observed decline in the labour share has been primarily caused by a reallocation effect across (large) firms, rather than by the average within-firm component of labour share. All these predictions are supported by US data, and similar patterns are found in other international data.

Barkai (2020) decomposed aggregate factor income into three elements: labour share, capital share and pure profits. He found that the fall in the labour share of income in the US was mirrored by a fall in the capital share, while pure profits increased from 3% of national income in 1985 to 16% in 2014. He linked the decline in labour share with market power, finding that the drop of the labour share was larger in industries where concentration rose the most in the same period.

CompNet researchers found that the evolution of the labour share in Europe was inversely associated with increased labour and market power, while initial capital intensity at the sector level had no effect (CompNet, 2020). But they also found that, once again, the process of substitution of labour with capital was very slow or even absent over time in the EU, unlike in the US.

These studies associate the fall of the labour share to increasing product market power, but a paper by Mertens (2019) found that labour market power had a significant negative impact on the labour share. He used firm-level data from the German manufacturing sector to investigate the potential sources of the fall of the labour share in that country. Only 30% of the decline in the labour share could be traced to increasing product and labour market power, but he suggested that labour market power was disproportionately more relevant than product market power. Mertens (2019) also argued that the remaining 70% was due to a general transition of firms to less labour-intensive production activities, and that increasing trade and economic integration seems to explain the bulk of these secular changes.

Azar et al. (2017) performed a comprehensive study of local labour markets in the US. They found that average labour market power was high, and that higher concentration was associated with lower wages. Using an instrumental variable approach, they also found that labour market power caused lower wages. Benmelech et al. (2018) built on Azar et al. (2017) and found that between 1977 and 2009 labour market power had increased in the US, and that it was negatively associated with wage levels, especially at high concentration levels. They also found that the negative correlation between labour market power and wages had been stronger when trade unions were weaker and in markets relatively more exposed to the import shock from China (measured as in Autor et al., 2013). Finally, where the labour market concentration was higher, the transmission of productivity gains to wage growth had been weaker.

De Loecker et al. (2020) also discussed the impact of rising markups on the decrease in the capital share, the decrease in low skilled wages, the decrease in labour market participation and the decrease in labour reallocation and US interstate migration. Eggertsson et al. (2018) developed a model with increased markups and used it to demonstrate that market power can explain a declining labour share, as well as other macroeconomic phenomena such as increasing profit shares, growth in the financial wealth-to-output ratio and increase in the Tobin's q without an associated increase in investment and a divergences between average and marginal return to capital. Their argument was that an increase in market power would lead directly to an increase in profit share through higher markups. As a result, Tobin's q and financial wealth increase. The increase in the share of pure profits would reduce both the labour and the capital share of income.

Therefore, it is hardly surprising that the reported increase in market power has implications that are not only restricted to the market where a firm operates, but also on the overall economy. Syverson (2019) reviewed recent empirical investigations and theoretical contributions on the relationship between the rise in market power and several macroeconomic puzzles. We need to look deeper at the connection between the documented decline in competition and the drop of investment rates, firm entry rates and the labour share, and the role played by intangibles and labour market power deeper if we are to solve the implications of rising market power on today's macroeconomic puzzles.

Relevance for Policy

We have reviewed some of the research on market power and its implications for the overall economy. We can conclude that, in the case of competition and market power, many of the policy-relevant forces are not visible if we only use macroeconomic data: De Loecker et al. (2020) found, for example, that the increase in the average markup level was driven by firms at the highest percentiles of the markup distribution. Van Reenen (2018) also pointed out that a full understanding of macroeconomic outcomes requires taking into account the role of firm heterogeneity in terms of markups as well as productivity levels. So, once again, the development of good-quality firm-level data can help us better understand the macro phenomena and improve economic policy.

Both in the US and in Europe, growth in market power has gained the attention of monetary policymakers. In an economic brief issued by the Federal Reserve Bank of Richmond, Sablik and Trachter (2019) highlighted the extent to which market power might become an issue for the Fed and other central banks. They argued, however, that higher markups should not necessarily worry the Fed: an increase could just mean that marginal costs had gone down, which would ultimately be welfare enhancing.

Rising market power, however, should concern the Federal Reserve due to its implications for employment, the second part of its dual mandate. We have seen that firms with high markups tend to hire fewer workers, which could increase unemployment. In addition, they might pay workers less.

In a competitive environment, firms with higher productivity levels would pass their efficiency gains to workers through higher wage growth. But in a world of increasing market power, some firms (typically the largest) keep their efficiency gains through higher profits rather than passing them to workers through higher wages. A (very) incomplete pass-through of efficiency gains to wage growth would potentially be deflationary, potentially in turn biasing monetary policy decisions. Low wage growth in a competitive environment could be a sign of slowing productivity and economic growth and an argument for expansionary monetary policy. But the same signal in non-competitive markets would weaken the case for expansionary monetary policy.

Rising market power can also hamper the transmission mechanism of monetary policy. Firms with higher markups tend to invest less in the US, depressing aggregate productivity growth. Midrigan et al. (2016) have argued that firms with higher markups were responsible for real interest rates being low. Therefore, in an economy in which there was rising market power, central banks might encounter the zero lower bound more often. If these firms invested less because of market power, and were able to capture more profits through markups, they may absorb interest rate changes as profits rather than higher investment. This means they would be less responsive to a monetary policy stimulus, making monetary policy as a whole less effective.

Though less pronounced than in the US, in the euro area falling competition and rising market power has also alerted the attention of monetary policy decision-makers. A study by McAdam et al. (2019) focused on the four core euro-area countries and argued that the adoption of the euro could explain the decline in market concentration observed in Europe pre-crisis. Peter Praet, formerly chief economist of the ECB, reinforced the argument that euro area firms do not seem to have rising markups.[2] While it may be a good sign that the business environment in the euro area is suffering less from bad competition dynamics, Europe has nevertheless not been able to develop its own superstar firms, all the while importing negative effects into its business environment through global firms headquartered in the US.

Conceptual Framework and Measurement Issues

If we are arguing for policy relevance, we cannot ignore the complex problem of how to measure market power. There is a healthy debate over the theoretical basis of the methods of estimating market power.[3]

Syverson (2019) has provided a comprehensive review of the different measures of market power that researchers and policymakers use. We will follow his logic and use it to build some state-of-the-art market power measurements.

Syverson (2019) defined market power as the ability of a firm to affect the price at which it sells its products. We can observe market

---

[2] *Market Power – A Complex Reality*, speech by Peter Praet, Member of the Executive Board of the European Central Bank, at the EIB/CompNet conference, Luxembourg, 18 March 2019.

[3] In Section 4.2, we have already discussed the three main measures of market power: concentration indexes, firm-level markups and price-cost margin, which we will use for this analysis.

power when a company can price its products above marginal cost. The magnitude of market power is linked to the gap between price and marginal cost – that is, its markup.

But markups are hard to measure directly, as mentioned in Chapter 4, section 2. They require information on prices and also on marginal costs, and firms do not report marginal costs. Several informal metrics have been used in the economic literature, such the number of firms in a market, profit rates and the costs to entry. All of them, however, have ambiguities.

The most used measure is concentration. Measures of market concentration summarise the share of market or industry activity accounted for by large firms. The two most common are the Hirschman–Herfindahl index (HHI), which is the sum of firms' squared market shares and the combined market shares of a set number of the largest firms.

These measures of concentration have one large advantage and several disadvantages. In their favour, they are easy to measure, because they require only information on revenues. But they do not provide information on profits and costs. Measures of concentration also require that we define a market, which is always contentious. Finally, and most importantly, Syverson (2019) argued that concentration is an *outcome*, and not a determinant of whether a market or industry is competitive.

Concentration can be associated with less competition, but also with more. In traditional models of monopolistic or oligopolistic competition in an industrial organisation, more concentration leads to less competition. But in modern models accounting for firm heterogeneity, there is a negative association between market or industry concentration and market power. For example, in Melitz and Ottaviano (2008) the pro-competitive effects of trade exposure offset rising concentration due to the exit of high-cost firms from the market (see Chapter 8). In this class of models, both consumer welfare and firm profits increase as a result of more competition. And so, using these models, market or industry concentration is an outcome that varies according to market characteristics. This result means concentration metrics are not a reliable way to measure market power.

A different approach derives directly from firm-level accounting data. Techniques have been developed in recent years to use balance sheet information to estimate directly the firm markup. The easiest way is to calculate the firm's price-cost margin. To do so, total revenues are used as a proxy for prices, and variable costs as a proxy for marginal costs. Clearly this measure relies on some strong assumptions.

We need a more sophisticated estimate of markups. De Loecker and Warzynski (2012) have pioneered what we know as the production approach, which estimates markups at the firm level, exploiting cost minimisation of an input variable of production.[4] Markups estimated through the production approach have been widely used in the economic research on this topic. But this method needs an explicit treatment of the production function and precise estimates of elasticities. This too is contentious: when input and output variables are measured in nominal terms, typical of balance-sheet, firm-level data, standard production function estimation techniques may lead to biased estimates of the output elasticities (De Loecker and Goldberg, 2013). We need to attempt to control for this bias.

Moreover, most firm-level markup measures following De Loecker and Warzynski (2012) also use cost of goods sold (COGS – the labour input and materials) as their main measure of variable input. But, over time, the relevance of COGS to the production function can change due to changes in technology. Covarrubias et al. (2019) have demonstrated an increase in the share of sales, general and administrative (SG&A) expenditures in total costs across all countries. We would expect this, because of the shift towards intangible capital. But this means the cost-share of COGS has been falling across countries, which implies rising markups – the result found by De Loecker et al. (2020) – as those are measured against this variable input.

But Covarrubias et al. (2019) showed that, especially for the EU15, profits did not rise because the decline in COGS associated with higher markups was fully offset by a rise in SG&A. Profits remain flat; operating income before depreciation equals sales minus COGS and SG&A. Only in the US was the the increase in markups associated with increasing profits. It then follows that the association between rising markups (measured on COGS) and rising market power might be

---

[4] See Section 4.2 for technical details.

imprecise for all countries, and would need to be thoroughly evaluated with additional indicators.

A final issue for markup estimation concerns the role of demand. Most theoretical models still rely on CES demand functions and monopolistic competition. These two assumptions together imply constant markups. This contrasts with our empirical evidence that heterogeneous firms charge heterogeneous markups. Arkolakis and Morlacco (2017) provided a review of alternatives to CES demand functions in international economics. Mrázová et al. (2018) provided a new theoretical model based on a constant revenue elasticity of marginal revenue (CREMR) demand function, consistent with productivity and sales distributions that have the same form in the cross section. They used their methodology to quantify misallocation at the microeconomic level, and to characterise markups. Finally, they used Indian firm-level data to show that their framework fits well in empirical applications. Frameworks of this kind are a promising new class of model for future research.

9.3 Productivity and Market Power

CompNet has worked intensely in the last years to develop and incorporate all widely accepted measures of market power in its datasets (Lopez-Garcia et al., 2018). In particular, the sixth and seventh vintage dataset contain markups estimated as in De Loecker and Warzynski (2012), at the one-digit and two-digit sector level, and based on both revenue and value added. We thus present some evidence on the trends in concentration across European countries, employing the most granular measure of markup available: estimated with production function at the two-digit sector level, based on value added. We also discuss Hirschman–Herfindahl indices and price-cost margins without capital costs, also provided by CompNet data.

Figure 9.1 shows the average change in firm concentration across European countries between 2009 and 2016. The data are reported as country-level averages of first differences of the 99th percentile ratio, at the one-digit sector level. The circles represent this cross-sector average across all one-digit sectors, with a short-dashed line showing fitted values. The squares and long-dashed line represent the change just for the manufacturing sector.

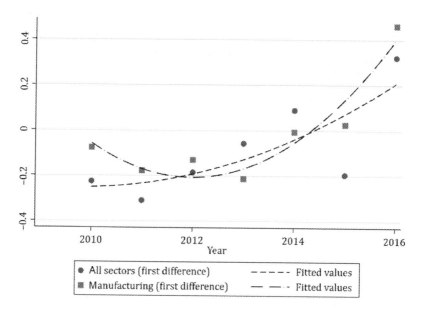

Figure 9.1 Evolution of firm market concentration: unweighted average of the first difference change across European countries, 2009–2016.

Source: CompNet (2020). First differences of the 99th percentile ratio, at the one-digit sector level

As discussed, this contrasts with the evidence in McAdam et al. (2019), which argued that concentration has been flat in the EU. On the contrary, CompNet (2020) shows that recently concentration has increased in Europe, particularly in the manufacturing sector.

Figure 9.2 looks at market concentration trends by country with respect to the European average, showing large differences across European countries, particularly for the manufacturing sector. In some countries, the path is strongly different between country and sector. For example, Spain faced a high increase in average concentration, but concentration in the manufacturing sector decreased. In these countries, the explanation is likely that concentration in manufacturing was already high, and that other macro sectors faced a strong increase in concentration (CompNet, 2020). In other countries, changes in concentration are mainly driven by changes in the manufacturing sector.

CompNet data can also highlight and analyse some of the main findings of the literature we have reviewed so far. For example, the

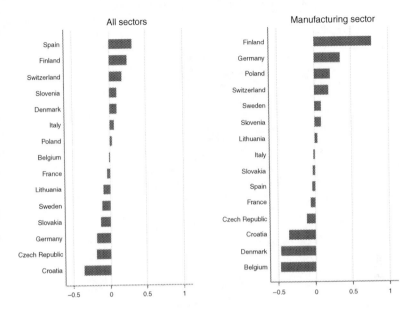

Figure 9.2 Firm market concentration by country: deviation from European average, 2009–2016.
Source: CompNet (2020). Percentage-point difference in concentration growth of a country, compared to the European average

connection between high market power and low investment rates (Gutiérrez and Philippon, 2017) and high market power and low wage levels (Azar et al., 2017; Benmelech et al., 2018; De Loecker et al., 2020).

Figure 9.3 shows the correlation between median markup (relative to country average, to make the measure comparable across countries) and median investment ratio in Europe after controlling for country and sector fixed effects. This relationship is negative in the US, but not in our sample of European countries. The figure implies that firms with higher markups had higher investment rates between 2004 and 2015.

Figure 9.4 shows the correlation between median markup relative to country average and median wages. There is a slight negative correlation between these two variables in our sample of European countries between 2004 and 2015, after controlling for country and sector fixed effects. This is in line with a similar empirical finding for the US (Azar et al., 2017; Benmelech et al., 2018; De Loecker et al., 2020).

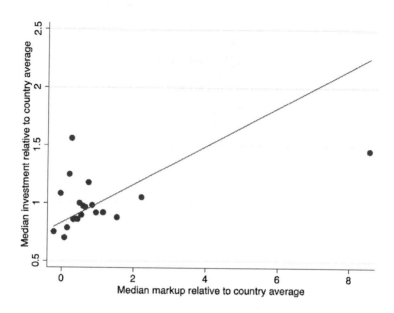

Figure 9.3 Correlation between median markup and median investment.
Source: Authors' elaboration of CompNet sixth vintage dataset

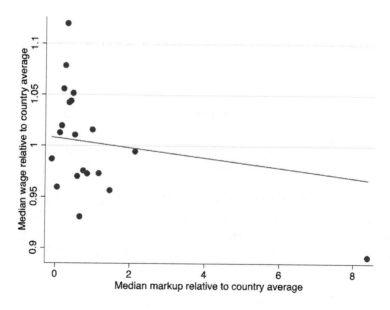

Figure 9.4 Correlation between median markup and median wage.
Source: Authors' elaboration of CompNet sixth vintage dataset

This reinforces our conclusion that there are different market power dynamics in the US and the EU. In particular, growing market power is correlated with decreasing investment in the US; not so in the EU. On the other hand, European countries and the US show a similar association between market power and lower wages, probably underlying similar dynamics in the observed fall in the labour share of income (as suggested by Autor et al., 2020; De Loecker et al., 2020).

Another important empirical observation is that heterogeneous firms charge heterogeneous markups. De Loecker et al. (2020) in particular found that both in the US and at the global level the rise of average markups was driven by the rise of markups of the firms at the highest percentiles of the markup distribution.

Thanks to the availability of information at each decile of the TFP distribution in CompNet sixth vintage dataset – the so-called joint distributions – we can show the average markup level at each decile in different European countries. For this analysis, we will focus on three different countries in terms of geography and size: France, the Netherlands and Hungary.

Figure 9.5 shows the median markup relative to country average at each decile of the TFP distribution. Firms at the highest percentiles of the TFP distribution on average have higher markups than those at low productivity deciles:

- France and the Netherlands have very similar median markup levels across the productivity distribution of firms. They are core countries in the EU and euro area, and the distribution of markups is quite concentrated, with median markups approximately stable across the productivity distribution.
- Hungary has a different distribution. It is not a member of the euro area and is exposed to German-led GVCs. The distribution is more dispersed, with markup levels disproportionately higher at the upper end and low at left tail of the productivity distribution.

Figure 9.6 shows these differences in more detail: the median markup level relative to country average for these three countries at the bottom (first decile), median and top (ninth decile) of the productivity distribution. In Hungary, there is a large difference between low- and high-productivity firms, which is not apparent in core euro area countries such as France and the Netherlands.

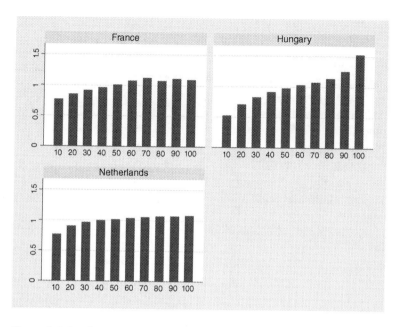

Figure 9.5 Median markup by TFP decile.
Source: Authors' elaboration of CompNet sixth vintage data.

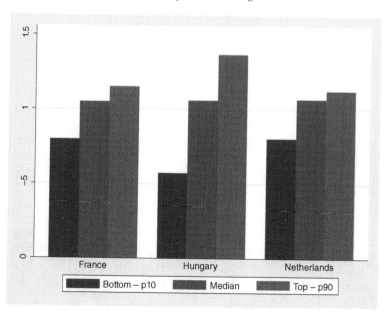

Figure 9.6 Median markup at bottom, median and top of TFP distribution.
Source: Authors' elaboration of CompNet sixth vintage dataset.

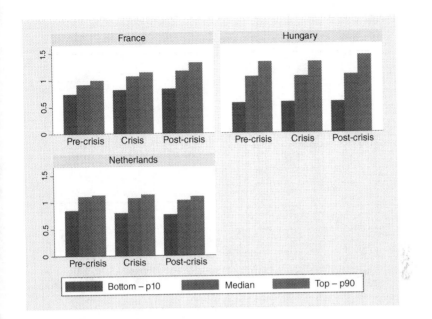

Figure 9.7 Median markup at bottom, median and top of TFP distribution, by period.
Source: Authors' elaboration of CompNet sixth vintage dataset

Using CompNet data, we can explore how markups have reacted to the Global Financial crisis – particularly after the 2008 demand shock – in European countries. Figure 9.7 shows median markup levels (relative to country average) at the bottom, median and top of the TFP distribution before, during and after the 2008 demand shock. We focus on the crisis years between 2008 and 2010 and France, Hungary and the Netherlands. The figure shows different patterns:

- France has median markup levels that increased on average after the demand shock and remained high in the recovery period. The increase is pronounced at the median, and even more so at the top of the TFP distribution. At the bottom of the productivity distribution, markups increased little during the crisis, and slightly decreased thereafter.

- The Netherlands shows evidence of a slight cleansing effect, with markups slightly decreasing after the crisis at all deciles of the TFP distribution.

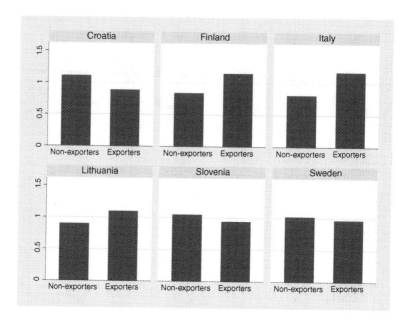

Figure 9.8 Median markup by exporter status.
Source: Authors' elaboration of CompNet sixth vintage data

- Hungarian firm markups remained flat after the crisis at the bottom and median of the TFP distribution but increased slightly at the top of the productivity distribution in the recovery period.

CompNet data also allow us to combine information on markups with trade data. We can therefore explore whether firms which engage in internationalisation activities – such as being exporters or participating in GVCs – are able to charge higher markups, as predicted by, for example, Morlacco (2019) for France and Gradzewicz and Muck (2019) for Poland.

Figures 9.8 and 9.9 show the median markup level (relative to country average) for firms engaged in exporting activities and participating in GVCs, respectively, as an average for 2004–2015 for six European countries that make trade data available in CompNet.

Both figures show no clear pattern on whether international firms can charge higher markups than domestic firms in European countries. This depends on the country under analysis:

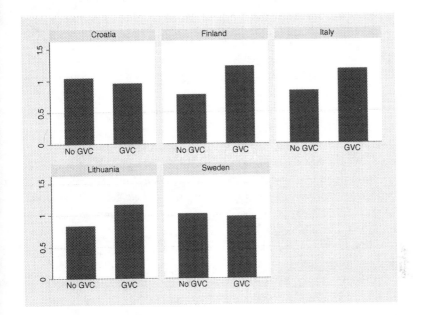

Figure 9.9 Median markup by GVC participation.
Source: Authors' elaboration of CompNet sixth vintage data

- In Finland, Italy and Lithuania, international firms charge higher markups than domestic firms.
- In Croatia, Slovenia and Sweden, this is reversed.

Further research is certainly needed to explore the determinants of this heterogeneity.

9.4 Conclusion

We have discussed the rise of market power in many sectors, a feature that is hotly debated in many countries, most obviously in the US. We do not yet have fully conclusive evidence, but in the EU market power does not seem to be rising to the same extent.

For countries or industries in which a rise in (measured) market power translates into an effective restriction of competition and increasing profits – as seems to be the case for the US – we see a significant slowdown of investment and business dynamism, and a fall in labour share and wages. This has policy implications. Obviously it reduces consumer welfare, creates low productivity growth and has severe implications for the transmission of monetary policy.

We should question the nature of this increase in market power. It may be the result of a reallocation of economic activities to the largest and most productive firms, which we can consider a healthy functioning of the market. If so, we may not need reform of competition policies.

One could argue that this is not a failure of existing competition policy, but a lack of adaptation to technological change. The prevalence of intangibles, the emergence of large economies of scale and, as a result, the lack of diffusion of technologies have led to a different competitive environment. This might explain the stylised facts we observe at the macro level.

The EU seems to be at least one step behind this process: most indicators show that competition is working properly, perhaps because technological change has been slower and less intense. Investment in intangibles in Europe is significantly smaller than in the US.[5]

We can debate, at least in Europe, whether industrial policies in the single market should precipitate the technological shocks and market outcomes that we have seen in the US, for example encouraging the emergence of "European champions" through mergers of competitors in the same sector. These policies might be useful in principle to boost European competitiveness, but they clearly risk consequences, especially distributional impacts, that would be harmful for consumers.

Finally, we must look at this debate in light of the new competitive environment emerging after the COVID-19 shock. Recent research (Hyun and Shin, 2020) shows that global connectedness and market power make firms more resilient to a domestic pandemic shock. US-listed firms with higher-than-average markups had a correspondingly higher weekly market value growth after controlling for explanatory variables. This confirms our intuition that the COVID-19 shock may generate winner-takes-all markets, especially in industries such as

---

[5] Corrado et al. (2018) use a newly revised and updated release of the INTAN-Invest dataset for 18 European countries and the US to analyse intangible investment diffusion within countries. They show that the total average share of intangibles as a share of GDP in 2002–2013 is larger in the US (8.8%) than the EU (7.2%). They also show that intangibles grew in the US after the financial crisis, while they remained flat in the EU.

technology and communication that already show the effect of rising market power. This raises the stakes for competition policy in the years to come.

Appendix 9.1: Profit Margins, Markups and Productivity

We can analyse market power in European countries in two further ways.

First, we consider the relationship between profit margins and market concentration (markups). We discussed how markup measures might suffer from technology shocks and the relevance of COGS as a share of total costs. Recall that a higher markup measured this way is not necessarily associated with higher market power. Looking at profits at the same time might help us understand these dynamics. This is certainly the case for Europe, where profits do not display a strong trend, compared to the US, where profits have been rising. Then we can look directly at the (complex) relationship between market power and firm-level productivity.

We can create a parametric specification assessing the relationship between profit margins and median markups at the sector level using CompNet data. We use regressions of the following form:

$$Profit_{s,c,t} = \alpha + \beta Markup_{s,c,t} + \gamma_c + \sigma_s + \tau_t + \epsilon_{s,c,t}, \qquad (9.1)$$

where $Profit_{s,c,t}$ is the profit margin in sector s of country c at year t, and $Markup_{s,c,t}$ is the median markup in sector s of country c at year t. γ_c, σ_s, and τ_t are country, sector and year fixed effects, respectively.

Results are reported in Table 9.1. Columns (1)–(3) show the results of regression 9.1 for firms at different percentiles of the profit distribution. A higher median markup translates into higher profit margins for firms at the bottom of the distribution, but slightly lower margin at the upper tail of the distribution. Although this result is consistent with the positive correlation between markups and profits (via productivity, as in Melitz and Ottaviano, 2008, and others), it also shows that there is no increase in the market power of the most productive (profitable) firms in the EU, a result consistent with other EU-related empirical evidence.

In columns (4) and (5), we include dummy variables for whether a certain sector is in the first quartile and in the fourth quartile of the

Table 9.1. *Profit margins and markups at sector level.*

	(1) log Profit p25	(2) log Profit p50	(3) log Profit p90	(4) log Profit p50	(5) log Profit p50
Markup	0.0865***	0.0608***	−0.0285***	0.0557***	0.0521***
	(0.0279)	(0.0110)	(0.00784)	(0.0120)	(0.0107)
Dummy Low HHI sector				0.134***	
				(0.0396)	
Markup*Low HHI sector				−0.000	
				(0.000)	
Dummy High HHI sector					−0.280***
					(0.0561)
Markup*High HHI sector					0.00633**
					(0.00285)
Observations	1,035	1,311	1,310	1,311	1,311
R-squared	0.650	0.787	0.641	0.788	0.793
Sector FEs	Yes	Yes	Yes	Yes	Yes
Country FEs	Yes	Yes	Yes	Yes	Yes
Year FEs	Yes	Yes	Yes	Yes	Yes

Source: CompNet's full sample.
Note: Robust standard errors are in parentheses.
* $p < 0.10$, ** $p < 0.05$, *** $p < 0.01$.

country's HHI distribution, meaning that the sector has low concentration or high concentration respectively"; furthermore, we include the interaction between these dummies and the median sectoral markup. This way, we can examine the cross-sectoral variation within a country and use it to assess whether markups in highly concentrated sectors translate into higher profit margins. The coefficient estimate of the interaction term in column (5) suggests that this is actually the case: in the most concentrated sectors in a country, higher markups translate into higher profit margins at the median of the distribution.

Bighelli et al. (2020) also used the CompNet micro-aggregated firm-level dataset and found the following:

- Market concentration at the European level increased after 2008.
- Rising concentration within European sectors was associated with increasing sector-level productivity in a changing market environment for which efficient firms increased market share.

They measured concentration aggregating the Herfindahl–Hirschman index at the European level using a new aggregation method based on country-level decompositions (Bighelli et al., 2020). This aggregation showed an increasing trend of concentration at the European level since 2008. This rise in concentration may demand a policy response, but from this result alone we do not know whether it is a signal of a less competitive market environment with higher markups and no increase in productivity, or whether it is simply the functioning of a competitive market.

To dig deeper, the authors computed productivity-size premiums by regressing productivity on firm size. Labour productivity increased by 15–18% when moving from one decile to the next in the size distribution. An increasing productivity-size premium over the last decade indicates that, in Europe, larger firms were becoming relatively more productive than their smaller counterparts, thus widening the productivity difference between large and small firms. This suggests the positive influence of competition, rewarding productive firms with higher market share.

The authors also examined the relationship between firm concentration and productivity (also known as the concentration–productivity nexus) by regressing sector-level HHI values on aggregate sector-level productivity. They found a positive association (regression coefficients between 0.39 and 0.46, statistically significant at the 0.01% level, robust to adding controls).

In particular, sector-level markups were neither significant nor led to a reduction in the coefficient on productivity. These results again support view that concentration is the effect of the success of productive firms.

Using the productivity decomposition presented by Olley and Pakes (1996b), concentration can be related to within firm productivity and allocative efficiency. The authors found a stronger and more precisely estimated positive association between the sector-level HHI values and allocative efficiency (recall, the covariance term). This also suggests that rising concentration in Europe primarily represents the outcome

Table 9.2. *Firm concentration and productivity.*

	(1) HHI	(2) HHI	(3) HHI	(4) HHI
Sector labour productivity	0.459*** (0.116)	0.379** (0.160)		
OP gap			0.00654*** (0.00137)	0.00748*** (0.00107)
Capital intensity	−0.0733 (0.0669)	−0.0558 (0.0648)	0.0199 (0.0583)	0.0124 (0.0547)
Median firm size	0.130 (0.0914)	0.168 (0.112)	0.109 (0.0938)	0.147 (0.112)
Weighted average markup	−0.399 (0.239)	−0.255 (0.203)	−0.317 (0.221)	−0.187 (0.149)
Intangible K intensity		−0.00305 (0.0250)		−0.00135 (0.0233)
Observations	6,643	4,145	6,643	4,145
Year FE	Yes	Yes	Yes	Yes
Sector-country FE	Yes	Yes	Yes	Yes
R-squared	0.873	0.881	0.880	0.889

Note: Robust standard errors are in parentheses.
* $p < 0.10$, ** $p < 0.05$, *** $p < 0.01$.

of the reallocation of market share from low-productivity to high-productivity firms. The analysis is robust to different concentration measures (the share of the 10 largest firms in revenue terms, for example) and alternative productivity measures such as TFP from a production function approach. Table 9.2 plots the regression analysis.

To summarise, this analysis yields two important findings:

- There is empirical evidence of increasing market concentration in Europe using a novel approach and a high-quality firm-level dataset.
- There is a positive and significant correlation between rising sector-level concentration and increases in sector-level productivity and allocative efficiency.

And so we can tentatively conclude that increasing market concentration in Europe is not necessarily a cause for concern, because on this evidence it is not related to a weaker competitive environment. This has important consequences for anti-trust and industrial policy.

10 | Conclusions

When we started writing this book in 2017, we would have hardly imagined the sheer amount of material at our disposal and the efforts that would have been needed to synthesize it. That's the price to be "paid" trying to follow up on a dynamic and highly productive network such as CompNet. But it is also a signal that firm-level analysis of productivity is a booming field in economics, and we are proud to have been able to show why this is so.

This book was designed to be a handbook – or a consultation device – in the field of firm productivity for students and practitioners, and it contains basic methodologies and applications of firm-level econometrics.

As we are now concluding this task, the sheer number of results presented and the very nature of the book have discouraged us to attempt in the final chapter a comprehensive summary of it. Still, we will point below to eight main take-aways most critical from the policy point of view. Four of them are general, three are more closely related to COVID impacts, the last is a call for better micro data.

10.1 The Firm-Level Perspective is Critical

As extensively mentioned over the entire book using "average" indicators is simply misleading in most instances, while firm-level analysis allows a much more targeted set of policies. Policy makers are by now aware that firm level data are there to be used if appropriately treated. Firm-level analysis is an essential tool to complement and integrate the macro-assessment and related policy response across the whole range of productivity drivers – from labour to trade, from finance to competition. Relying on macro-indicators only is simply unthinkable at the present stage of knowledge and data availability. The great advantage of the CompNet dataset is that it is built in such a fashion to be able to be used – as it is, and directly – to derive at the very least a first set of granular stylised facts to inform the policy considerations. The fact that all the variables computed – mostly productivity indicators and their most commonly analysed drivers – are comparable across countries already gives an incredible advantage with respect to other sources of firm-level information as it allows direct benchmarking of performance and structural indicators.

Moreover, as mentioned several times, the dataset also contains a large number of joint distributions – i.e., correlations of pairs of variables over their respective distribution. This allows to ascertain the extent in which relevant correlations – e.g., productivity versus labour cost – vary across different firms segments, and in this case enables the researcher or policy analyst to respond to questions such as: are larger (or more productive) firms paying higher wages? And if so how much does such correlation differs across countries and sectors? Again, this is an important benchmark figure which allows to compare the underlying structure of two or more sectors/regions/countries.

In the following, we present three specific cases for which the firm level perspective is essential, e.g. for assessing competitiveness, financial constraints and sensitivity to exchange rate shocks.

10.2 Average Unit Labor Costs (ULC) Can be Misleading for Competitiveness Analysis

Take the case of looking at the competitiveness of a sector or a country by examining its unit labour cost (ULC) – the ratio between wages and productivity. Let's suppose that ULC are high and rising on average, i.e., that average competitiveness of the economy is worsening. What to do? Since productivity (the denominator) is hard to influence in the short run, should we just simply recommend lower wages across the board? Well, yes, if you would have still been in the "only macro" world of a few decades ago. Doing so, however, would ignore that nowadays you have plenty of firm-level information which tells us that the ULC tends to be very different between highly productive and low productive firms. This calls for a very differentiated policy advice. Wage costs must represent a matter of concern only for those segments of the firm distribution in which they are not in line with productivity trends. Higher wages are in fact a good proxy for relative skills of the labour, and when they bring about higher firm performance, they should *not* be corrected but rather encouraged.

The CompNet dataset includes detailed analysis of such trends by countries and by sectors, allowing appropriate fine-tuning of policies, which can now be accurately guided by solid cross-country bench-marking. The policy makers should carefully assess how and whether labor costs match firms' productivity all across the firms' productivity distribution and intervene within the firms segments where divergences are judged as unsustainable, rather than across the board.

10.3 Financial Constraints have a Strong Micro Foundation

One important feature of firm-level analysis is that it allows analysts to match different datasets providing important information on how individual firm performance is directly influenced by specific structural features of the economy. Take the case of the availability of financing. In frictionless markets, financing – from banks and markets – should flow seamlessly to most promising ventures and firms. As we know, this is not always the case, because of institutional barriers, bank management inefficiencies, cyclical conditions or shocks affecting the economy and alike. But, how do we measure the extent to which credit is "constrained"? In the CompNet dataset, as shown in Chapter 6, performance indicators of the firms are matched with their respective response to a periodical survey conducted by the ECB on credit availability (SAFE) as experienced by potential borrowers. Such matching allows to establish how financial constraints vary across firms, distinguished by size, type and geographical locations. This obviously allows much more targeted interventions than any possible alternative average figures. For instance, following the shock of the Global Financial Crisis, it allows to establish whether and where credit constraints may have persisted – for the most or the least productive firms, in which location, in which sectors and so on – offering a solid basis for further investigation on causes and needed interventions.

10.4 Smaller and Less Productive Firms are More Exposed to Exchange Rate Shocks

There is an extensive literature on measuring the extent to which exchange rate fluctuations affect trade. Using panel data at the country level, estimates range from about -0.5 to -0.8, meaning that a 10%

appreciation of the real effective exchange rate is predicted to reduce exports of the average firm by 5% to 8%. However, the micro-founded research we have presented show that these figures hide rather strong heterogeneity across firms within sectors and countries. In particular, the export elasticity to the exchange rate for the least productive firms within each given sector, country and year is three to eight times higher than for the most productive firms in the same sector, country and year, depending on the elasticity measure adopted. This implies that the least productive European firms are on average more vulnerable to movements in the real effective exchange rate (REER) than the most productive firms. The latter's exports are much less sensitive to changes in the REER. Since export elasticity relative to REER is inversely correlated with size and productivity, policy makers of European countries with relatively high density of low productive firms will have to consider that on average their firms are more vulnerable to real effective exchange rate variations than countries with a small density of low productive firms. Such highly differentiated response to exchange rate movements has also substantial implications for the transmission mechanism of monetary policy, to the extent that the latter has a direct impact of exchange rate fluctuations. The result is therefore that the firm-level view on such matters is critical for solidly based policy making, including an evaluation of policies aimed at forcing the exit of least productive firms from the market.

As we are at present in the midst of recovering from the impact of the COVID pandemic, we have selected three applications which have high relevance for that.

10.5 The Fear of Creating Zombie Firms did not Materialize

The tremendous efforts by government, central banks and international organisations to dampen the impact of the epidemic on employment and incomes has raised yet again the debate on the risk of creating inefficiencies in the economy by allowing undeserving firms to survive. Memories are fresh of developments during the Euro area crisis at the beginning of the second decade of this century, when weak banks – strongly supported by government actions – were found to be more likely to extend credit to distressed firms as they were facing difficulties in raising capital to meet stricter capital requirements. This resulted in a serious misallocation of capital which increased the failure rate of healthy firms and reduced the failure rate of distressed firms (Schivardi et al., 2021).

While many agree that capital misallocation may have occurred, there is an increasing consensus that the overall impacts may have been overstated. On the one hand, productivity growth may have not been driven down because of that, as previously feared (Schivardi et al., 2021). On the other, some evidence using the same data for Finland, collected within the CompNet initiative, appear to show that a number of firms identified as zombies in an initial period may have not remained as such at later stage. Their negative profits for a number of years – one of the identification criteria for defining their status – may have turned out to be a temporary phenomenon later compensated by much better performance. Such developments call for a more careful assessment of the definition of zombies as well as of their overall impacts on aggregate productivity patterns, not always necessarily negative, as shown by extending the preceding analysis to a larger number of countries (Nurmi et al., 2020).

10.6 There is a Need to Preserve Well Functioning Global Value Chains (*GVCs*)

The discussion of COVID, a virus which spread worldwide, raises the issue of whether we are going to see major changes in the globalisation patterns prevailing in the last couple of decades, and therefore whether the re-thinking forced by the US-initiated trade wars will be further exacerbated. CompNet research presented in this book has confirmed the rather strong and positive impacts on firm performance that come from export activity and in general from globalisation. First, being able to export is limited to a small share of producers as there are important costs associated to entering export markets. This implies that analysing the top firms' export performance and outlook allows us to get a very good picture of what happens at the aggregate trade level. This is yet another advantage of going granular.

Firms acceding export markets are typically highly productive and enjoy a rather large productivity premium against those serving only the local market. Such premia tend also to increase with the complexity of internationalization activity: firms participating in GVCs are more productive than firms only exporting, which in turn are more productive than firms only serving their local market. In studying such patterns over time, Chapter 8 has shown that premia for exporting firms decreased in response to the 2009 trade collapse, but those for firms involved in more sophisticated trade linkages reacted less negatively and sometimes even positively to the demand shock. Very importantly, we have reported that there is evidence of causality between firms' innovation and internationalization activities. This implies that innovation policies are a major driver of trade and economic growth.

In terms of policy implications, the evidence discussed and presented generally highlights the need for European countries to preserve the steps undertaken in trade liberalization over the last 20 years, since trade is a major driver of economic growth. This entails supporting trade agreements under discussion at the European Union level (for example, with Japan and Latin American countries, as well as with the post-Brexit United Kingdom) as they are necessary to further reduce trade costs, both price and non-price. This is especially relevant as anger against globalisation increases, scepticism assumes central stance in diplomatic negotiations and threats of "trade wars" unfold.

10.7 In Europe Higher Firm Concentration

As the COVID shock is decimating smaller firms, the consensus is that, at least in the short run, firms concentration will further increase, with associated higher markup, monopoly power and ultimately negative welfare impacts on consumers. The issue is complex, and past literature has been divided both in the US and in Europe on measuring firms concentration and markups as well as assessing the impact of such developments on productivity and consumer welfare. CompNet evidence we have presented in Chapter 9 would suggest that, yes, firms' concentration in Europe is actually increasing, but it would seem to be of a different nature than in the US. There, as shown by the work of Covarrubias et al. (2019), concentration actually translates into an effective restriction of competition and increasing profits, together with a significant slowdown of investment, business dynamism, fall in labour share and wages and eventually lower consumers' welfare and low productivity growth. Ultimately, this would be the result of a failure of US competition policies. The picture we gather for Europe would be rather different. Higher concentration would seem to be led by "good" market forces reallocating resources towards largest and most productive firms, thus driving up aggregate productivity.

10.8 We Need Better and More Available Data

All of the preceding gives a sense of the immense value added that firm-level analysis can provide to research and policy making. CompNet in the last decade has made tremendous efforts to improve the quality and depth of its dataset and has multiplied evidence on the great advantage for research and policy to have, at the very least as a complement, a granular view. More efforts are needed, however, particularly on the data front. National statistical institutes (NSIs) are sitting on an immense treasure of firm-level information, which is – sadly – only very marginally used, despite its huge potential. Take the case of the COVID crisis and the huge need of information in order to act promptly and correctly. NSIs made tremendous efforts during 2020 to gather additional info also via ad hoc surveys on a wide range of issues, health, government programs, work practices, credit availability and so on. But all of this was mostly done at the national level with little coordination of efforts across Europe. Most importantly, such efforts – even when they are made – are severely hampered by (i) an access to information by researchers, which is overall inadequate; and (ii) comparability of the information across countries, which tends to be limited.

Data access regulations vary tremendously across countries, cross-country homogenisation takes time and there is not a centralised unit in charge of coordinating efforts when timeliness of execution is of the essence. This book has amply shown that Europe policy making and research will gain immensely from a much larger use of firm level information. Major European Institutions and NSIs should therefore diligently and more convincingly work to improving the quality and the access to such granular information. Even here a truly common internal market, for firm level data this time, would be of tremendous benefit to Europe as well.

Bibliography

Abowd, J., F. Kramarz and S. Woodcock. Econometric analyses of linked employer-employee data. In László Mátyás and Patrick Sevestre, editors, *The Econometrics of Panel Data*, pages 727–760. Springer, 2008.

Acemoglu, D. and P. Restrepo. Robots and jobs: evidence from US labor markets. *Journal of Political Economy*, 128(6):2188–2244, 2020.

Acharya, V. V., T. Eisert, C. Eufinger and C. Hirsch. Whatever it takes: the real effects of unconventional monetary policy. *Review of Financial Studies*, 32(9):3366–3411, 01 2019.

Ackerberg, D., L. C. Benkard, S. Berry and A. Pakes. Econometric tools for analyzing market outcomes. In J. Heckman and E. Leamer, editors, *Handbook of Econometrics*, volume 6, chapter 63. Elsevier, 1 edition, 4171–4276, 2007.

Ackerberg, D., K. Caves and G. Frazer. Identification properties of recent production function estimators. *Econometrica*, 83(6):2411–2451, November 2015.

Aglio, D. and F. di Mauro. Decentralisation of collective bargaining: a path to productivity? IWH-CompNet Discussion Papers 3, Halle Institute for Economic Research (IWH), 2020.

Akcigit, U. and S. T. Ates. Ten facts on declining business dynamism and lessons from endogenous growth theory. *American Economic Journal: Macroeconomics*, 13(1):257–298, 2021.

Alfaro, L., P. Antras, D. Chor and P. Conconi. Internalizing global value chains: a firm-level analysis. *Journal of Political Economy*, 127(2): 508–559, 2019.

Altomonte, C. and T. Aquilante. The EU-EFIGE/Bruegel-Unicredit dataset. Working Paper Series Bruegel 753, Bruegel, 2012.

Altomonte, C., M. Nicolini, A. Rungi and L. Ogliari. Assessing the competitive behaviour of firms in the single market: a micro-based approach. European Economy – Economic Papers 2008–2015 409, Directorate General Economic and Financial Affairs (DG ECFIN), European Commission, May 2010.

Altomonte, C., F. di Mauro, G. I. Ottaviano, A. Rungi and V. Vicard. Global value chains during the Great Trade Collapse: a bullwhip effect? Working Paper Series 1412, ECB, 2011a.

Altomonte, C., G. B. Navaretti, F. di Mauro and G. Ottaviano. Assessing competitiveness – how firm-level data can help. Policy Contributions 643, Bruegel, 2011b.

Altomonte, C., T. Aquilante and G. Ottaviano. The triggers of competitiveness. The EFIGE cross-country report. Bruegel, 2012.

Altomonte, C., T. Aquilante, G. Békés and G. I. Ottaviano. Internationalization and innovation of firms: evidence and policy. *Economic Policy*, 28(76):663–700, 08 2014.

Altomonte, C., F. Biondi and V. Negri. The Competitiveness of European Industry in the Digital Era, chapter 3, pages 53–78. In *Remaking Europe: The Manufacturing as an Engine for Growth*. Bruegel Blueprint Series XXVI, Bruegel, www.bruegel.org/wp-content/uploads/2017/09/Remaking_Europe_blueprint.pdf, 2017.

Altomonte, C., L. Bonacorsi and I. Colantone. Trade and growth in the age of global value chains. Working Paper 97, Bocconi University, 2018a.

Altomonte, C., D. Favoino, M. Morlacco and T. Sonno. Markups and productivity under heterogeneous financial frictions. BAFFI CAREFIN Working Papers 100, BAFFI CAREFIN, Centre for Applied Research on International Markets Banking Finance and Regulation, Universita' Bocconi, Milano, Italy, 2018b.

Altomonte, C., F. di Mauro, and S. Inferrera. EU firms' participation in GVC: bliss or curse after COVID? CompNet Policy Briefs, 2020.

Amador, J. and F. di Mauro. *The Age of Global Value Chains: Maps and Policy Issues*. VoxEU.org eBook, 2015.

Andrews, D. and F. Cingano. Public policy and resource allocation: evidence from firms in OECD countries. *Economic Policy*, 29(78):253–296, 11 2014.

Andrews, D. and F. Petroulakis. Breaking the shackles: zombie firms, weak banks and depressed restructuring in Europe. OECD Economics Department Working Paper, (1433), 2017.

Andrews, D., C. Criscuolo and P. N. Gal. The best versus the rest: the global productivity slowdown, divergence across firms and the role of public policy. OECD Productivity Working Papers 5, OECD Publishing, December 2016.

Antoni, M., M. Koetter, S. Müller and T. Sondershaus. Do asset purchase programmes shape industry dynamics? Evidence from the ECB's SMP on plant entries and exits. Technical report, IWH Discussion Papers, 2019.

Antràs, P. Conceptual aspects of global value chains. *World Bank Economic Review*, 34(3):551–574, 2020.

Antràs, P. and D. Chor. Organizing the global value chain. *Econometrica*, 81(6):2127–2204, November 2013.

Arkolakis, C. and M. Morlacco. Variable demand elasticity, markups, and pass-through. Technical report, Yale University, August 2017.

Atkin, D., A. K. Khandelwal and A. Osman. Exporting and firm performance: evidence from a randomized experiment. *Quarterly Journal of Economics*, 132(2):551–615, 02 2017.

Autor, D., D. Dorn, G. Hanson and K. Majlesi. Importing political polarization? The electoral consequences of rising trade exposure. NBER working papers, National Bureau of Economic Research, Inc, September 2016.

Autor, D., D. Dorn and G. Hanson. When work disappears: manufacturing decline and the falling marriage market value of young men. *American Economic Review: Insights*, 1(2):161–178, September 2019.

Autor, D., D. Dorn, L. F. Katz, C. Patterson and J. Van Reenen. The fall of the labor share and the rise of superstar firms. *Quarterly Journal of Economics*, 135(2):645–709, 02 2020.

Autor, D. H., D. Dorn and G. H. Hanson. The China syndrome: local labor market effects of import competition in the United States. *American Economic Review*, 103(6):2121–2168, October 2013.

Autor, D. H., D. Dorn, G. H. Hanson and J. Song. Trade adjustment: worker-level evidence. *Quarterly Journal of Economics*, 129(4):1799–1860, 2014.

Azar, J., I. Marinescu and M. I. Steinbaum. Labor market concentration. Working Paper 24147, National Bureau of Economic Research, December 2017.

Baily, M. N., C. R. Hulten and D. Campbell. Productivity dynamics in manufacturing plants. *Brookings Papers on Economic Activity: Microeconomics*, 4:187–267, 1992.

Bajgar, M., G. Berlingieri, S. Calligaris, C. Criscuolo and J. Timmis. Industry concentration in Europe and North America. Working Paper 18, OECD, 2019.

Baldwin, R. *The Great Convergence: Information Technology and the New Globalization.* Harvard University Press, 2016.

    The Globotics Upheaval: Globalization, Robotics, and the Future of Work. Weidenfeld & Nicolson, 2020.

Baldwin, R. E. and B. W. Di Mauro. *Economics in the Time of COVID-19.* CEPR Press, 2020.

Barkai, S. Declining labor and capital shares. *Journal of Finance*, 75(5):2421–2463, 2020.

Barnett, A., B. Broadbent, A. Chiu, J. Franklin and H. Miller. Impaired capital reallocation and productivity. *National Institute Economic Review*, 228(1):R35–R48, 2014.

Bartelsman, E., J. Haltiwanger and S. Scarpetta. Microeconomic evidence of creative destruction in industrial and developing countries. World Bank, Policy Research Working Paper, (3464), December 2004.

Bartelsman, E., S. Scarpetta and F. Schivardi. Comparative analysis of firm demographics and survival: evidence from micro-level sources in OECD countries. *Industrial and Corporate Change*, 14(3):365–391, 04 2005.

Bartelsman, E., J. Haltiwanger and S. Scarpetta. Cross-country differences in productivity: the role of allocation and selection. *American Economic Review*, 103(1):305–334, February 2013.

Bartelsman, E., P. Lopez-Garcia and G. Presidente. Cyclical and stuctural variation in resource reallocation: evidence for Europe. Tinbergen Institute Discussion Papers 18-057/VI, Tinbergen Institute, June 2018.

Bartelsman, E. J. and M. Doms. Understanding productivity: lessons from longitudinal microdata. *Journal of Economic Literature*, 38(3):569–594, September 2000.

Bartelsman, E. J., P. A. Gautier and J. De Wind. Employment protection, technology choice and worker allocation. *International Economic Review*, 57(3):787–826, 2016.

Beck, T., A. Demirguc-Kunt, L. Laeven and V. Maksimovic. The determinants of financing obstacles. *Journal of International Money and Finance*, 25(6):932–952, 2006.

Békés, G., L. Halpern, M. Koren and B. Muraközy. Still standing: how European firms weathered the crisis. The third EFIGE policy report. Number 661 in Blueprints. Bruegel, 2011.

Belotti, F., A. Borin and M. Mancini. Icio: economic analysis with inter-country input–output tables in stata. World Bank Policy Research Working Paper 9156, World Bank, 2020.

Benmelech, E., N. K. Bergman and H. Kim. Strong employers and weak employees: how does employer concentration affect wages? Working Papers 18-15, Center for Economic Studies, US Census Bureau, April 2018.

Berlingieri, G., P. Blanchenay, S. Calligaris and C. Criscuolo. The Multiprod project: a comprehensive overview. OECD Science, Technology and Industry Working Papers 2017/04, OECD Publishing, May 2017.

Bernard, A. B., J. Eaton, J. B. Jensen and S. Kortum. Plants and productivity in international trade. *American Economic Review*, 93(4):1268–1290, September 2003.

Bernard, A. B., J. B. Jensen, S. J. Redding and P. K. Schott. Firms in international trade. *Journal of Economic Perspectives*, 21(3):105–130, September 2007.

Bernard, A. B., S. J. Redding and P. K. Schott. Multiple-products firms and product switching. *American Economic Review*, 100(1):70–97, 2010.

Bernard, A. B., J. B. Jensen, S. J. Redding and P. K. Schott. The empirics of firm heterogeneity and international trade. NBER Working Paper, (17627), November 2011a.

Bernard, A. B., S. J. Redding and P. K. Schott. Multiproduct firms and trade liberalization. *Quarterly Journal of Economics*, 126:1271–1318, 2011b.

Bernard, A. B., I. V. Beveren and H. Vandenbussche. Multi-product exporters and the margins of trade. *Japanese Economic Review*, 65(2):142–157, June 2014.

Bernard, A. B., E. A. Bøler and S. Dhingra. Firm-to-firm connections in Colombian imports. CEP Discussion Paper 1543, Centre for Economic Performance, 2018.

Berthou, A. and E. Dhyne. Exchange rate movements, firm-level exports and heterogeneity. Working Paper Research 334, National Bank of Belgium, 2018.

Berthou, A. and F. di Mauro. The exchange rate, asymmetric shocks and asymmetric distributions. Technical report, VoxEU.org, 2015.

Berthou, A., E. Dhyne, M. Bugamelli, et al. Assessing European firms' exports and productivity distributions: the compnet trade module. ECB Working Paper, (1788), May 2015.

Berthou, A., J. J.-H. Chung, K. Manova and C. Sandoz Dit Bragard. Productivity, (mis)allocation and trade. Discussion Paper DP14203, CEPR, 2019.

Besley, T., I. Roland and J. V. Reenen. The aggregate consequences of default risk: evidence from firm-level data. NBER Working Paper, (26686), January 2020.

Bighelli, T., F. di Mauro, M. Melitz and M. Mertens. Firm concentration and aggregate productivity. Firm Productivity Report, 2020.

Bloom, N. and J. Van Reenen. Measuring and explaining management practices across firms and countries. *Quarterly Journal of Economics*, 122(4):1351–1408, November 2007.

Bloom, N., M. Draca and J. Van Reenen. Trade induced technical change? The impact of Chinese imports on innovation, IT and productivity. *Review of Economic Studies*, 83(1):87–117, 09 2015.

Bobbold, T. A comparison of gross output and value-added methods of productivity estimations. Research Memorandum GA 511, Productivity Commission, Australian Government, November 2003.

Boehm, C. E., A. Flaaen and N. Pandalai-Nayar. Multinationals offshoring, and the decline of U.S. manufacturing. Working Papers 17–22, Center for Economic Studies, U.S. Census Bureau, January 2017.

Boeri, T. and H. Brücker. Short-time work benefits revisited: some lessons from the great recession. IZA Discussion Papers 5635, Institute of Labor Economics (IZA), 2011.

Bond, S. and M. Söderbom. Adjustment costs and the identification of Cobb–Douglas. Institute for Fiscal Studies, Working Paper Series, 05/04, 2005.

Bond, S. R. and C. Meghir. Dynamic investment models and the firm's financial policy. *Review of Economic Studies*, 61(2):197–222, 1994.

Bond, S. R. and M. Soderbom. Conditional investment – cash flow sensitivities and financing constraints. *Journal of the European Economic Association*, 11(1):112–136, 2013.

Bond, S. R., J. A. Elston, J. Mairesse, and B. Mulkay. Financial factors and investment in Belgium, France, Germany, and the United Kingdom: a comparison using company panel data. *Review of Economics and Statistics*, 85(1):153–165, 2003.

Bonfiglioli, A., R. Crinò, H. Fadinger and G. Gancia. Robot imports and firm-level outcomes. CESifo Working Paper Series 8741, CESifo, 2020.

Bougheas, S., P. Mizen and C. Yalcin. Access to external finance: theory and evidence on the impact of monetary policy and firm-specific characteristics. *Journal of Banking and Finance*, 30(1):199–227, 2006.

Byiers, B., J. Rand, F. Tarp and J. S. Bentzen. Credit demand in Mozambican manufacturing. *Journal of International Development*, 22(1):37–55, 2010.

Caballero, R. J., T. Hoshi and A. K. Kashyap. Zombie lending and depressed restructuring in Japan. *American Economic Review*, 98(5):1943–77, 2008.

Caliendo, L., F. Monte and E. Rossi-Hansberg. The anatomy of French production hierarchies. *Journal of Political Economy*, 123(4):809–852, 2015.

Caliendo, L., M. Dvorkin and F. Parro. Trade and labor market dynamics: general equilibrium analysis of the China trade shock. *Econometrica*, 87(3):741–835, 2019.

Calligaris, S., M. D. Gatto, F. Hassan, G. I. P. Ottaviano and F. Schivardi. The productivity puzzle and misallocation: an Italian perspective. CEP Discussion Paper, (1520), December 2017.

Caselli, M. and S. Schiavo. Markups, import competition and exporting. *World Economy*, 43(5):1309–1326, 2020.

Chadha, J. S., A. Kara and P. Labonne. The financial foundations of the productivity puzzle. *National Institute Economic Review*, 241(1):R48–R57, 2017.

Chirinko, B. Business fixed investment spending: modelling strategies, empirical results and policy implications. *Journal of Economic Literature*, 31:1875–1911, 1993.

Clarke, G. R., R. Cull and G. Kisunko. External finance and firm survival in the aftermath of the crisis: evidence from eastern Europe and central Asia. *Journal of Comparative Economics*, 40(3):372–392, 2012.

Colantone, I. and P. Stanig. The trade origins of economic nationalism: import competition and voting behavior in western Europe. *American Journal of Political Science*, 62(4):936–953, 2018a.

Global competition and Brexit. *American Political Science Review*, 112(2):201–218, 2018b.

Colantone, I., R. Crinò and L. Ogliari. Globalization and mental distress. *Journal of International Economics*, 119(C):181–207, 2019.

CompNet. European firms after the crisis. new insights from the 5th vintage of the CompNet firm-level-based database. ECB Working Paper, September 2016.

Assessing the reliability of the CompNet micro-aggregated dataset for policy analysis and research: coverage, representativeness and cross-EU comparability. Technical report, CompNet, 2018.

Firm productivity report. Annual Report 05/20, CompNet, May 2020.

Corrado, C., J. Haskel, C. Jona-Lasinio and M. Iommi. Intangible investment in the EU and US before and since the great recession and its contribution to productivity growth. *Journal of Infrastructure, Policy and Development*, 2(1):11–36, 2018.

Covarrubias, M., G. Gutiérrez and T. Philippon. From good to bad concentration? U.S. industries over the past 30 years. In *NBER Macroeconomics Annual 2019*, volume 34, pages 1–46, NBER Chapters. National Bureau of Economic Research, Inc, December 2019.

Criscuolo, C., P. N. Gal and C. Menon. The dynamics of employment growth: new evidence from 18 countries. OECD Science, Technology and Industry Policy Papers 14, OECD Publishing, May 2014.

Crouzet, N. and J. C. Eberly. Understanding weak capital investment: the role of market concentration and intangibles. Working Paper 25869, National Bureau of Economic Research, May 2019.

Davis, S. and J. Haltiwanger. Gross job creation, gross job destruction, and employment reallocation. *Quarterly Journal of Economics*, 107(3):819–863, 1992.

De Loecker, J. Do exports generate higher productivity? Evidence from Slovenia. *Journal of International Economics*, 73(1):69–98, 2007.

Product differentiation, multiproduct firms, and estimating the impact of trade liberalization on productivity. *Econometrica*, 79(5):1407–1451, September 2011.

De Loecker, J. and J. Eeckhout. The rise of market power and the macroeconomic implications. NBER Working Papers 23687, National Bureau of Economic Research, Inc, August 2017.

Global market power. NBER Working Papers 24768, National Bureau of Economic Research, Inc, June 2018.

De Loecker, J. and P. K. Goldberg. Firm performance in a global market. NBER Working Paper, (19308), August 2013.

De Loecker, J. and F. Warzynski. Markups and firm-level export status. *American Economic Review*, 102(6):2437–2471, 2012.

De Loecker, J., P. Goldberg, A. Khandelwal and N. Pavcnik. Prices, markups and trade reform. *Econometrica*, 84(2):445–510, 2016.

De Loecker, J., J. Eeckhout and G. Unger. The rise of market power and the macroeconomic implications. *Quarterly Journal of Economics*, 135(2):561–644, 01 2020.

Decker, R., J. Haltiwanger, R. Jarmin and J. Miranda. The role of entrepreneurship in US job creation and economic dynamism. *Journal of Economic Perspectives*, 28(3):3–24, September 2014.

Del Prete, D. and A. Rungi. Organizing the global value chain: a firm-level test. *Journal of International Economics*, 109(C):16–30, 2017.

Demian, V. and F. di Mauro. The exchange rate, asymmetric shocks and asymmetric distributions. Working Paper Series 1801, ECB, 2015.

Desnoyers-James, I., S. Calligaris and F. Calvino. DynEmp and MultiProd: metadata. Working Paper 2019/03, OECD, 2019.

Di Giovanni, J., A. Levchenko and I. Mejean. Firms, destinations, and aggregate fluctuations. Working Paper 20061, National Bureau of Economic Research, April 2014.

di Mauro, F. and M. Ronchi. Wage bargaining regimes and firms' adjustments to the great recession. Discussion Paper Series 1/2017, IWH-CompNet, 2017.

Di Mauro, F., F. Hassan and G. I. P. Ottaviano. Financial markets and the allocation of capital: the role of productivity. CEP Discussion Papers dp1555, Centre for Economic Performance, LSE, July 2018.

Dobbelaere, S. and J. Mairesse. Panel data estimates of the production function and product and labor market imperfections. *Journal of Applied Econometrics*, 28:1–46, 2013.

Dustmann, C., A. Lindner, U. Schömberg, M. Umkehrer and P. vom Berge. Reallocation effects of the minimum wage. Discussion Paper Series CDP 07/20, CReAM, 2020.

Duval, R. A., G. H. Hong and Y. Timmer. Financial frictions and the great productivity slowdown. IMF Working Paper, (17/129), May 2017.

Eggertsson, G. B., J. A. Robbins and E. G. Wold. Kaldor and Piketty's facts: the rise of monopoly power in the United States. Working Paper 24287, National Bureau of Economic Research, February 2018.

Elsby, M., B. Hobijn and A. Sahin. The decline of the U.S. labor share. *Brookings Papers on Economic Activity*, 44(2 (Fall)):1–63, 2013.

Fazzari, S. M., R. G. Hubbard and B. Petersen. Financing constraints and corporate investment. *Brookings Papers on Economic Activity*, 19(1):141–206, 1988.

Fernández, C., R. García, P. Lopez-Garcia, et al. Firm growth in Europe: an overview based on the CompNet labour module. ECB Working Paper, (2048), April 2017.

Ferrando, A. and N. Griesshaber. Financing obstacles among euro area firms: who suffers the most? ECB Working Paper, (1293), 2011.

Ferrando, A., M. Iudice, C. Altomonte, et al. Assessing the financial and financing conditions of firms in Europe: the financial module in CompNet. ECB Working Paper, (1836), August 2015.

Ferrando, A., I. Ganoulis and C. Preuss. What were they thinking? Firms' expectations since the financial crisis. *Review of Behavioral Finance*, 13(4):370–385, 2021.

Foster, L., J. Haltiwanger and C. Krizan. Aggregate productivity growth: lessons from microeconomic evidence. In *New Developments in Productivity Analysis*, pages 303–372. National Bureau of Economic Research, Inc, 2001.

Foster, L., J. Haltiwanger and C. J. Krizan. Market selection, reallocation, and restructuring in the U.S. retail trade sector in the 1990s. *Review of Economics and Statistics*, 88(4):748–758, November 2006.

Foster, L., J. Haltiwanger and C. Syverson. Reallocation, firm turnover, and efficiency: selection on productivity or profitability? *American Economic Review*, 98(1):394–425, 2008.

Foster, L., C. Grim and J. Haltiwanger. Reallocation in the great recession: cleansing or not? *Journal of Labor Economics*, 34(S1):S293–S331, 2016.

Frankel, J. A. and D. H. Romer. Does trade cause growth? *American Economic Review*, 89(3):379–399, June 1999. doi: 10.1257/aer.89.3. 379. URL www.aeaweb.org/articles?id=10.1257/aer.89.3.379.

Friedrich, B. Trade shocks, firm hierarchies and wage inequality. Economics working papers, Department of Economics and Business Economics, Aarhus University, 2015.

Gabaix, X. The granular origins of aggregate fluctuations. *Econometrica*, 79(3):733–772, 2011.

Gamberoni, E., C. Giordano and P. Lopez-Garcia. Capital and labour (mis)allocation in the euro area: some stylized facts and determinants. Working Paper Series 1981, European Central Bank, November 2016.

Gamberoni, E., C. Gartner, C. Giordano and P. Lopez-Garcia. Is corruption efficiency-enhancing? A case study of the central and eastern European region. *European Journal of Comparative Economics*, 15(1):119–164, June 2018.

Giupponi, G. and C. Landais. Subsidizing labor hoarding in recessions: the employment & welfare effects of short time work. CEP Discussion Papers dp1585, Centre for Economic Performance, LSE, Dec. 2018.

Gopinath, G., S. Kalemli-Ozcan, L. Karabarbounis and C. Villegas-Sanchez. Capital allocation and productivity in south Europe. *Quarterly Journal of Economics*, 132(4):1915–1967, 2017.

Gradzewicz, M. and J. Mućk. Globalization and the fall of markups. Technical report, 2019.

Grubel, H. and P. Lloyd. *Intra-Industry Trade: The Theory and Measurement of International Trade in Differentiated Products*. Macmillan Press, 1975.

Guariglia, A. Internal financial constraints, external financial constraints, and investment choice: evidence from a panel of UK firms. *Journal of Banking and Finance*, 32(9):1795–1809, 2008.

Guariglia, A. and S. Mateut. Inventory investment, global engagement, and financial constraints in the UK: evidence from micro data. *Journal of Macroeconomics*, 32(1):239–250, 2010.

Gutiérrez, G. and T. Philippon. Investment-less growth: an empirical investigation. Working Paper 22897, National Bureau of Economic Research, December 2016.

Declining competition and investment in the U.S. Working Paper 23583, National Bureau of Economic Research, July 2017.

Hadlock, C. J. and J. R. Pierce. New evidence on measuring financial constraints: moving beyond the KZ index. *Review of Financial Studies*, 23(5):1909–1940, 2010.

Haltiwanger, J., R. Kulick and C. Syverson. Misallocation measures: the distortion that ate the residual. Working Paper 24199, National Bureau of Economic Research, January 2018.

Haskel, J. and S. Westlake. *Capitalism without Capital: The Rise of the Intangible Economy*. Princeton University Press, 2018.

Heckscher, E. and B. Ohlin. *Interregional and Internation Trade*. Harvard University Press, 1933.

Heil, M. Finance and productivity: a literature review. Economics Department Working Paper 1374, OECD, 2017.

Helpman, E. and P. Krugman. *Market Structure and Foreign Trade: Increasing Returns, Imperfect Competition, and the International Economy*. MIT Press, Cambridge, 1975.

Helpman, E., M. J. Melitz and S. R. Yeaple. Export versus FDI with heterogeneous firms. *American Economic Review*, 94(1):300–316, March 2004.

Hoch, I. Estimation of production function parameters combining time-series and cross-section data. *Econometrica*, 30(1):34–53, January 1962.

Hopenhayn, H., J. Neira and R. Singhania. From population growth to firm demographics: implications for concentration, entrepreneurship and the labor share. Working Paper 25382, National Bureau of Economic Research, December 2018.

Hopenhayn, H. A. Firms, misallocation, and aggregate productivity: a review. *Annual Review of Economics*, 6(1):735–770, 2014.

Hsieh, C.-T. and P. J. Klenow. Misallocation and manufacturing TFP in China and India. *Quarterly Journal of Economics*, 124(4):1403–1448, November 2009.

Huang, Z. Evidence of a bank lending channel in the UK. *Journal of Banking and Finance*, 27(3):491–510, 2003.

Hubbard, R. Capital-market imperfections and investment. *Journal of Economic Literature*, 36(1):193–225, 1998.

Hulten, C. R. Total factor productivity: a short biography. In C. R. Hulten, E. R. Dean and M. J. Harper, editors, *New Developments in Productivity Analysis*, chapter 1, pages 1–54. University of Chicago Press, January 2001.

Hyatt, H. and J. R. Spletzer. The recent decline of single quarter jobs. IZA Discussion Papers 8805, Institute of Labor Economics (IZA), 2015.

Hyun, J., D. Kim and S.-R. Shin. The role of global connectedness and market power in crises: firm-level evidence from the COVID-19 pandemic. *COVID Economics: Vetted and Real-Time Papers*, 49:148–171, 2020.

Israel, J. M., V. Damia, R. Bonci and G. Watfe. The analytical credit dataset: a magnifying glass for analysing credit in the euro area. ECB Occasional Paper, (187), 2017.

Jäger, K. EU KLEMS growth and productivity accounts 2017 release, statistical module. The Conference Board, 2017.

Jiménez, G., S. Ongena, J.-L. Peydró and J. Saurina. Hazardous times for monetary policy: what do twenty-three million bank loans say about the effects of monetary policy on credit risk-taking? *Econometrica*, 82(2):463–505, 2014.

Kalemli-Ozcan, S., B. Sorensen, C. Villegas-Sanchez, V. Volosovych and S. Yesiltas. How to construct nationally representative firm level data from the ORBIS global database: new facts and aggregate implications. Working Paper 21558, National Bureau of Economic Research, 2015.

Kaplan, S. N. and L. Zingales. Do investment-cash flow sensitivities provide useful measures of financing constraints?. *Quarterly Journal of Economics*, 112(1):169–215, 1997.

Karabarbounis, L. and B. Neiman. The global decline of the labor share. *Quarterly Journal of Economics*, 129(1):61–103, 10 2013.

Kashyap, A. K., J. C. Stein and D. Wilcox. Monetary policy and credit conditions: evidence from the composition of external finance. *American Economic Review*, 83(1):78–98, 1993.

Katayama, H., S. Lu and J. R. Tybout. Firm-level productivity studies: illusions and a solution. *International Journal of Industrial Organization*, 27:403–413, 2009.

Kaymak, B. and I. Schott. Corporate tax cuts and the decline of the labor share. Technical report, 2018.

Klette, T. J. and Z. Griliches. The inconsistency of common scale estimators when output prices are unobserved and endogenous. *Journal of Applied Econometrics*, 11(4):343–361, 1996.

Koopman, R., Z. Wang and S.-J. Wei. Tracing value-added and double counting in gross exports. *American Economic Review*, 104(2):459–94, February 2014.

Krugman, P. Scale economies, product differentiation, and the pattern of trade. *American Economic Review*, 70(5):950–59, 1980.

Increasing returns and economic geography. *Journal of Political Economy*, 99(3):483–99, 1991.

Krugman, P. R. Increasing returns, monopolistic competition, and international trade. *Journal of International Economics*, 9(4):469–479, 1979.

Krusell, P., T. Mukoyama, R. Rogerson and A. Sahin. Gross worker flows over the business cycle. *American Economic Review*, 107(11):3447–3476, November 2017.

Laeven, L., G. Schepens and I. Schnabel. Zombification in Europe in times of pandemic. VoxEU.org 11, October 2020.

Lawrence, R. Z. Recent declines in labor's share in us income: a preliminary neoclassical account. Working Paper 21296, National Bureau of Economic Research, June 2015.

Lerner, A. P. The concept of monopoly and the measurement of monopoly power. *Review of Economic Studies*, 1(3):157–175, June 1934.

Levinshon, J. and A. Petrin. Estimating production functions using inputs to control for unobservables. *Review of Economic Studies*, 70(2):317–341, April 2003.

Lopez-Garcia, P., D. Aglio, R. Bräuer, et al. CompNet's 6th vintage of data: novelties and main stylised facts. CompNet Cross-Country Report, 2018.

Love, I. Financial development and financing constraints: international evidence from the structural investment model. *Review of Financial Studies*, 16(3):765–791, 2003.

Manaresi, F. and N. Pierri. Credit constraints and firm productivity: evidence from Italy. Mo.Fi.R. Working Paper, (137), 2017.

Marschak, J. and W. H. Andrews. Random simultaneous equations and the theory of production. *Econometrica*, 12(3/4):143–205, July–October 1944.

Martincus, C. V. and J. Carballo. Beyond the average effects: the distributional impacts of export promotion programs in developing countries. *Journal of Development Economics*, 92(2):201–214, 2010.

Mayer, T. and G. P. Ottaviano. The happy few: the internationalisation of European firms. *Bruegel Blueprint*, 3, 2007.

Mayer, T., M. Melitz and G. Ottaviano. Market size, competition, and the product mix of exporters. *American Economic Review*, 104(2):594–536, 2014.

McAdam, P., F. Petroulakis, I. Vansteenkiste, M. C. Cavalleri, A. Eliet and A. Soares. Concentration, market power and dynamism in the euro area. Working Paper Series 2253, European Central Bank, March 2019.

McGowan, M. A., D. Andrews and V. Millot. Insolvency regimes, technology diffusion and productivity growth. OECD Working Paper, (1425), 2017.

Melitz, M. The impact of trade on intra-industry reallocations and aggregate industry productivity. *Econometrica*, 71(6):1695–1725, November 2003.

Melitz, M. and S. Polanec. Dynamic Olley–Pakes productivity decomposition with entry and exit. *RAND Journal of Economics*, 46(2):362–375, 2015.

Melitz, M. J. and G. I. P. Ottaviano. Market size, trade, and productivity. *Review of Economic Studies*, 75(1):295–316, 01 2008.

Merler, S. The financial side of the productivity slowdown. *Bruegel Blog Post*, January 2018.

Mertens, M. Micro-mechanisms behind declining labor shares: market power, production processes, and global competition. No. 3/2019. IWH-CompNet Discussion Papers, 2019.

Midrigan, V., T. Philippon and C. Jones. Beyond the liquidity trap: the secular stagnation of investment. Technical report, 2016.

Mollisi, V. and G. Rovigatti. Theory and practice of TFP estimation: the control function approach using STATA. *STATA Journal*, 18(3):618–662, 2018.

Morlacco, M. Market power in input markets: theory and evidence from French manufacturing. Job market paper, Yale University, November 2019.

Mrázová, M., J. P. Neary and M. Parenti. Sales and markup dispersion: theory and empirics. Technical report, 2018.

Mulier, K., K. Schoors and B. Merlevede. Investment-cash flow sensitivity and financial constraints: evidence from unquoted European SMEs. *Journal of Banking & Finance*, 73:182–197, 2016.

Mundlak, Y. Empirical production function free of management bias. *Journal of Farm Economics*, 43:44–56, February 1961.

Nurmi, S., J. Vanhala and M. Virén. The life and death of zombies – evidence from government subsidies to firms. Research Discussion Papers 8/2020, Bank of Finland, May 2020.

OECD. The future of productivity. In *Joint Economics Department and the Directorate for Science, Technology and Innovation Policy Note*. OECD Publishing, Paris, 2015.

Job Retention Schemes during the COVID-19 Lockdown and Beyond. OECD Publishing, 2020.

Olley, G. S. and A. Pakes. The dynamics of productivity in the telecommunications equipment industry. *Econometrica*, 64(6):1263–1297, November 1996a.

The dynamics of productivity in the telecommunications equipment industry. Technical report, National Bureau of Economic Research, 1996b.

O'Toole, C. M., C. Newman and T. Hennessy. Financial constraints and agricultural investment: effects of the Irish financial crisis. *Journal of Agricultural Economics*, 65(1):152–176, 2014.

Petrin, A. and J. Sivadasan. Estimating lost output from allocative inefficiency, with an application to Chile and firing costs. *Review of Economics and Statistics*, 95(1):286–301, 2013.

Philippon, T. *The Great Reversal: How America Gave Up on Free Markets*. Belknap Press of Harvard University Press, Cambridge, 2019.

Ricardo, D. *On the Principles of Political Economy and Taxation*. John Murray, 1817.

Rostagno, M., C. Altavilla, G. Carboni, et al. A tale of two decades: the ECB's monetary policy at 20. Working Paper Series 2346, ECB, December 2019.

Sablik, T. and N. Trachter. Are markets becoming less competitive? Economic Brief 19-06, Federal Reserve Bank of Richmond, June 2019.

Sapir, A., P. Aghion, G. Bertola, et al. *An Agenda for a Growing Europe: The Sapir Report*. Oxford University Press, 2004.

Schivardi, F., E. Sette and G. Tabellini. Identifying the real effects of zombie lending. *Review of Corporate Finance Studies*, 9(3):569–592, 2020.

Schivardi, F., E. Sette and G. Tabellini. Credit misallocation during the European financial crisis. *Economic Journal*, 2021, doi: 10.1093/ej/ueab039

Sforza, A. Shocks and the organization of the firm: who pays the bill? CESifo Working Paper Series 8084, CESifo Group Munich, 2020.

Smeets, V. and F. Warzynski. Estimating productivity with multi-product firms, pricing heterogeneity and the role of international trade. *Journal of International Economics*, 90(2):237–244, 2013.

Solow, R. M. Technical change and the aggregate production function. *Review of Economics and Statistics*, 39(3):312–320, August 1957.

Syverson, C. Product substitutability and productivity dispersion. *Review of Economics and Statistics*, 86(2):534–550, May 2004.

What determines productivity? *Journal of Economic Literature*, 49(2): 326–365, 2011.

Macroeconomics and market power: context, implications, and open questions. *Journal of Economic Perspectives*, 33(3):23–43, August 2019.

Syverson, C. and F. di Mauro. The COVID crisis and productivity growth. VoxEU.org 16 April 2020, 2020.

Timmer, M. P., E. Dietzenbacher, B. Los, R. Stehrer and G. J. de Vries. An illustrated user guide to the world input-output database: the case of global automotive production. *Review of International Economics*, 23(3):575–605, 2015.

Tybout, J. R. Plant- and firm-level evidence on "new" trade theories. No. 8418, NBER Working Papers, National Bureau of Economic Research, Inc., 2021.

UNCTAD. *World Investment Report 2013 – Global Value Chains: Investment and Trade for Development*. UNCTAD, Geneva, 2013.

Van Ark, B. and K. Jäger. Recent trends in Europe's output and productivity growth performance at the sector level, 2002–2015. *International Productivity Monitor*, 33:8–23, Fall 2017.

Van Beveren, I. Total factor productivity estimation: a practical review. *Journal of Economic Surveys*, 26(1):98–128, 2012.

Van Biesebroeck, J. Exporting raises productivity in sub-Saharan African manufacturing firms. *Journal of International Economics*, 67(2):373–391, 2005.

Robustness of productivity estimates. *Journal of Industrial Economics*, 55(3):529–569, 2007.

Van Reenen, J. Increasing differences between firms: market power and the macro-economy. CEP Discussion Papers dp1576, Centre for Economic Performance, LSE, September 2018.

Wang, Z., S.-J. Wei, X. Yu and K. Zhu. Measures of participation in global value chains and global business cycles. NBER Working Papers 23222, National Bureau of Economic Research, Inc, March 2017.

Wedervang, F. *Development of a Population of Industrial Firms*. Scandinavian University Books, Oslo, 1965.

Whited, T. Debt, liquidity constraints, and corporate investment: evidence from panel data. *Journal of Finance*, 47(4):1425–1460, 1992.

Whited, T. M. and G. Wu. Financial constraints risk. *Review of Financial Studies*, 19(2):531–559, 2006.

Wooldridge, J. M. On estimating firm-level production functions using proxy variables to control for unobservables. *Economics Letters*, 104:112–114, 2009.

World Bank. *World Development Report 2020 – Trading for Development in the Age of Global Value Chains*. World Bank, 2020.

Zheng, G., D. Hoang and G. Pacheco. Benchmarking New Zealand's frontier firms. New Zealand Productivity Commission, New Zealand, 2021.

Index

Printed in the United States
by Baker & Taylor Publisher Services